THE HIDDEN HOLMES

T H E HIDDEN H O L M E S

A
SHERLOCK
HOLMES
COMPANION

*A Serious Rereading of the Stories and
Novels by Sir Arthur Conan Doyle with
Analyses and Commentary*

by

IRA J. FISTELL

To the girl I met on the first day of high school—the most beautiful girl I have ever seen. She's the one with the sparkling eyes and the melting smile, not to mention the perfect figure. Talk about having it all—not only was this girl Hollywood starlet pretty, she was always at the top of our class academically: she had a warm personality, a terrific sense of humor, a wonderful imagination, and to top it all off she had more compassion and caring for other people than anyone else I have ever met. In short, I knew that I had met my dream girl.

But after a happy senior year in high school, she went away to college in the East, I stayed in Chicago, and we soon lost touch. I spent a long time looking for another girl like her, but never found one. Now I know why—there isn't anyone like her. I never forgot her: she was always there in the back of my mind.

And then one day many years later I came to a reunion party, and as I walked in the door someone said to me, "Your old girl friend is here!" A miracle followed: we came together again, and since then we have been virtually inseparable.

So, on this the occasion of the publication of *The Hidden Holmes*, which I could never have written without her inspiration and help, I am dedicating this book to the most important person in my entire world—my life companion and beloved partner,

Dr. Rachel Oriel Berg

Contents

Introduction ix

PART 1: THE HOLMES SHORT STORIES

Chapter 1: Reading the Short Stories 3

Chapter 2: The Adventures of Sherlock Holmes 8

Chapter 3: The Memoirs of Sherlock Holmes 27

Chapter 4: The Return of Sherlock Holmes 39

Chapter 5: His Last Bow 60

Chapter 6: The Case-Book of Sherlock Holmes 73

Chapter 7: Essays on the Short Stories 91

PART 2: THE FOUR SHERLOCK HOLMES NOVELS

Chapter 8: A Study in Scarlet 127

Chapter 9: The Sign of the Four 156

Chapter 10: The Valley of Fear 200

Chapter 11: The Hound of the Baskervilles 246

About the Author 315

Introduction

THIS BOOK WAS DESIGNED AS A COMPANION TO THE SIXTY SHERLOCK
Holmes stories and novels written by Sir Arthur Conan Doyle, and
it contains a good deal of commentary. Also, especially in the short
stories, the names of the perpetrators (or generally bad persons) are
disclosed. Therefore, I urge any reader of this volume who is not
quite familiar with the texts to *read the stories before tackling my analyses.* In that way you will get the most satisfaction, both from Sir
Arthur's work and my own.

As to other works about the Holmes canon—Les Klinger's *The
New Annotated Sherlock Holmes* (published in 2006 by W.W. Norton,
in both New York and London, and in two volumes) is probably
the most interesting and informative one now in print. There are,
however, many, many other books about the Doyle stories which can
provide many, many hours of fun to people interested in the great
detective. Be warned, however. No other book I know
of takes the same approach as this one. I believe I
am the first to treat the Holmes stories as serious
literature—not merely as trivial entertainment.
Dr. Doyle's works deserve to be read carefully
and thoughtfully.

This book will show you what I mean. Read
the stories first, and then read on!

A REREADING OF THE CANON

In the preface to my book on Mark Twain—*Ira Fistell's Mark Twain: Three Encounters*—I wrote, "I will probably never write a similar book about any other author."[*]

To the degree that this present work is not so much about the relationship between the life of Sir Arthur Conan Doyle and his Sherlock Holmes novels and short stories, that statement continues to be true. However, it is false insofar as the present volume aims to explore and to explicate the Holmes tales, which I have found to be much deeper and more complicated than has previously been recognized. The canon contains much deep thought, critical examination of Victorian / Edwardian British society, and layers of meaning far beyond what casual readers of these works have realized. With my analysis I hope to demonstrate that Doyle was indeed much more than a gifted storyteller: he was also a master of language and a better literary craftsman than he generally is credited with being.

Of course, the author himself was keenly aware that the popularity of Sherlock Holmes might detract from his literary reputation. He feared that his historical novels in particular, which he considered his best and most important works, would be taken less seriously if he were seen simply as a writer of popular fiction. The great irony is that much of the Holmes canon demonstrates Sir Arthur's deeper concerns about the society in which he lived, as well as his great talent for structure, brilliant characterization, and superior use of the English language. Just as Mark Twain was far more than a great humorist, Conan Doyle was far more than just a great teller of tales.

Nor is Doyle's wonderful facility in entertaining his readers any less important than his other merits as a writer. It is now well over 100 years since Holmes and Watson made their first appearance in print, and it may not be any exaggeration to remark that the stories Dr. Doyle created may have entertained a million people for each of

---

[*] This book was published in 2012, and it is available from Xlibris Corporation (xlibris.com or amazon.com).

those years. Few if any writers can approach Doyle's truly remarkable talent for enthralling readers literally around the world.

Time magazine, in a special edition published on July 24, 2013, paid tribute to "The One Hundred Most Influential People Who Never Lived," and Sherlock Holmes was a prominent member of that exclusive society. It is possible—indeed, likely—that Holmes is the most depicted fictional character ever created. He appears in every form of mass media, from cartoons and stage performances through radio, television, motion pictures—even music. His name is recognized by untold numbers of people who have never read a word about him: it is synonymous with the idea of a detective. John Lennon may have exaggerated when he remarked that the Beatles were more popular than Jesus Christ, but to say the same thing about Holmes may very well be the literal truth.

And still, Conan Doyle is often overlooked when one considers the great writers of his time. Case in point: a few years ago, a house in which Doyle had lived was about to be turned into a rooming house. There was a public outcry against the local authorities who intended to allow this desecration, and someone in a position of authority responded with this gem of a putdown: "Doyle was not one of the great English writers, like Dickens, for example."

That made my blood boil. As an English teacher (among my other careers) I have read and taught both Doyle and Dickens, and in my opinion a conscientious and careful reading of Doyle's work reveals him to be every bit the equal of Dickens in facility, but far deeper in thought and more skilled in the craft of writing than his rival. I hope to demonstrate during this study of the Holmes canon that Conan Doyle deserves to be recognized not only beside Dickens, but as the peer of any other British writer of the late Victorian / Edwardian period.

Note that I cite only the Holmes works here. I have made no effort to write about the author's historical novels, or even about his many other short stories outside the Holmes canon—although the Brigadier Gerard series and the Professor Challenger stories are favorites with me. After all, it was the Holmes stories that established the author's immense success, and among them one can find ample evidence of their creator's greatness.

However Sir Arthur himself may have felt about the Holmes canon, I am confident that these stories and novels contain ample evidence of Doyle's stature as both a thinker and a writer: one just has to read the materials with care and without the preconception that Holmes is (as Christopher Morley inaccurately put it) "pure anesthesia." Doyle's wonderful ability as a storyteller is testimony to his greatness, but it is far from being his only—or, for that matter, greatest—merit. In this book I hope to convince the world that Sir Arthur had much else on his mind, and that the Holmes canon is full of social criticism, sympathy for the underclasses and women, and apparent disdain for the smug self-satisfaction which marked England in the late Victorian and Edwardian years.

Nor is presenting a positive reinterpretation of Conan Doyle's literary accomplishments my only purpose in writing this book. I hope to expose the reader to some tools which I have found to be of great importance in the art of reading and comprehending written English, whether fiction or non-fiction, whether long novel or short essay, whether historical or contemporary. These tools include first and foremost the technique of finding the structure of the text in question.

Every human creation—whether it is a building, a bridge, a book, a piece of music, a painting, or what have you—must have a structure which holds it together, or else it becomes meaningless, useless, and chaotic. In the case of writing, the author chooses the structure which he believes will best present what he is trying to say: in turn, when the reader finds and understands the structure, he holds the key to receiving the author's message. Other techniques which I have found to be useful in interpreting written works are the author's skill in the use of language and in the creation of characters and dialogue; the use of proper nouns to convey meaning; and the triple devices of satire, irony, and humor, and how they may be used to elaborate the author's meaning. A message may be more effective when by indirection it involves the reader in its presentation rather than preaching the message directly.

Let us now proceed to a discussion of the Holmes canon. What does it consist of, and how does it work?

GENERAL COMMENTS ON THE CANON

Arthur Conan Doyle conceived the idea of a scientific detective while still quite a young man. Born in 1859, he already had behind him a career in medicine, including time serving as surgeon's clerk to Dr. Joseph Bell, one of his professors at the University of Edinburgh; as a surgeon on a whaling ship in 1880 and on a passenger liner a year and half later; and as a general practitioner at South Sea, Portsmouth. Simultaneously, he was writing for money. His first published story, "The Mystery of Sasassa Valley," appeared in a magazine when he was just twenty years old, and over the next five or six years he wrote and published additional stories and some non-fiction. In 1885 he married Louisa Hawkins, the sister of a former patient.

Soon he began to write a detective story featuring "Sherrinford Holmes" and "Ormond Sacker"—roommates at 221B Baker Street, London. One inspiration for the scientific detective was Doyle's former professor, Dr. Bell, whose use of observation and deduction in diagnosing illness had impressed his former clerk. Another principal source was the work of Edgar A. Poe, the American author of what is generally conceded to be the first modern detective story, "The Murders in the Rue Morgue," which had appeared in 1841. Doyle finished the first Sherlock (no longer Sherrinford) Holmes story, the novel *A Study in Scarlet*, in 1886, when he was twenty-seven, but had to wait a year to see it published in *Beeton's Christmas Annual*, late in 1887. The author had by this time turned "Ormond Sacker" into John H. Watson, MD, and the canon now began.

Over the next forty years, Dr. Doyle wrote and published three more novels and fifty-six short stories featuring Sherlock Holmes. Nobody in his right mind would argue that they are all of the highest quality, but a surprising number of them reach that level. And no other detective story writer—not even the immensely popular Agatha Christie—surpasses Conan Doyle and his Holmes stories in the public's affection, which is surely a sign of reader satisfaction.

What accounts for the truly amazing world-wide popularity of the Holmes stories?

First, I think, we must recognize Doyle's debt to Poe, who was the first modern writer to publish a detective story, and who created, from the beginning, many of the characteristics of the genre. Not the least of these was Poe's use of narration by a nameless friend and companion of C. Auguste Dupin, his detective. Doyle was smart enough to not only use this device—which keeps the detective's thought process secret from the reader until the case is solved, thus holding the reader's attention while not giving away the solution too soon—but to improve on it.

In place of Poe's nameless and characterless narrator, Doyle created in his very first attempt at a detective story the very real personality of Dr. Watson. Watson stands between the brilliant, enigmatic, and sometimes impossible Holmes and the reader, in a way that Dupin's nameless companion never could. Holmes says in *A Study in Scarlet* that "Dupin was a very inferior fellow." I would argue that it was not Poe's detective who was inferior, but his narrator, to whom we can never really get close. Watson, a fully drawn personality with brains and feelings, is in a large measure responsible for the enormous appeal of Doyle's stories.

The proof of this pudding is to be found in the three late Holmes tales in which Watson is either absent altogether or appears as a character in the story but is not the narrator. None of these ("The Blanched Solder," and "The Lion's Mane"—both told in the first person by Holmes himself—and "The Mazarin Stone," which has no narrator at all but is told in the third person) are nearly as effective or as reader friendly as the rest of the canon. In them, Doyle appears to have been experimenting, abandoning the tried and true framing formula, which he had introduced in the first of these tales, *A Study in Scarlet*. Perhaps he found himself tired of reusing the same design after more than three decades of composing Holmes adventures, but whatever his thinking, the Watsonless stories clearly lack the usual magic. Watson's presence allows Holmes's stature to become exalted—for as Watson himself often remarks after hearing the detective's explanations of his thinking, "It is all so absurdly simple!"

Other reasons for the immense success of the Holmes stories, as I see it, are Dr. Doyle's sometimes completely original plots (although like other detective story writers, he does sometimes rework the same basic ideas in different ways); his wonderful talent for creating characters; and above all his unexcelled facility in the use of the English language as a medium for recounting stories. Few if any other writers have entertained so many readers so well for so long: even after more than a century and a quarter, there seems to be no end in sight for Dr. Doyle's hegemony as a first-order writer of detective stories. Indeed, Sherlock Holmes and Dr. Watson will probably be enthralling our great-grandchildren, just as they entertained our great-grandparents.

Yet the debut of the great detective and several members of his supporting cast—Watson; the long-suffering landlady, Mrs. Hudson; Scotland Yard Inspectors Gregson and Lestrade—caused no literary earthquake when *A Study in Scarlet* first appeared in 1887. It is possible that the Holmes canon might have ended with that single story had it not been for some good luck.

In 1889, two years after *A Study in Scarlet* finally appeared in print, the American publishing house of J. B. Lippincott was to begin publication of a British edition of its popular American magazine. The idea was to use an English editor and English writers to create English sales. The managing editor of the American magazine was a man named Joseph M. Stoddart. His firm linked up with Ward, Lock, and Co., publishers of <u>Beeton's Christmas Annual</u>, in which *Scarlet* had appeared. Stoddart hired away from Ward, Lock their chief editor and principal manuscript reader, G. T. Bettany. Bettany had advised his firm to buy *Study in Scarlet*—but it was not

Mr. Bettany but his wife who had liked the story and urged her husband to acquire it.

In a very real sense, then, Mrs. Bettany may be considered the godmother of Sherlock Holmes—if not for her support, he might never have been noticed.

In any case, George Bettany now talked up "his" discovery—Conan Doyle—to his new boss, Stoddart. Stoddart, in turn, set up a luncheon meeting at the posh Langham Hotel in London, inviting both Dr. Doyle and another young writer, an Irishman by the mellifluous name of Oscar Fingal O'Flaherty Wills Wilde. Stoddart's object was to explore the commissioning of new works from these two literary lion cubs.

That was probably the most productive literary lunch in history: it resulted in both Doyle and Wilde agreeing to write for Lippincott's. Wilde's contribution turned out to be *The Picture of Dorian Gray*, certainly one of the best horror stories ever written in English. For his part, Doyle produced a sequel to *A Study in Scarlet*, featuring Sherlock Holmes and Dr. Watson in a deeper, finer book entitled *The Sign of the Four*. The author agreed a to contract calling for a manuscript of not less than 40,000 words to be delivered by January, 1890. Doyle was promised a fee of a hundred pounds sterling—four times what he had earned from *Scarlet* three years before. Doyle worked rapidly: he actually completed the book in just a month, though it was not to be published until October, 1890. Unlike its predecessor, *Sign* was an immediate hit.

Its success caught the attention of a publisher named George Newnes, who was planning to introduce a new monthly English magazine to be called *The Strand*. He approached Dr. Doyle with an offer to buy six short stories featuring Sherlock Holmes, to appear at the rate of one per month for the rest of 1891. The author accepted, and the first Holmes short story, "A Scandal in Bohemia," appeared in *The Strand* issue of July 1891. As the popularity of the new series became apparent, Mr. Newnes asked the author for another six stories. Doyle agreed, and both the author and his unique detective character were on their way to immortality. The first dozen stories were collected and published in book form by Newnes in October 1892, as *The Adventures of Sherlock Holmes*. The publisher asked for more Holmes shorts, and Doyle delivered another twelve tales which appeared in *The Strand* beginning with the issue of December 1892. All but one of these were also published by Newnes in December 1893, as *The Memoirs of Sherlock Holmes*.

The association between Arthur Conan Doyle and *The Strand* continued for the rest of the author's long career, and it was greatly profitable for both. *The Strand* gave Dr. Doyle a vehicle for virtually anything he wrote, while the magazine found itself in demand every month as readers lined up to get the newest Holmes story. It was a match made in publishing heaven. All fifty-six of Doyle's Holmes short stories, plus serial versions of the two later Holmes novels (*The Hound of the Baskervilles* and *The Valley of Fear*) first reached the public through the pages of *The Strand*.

But enough of these preliminary remarks. Let us proceed to the meat of this book—a close reading and analysis of the entire Sherlock Holmes canon. I have chosen to begin with the short stories, because I believe that they contain much material and many examples of things which will be found in our later study of the greatest Holmes tales—the novels, especially the last three: *The Sign of the Four*, *The Valley of Fear*, and *The Hound of the Baskervilles*.

Let us turn, then, to those fifty-six short stories. I think that you will find the study of these works an adventure in literature which will surprise and, I hope, delight you.

PART 1

The Holmes Short Stories

CHAPTER 1

Reading the Short Stories

THE SHORT STORY WAS THE ORIGINAL FORMAT FOR DETECTIVE AND MYSTERY fiction. Poe, of course, created the modern detective story in 1841, and all of his work in the genre (including not only the "Rue Morgue" tale, but "The Purloined Letter," "The Mystery of Marie Roget," and "The Gold Bug") was done in the short story format. After Poe's death, however, Wilkie Collins and Charles Dickens used the long prose form, the novel, for their explorations of the type. So did Katherine Anne Green, in the first detective story written by a woman (*The Leavenworth Case*) and Mark Twain (*Pudd'nhead Wilson*). It remained for Dr. Doyle to resurrect the detective short story, and his work in this form remains unsurpassed.

The magazine market, of course, provided the impetus for the creation of the short story: today, with that market having suffered a severe decline, the novel has again become the primary format for detective literature. The exception to this rule of thumb is the collection of magazine-inspired short stories into book form, and this was done with all of the Sherlock Holmes shorts after serialization. There are five volumes of Holmes short stories:

The Adventures and *The Memoirs*, already mentioned, which between them contain twenty-three of the fifty-six stories in existence; *The Return of Sherlock Holmes* (containing thirteen), *His Last Bow* (eight) and *The Case Book of Sherlock Holmes*, which presents all twelve of the tales Doyle wrote about the detective after 1915. I will discuss each of the fifty-six stories one by one, after a few general comments which apply to all five volumes of Holmes shorts.

LENGTH

Given that all the stories were written for *The Strand*, they vary in length to a surprising degree. True, most of the stories run to about 6,000 words; the shortest, however—"The Veiled Lodger," from the *Casebook*—is only about 4,000 words long, while at least three of the tales run above 9,000 words. The longest story (I was surprised to discover this) is "The Naval Treaty," from the *Memoirs*, which tops 10,000 words in length.

Most of the stories are self-contained in single issues of *The Strand*, but five were spread out over two: "The Naval Treaty" is one them (October / November 1893). The other four all date from 1908 or later. They are "Wisteria Lodge" (September / October 1908) and "The Red Circle" (March / April 1911)—both from *His Last Bow*—and two stories from *The Casebook*: "Thor Bridge," (February / March 1922) and "The Illustrious Client" (February / March 1925). Like *Whittaker's Almanac*, mentioned in *The Valley of Fear*, some of the Holmes stories get more garrulous towards the end.

While *The Strand* was the exclusive British publisher of Holmes short stories, several firms published the stories in America: *Collier's Weekly*, *Hearst's International*, *Liberty Magazine* and *Harper's Weekly*, to name a few.

STRUCTURE

Nothing is more important in the study of literature than the structure which the author creates to hold his story together as well as to present and clarify the meaning of what he has written. In writing the Holmes short stories, Dr. Doyle for the most part employed two structural patterns, which for want of a better idea I have designated as "Type A" and "Type B." While similar, they are distinguishable by the fact that Type A stories show a four-part structure, while Type B stories have only three parts.

The Type A story characteristically begins with an introduction which may range in length from a couple of paragraphs to two or more pages. Often these opening sections include Watsonian references, always tantalizing, to other Holmes investigations of which we remain otherwise ignorant. (My favorite has always been the story of the politician, the lighthouse, and the trained cormorant. Just what did the politician train the bird to do at the lighthouse? Or can the three subjects be integrated in some other way?)

In the Type A introduction, we also hear occasional details about Watson's past. "I know that country, Holmes," Watson says when Holmes talks about Lamberly, Sussex, in "The Sussex Vampire." Here too we hear details of Watson's home life and of his professional work, or about his views of Holmes and his peculiarities. In a Type A story, the action really does not begin until the second section of the story, in which Holmes is introduced to the case. Often this is the result of a visit from the would-be client; sometimes it comes about by a request from Scotland Yard or some other agency looking for Holmes's assistance. On one memorable occasion, it is Watson himself who delivers the client to Holmes—the case of the young engineer, Victor Hatherly, who has lost his thumb.

Most often the scene of a Type A second section is Baker Street. This part of the story is often when Holmes begins his investigation, especially if he needs data or recalls a similar incident. In the third section of the typical Type A structure, Holmes—often but not always accompanied by Watson—makes an on-site investigation, sometimes at the scene of the crime, sometimes elsewhere. Usually, by the end of a third section, Holmes has solved the case in his mind, but has yet to capture the perpetrator (whose identity the reader generally does not know yet).

The fourth and final section of a Type A Holmes short story is generally devoted to the capture of the perpetrator, or at least the disclosure of his/her identity, followed by an account, either from Holmes or from the criminal himself, of how the case was solved.

The Type B story has much in common with the Type A structure, but it has only three sections instead of four. Typically, the Type B story begins with a dramatic intrusion into the Baker Street rooms—sometimes by a client (for example, the unexcelled "stunning and startling appearance" of Dr. Thorneycroft Huxtable in "The Priory School"); sometimes by an official of the law seeking Holmes's immediate aid (see Stanley Hopkins's message calling the detective to The Abbey Grange at four o'clock in the morning); sometimes by a messenger (for example, Steve Dixie, the bruiser, sent by Barney Stockdale to warn Holmes off the case in "The Three Gables.") After the dramatic opening, the foreshortened Type B story proceeds along the same path as its Type A counterpart. Section one continues with the statement of the problem and the introduction of the person or people who want it solved. In section two Holmes makes his on-site investigation, with or without Watson's presence, and gathers the information he needs to solve the case. In section three we get to know the solution and the identity and / or fate of the perpetrator, and finally the story of how the case was resolved.

One or the other of these two structural patterns is to be found in nearly all of the Holmes short stories, although the relative lengths of the sections may change depending on the complexity of the investigation. The principal deviations from the basic structural patterns are to be found in "The Final Problem," where Holmes is the pursued rather than the pursuer; in "His Last Bow," in which there is no detection; and in the three late stories in which Watson is not the narrator. I will discuss each of these tales in their proper places as we go through the five volumes of short stories in which Holmes appears.

THE CATALOG

In what follows, I have compiled a catalogue of the fifty-six short stories. For each, I give the date and vehicle of first publication; the structural type; the crime(s), if any; the criminal and / or unpleasant person or persons in the story; the names of the officer(s) of the law involved, if any; and the approximate length of the story. Following this basic data, I present my personal comments on the tale and its characters. In some cases, I have a great deal to say; in others, just a few words suffice. After the catalogue has been completed, I will discuss a number of themes which I find important: these themes run throughout the short stories, and we should be on the lookout for them when we get to the study of Holmes novels.

The Adventures of Sherlock Holmes

This collection was first published in book form by Newnes in 1892.

"A SCANDAL IN BOHEMIA"

First publication: The Strand Magazine, July 1891
Structural type: A (four-part structure)
Crime: None
Evildoers: The King (?), Irene Adler (?)
Official police: None
Length: Approximately 7,800 words

Having never attempted a Sherlock Holmes short story, Dr. Doyle produced one of the best on his first try. Superficially, this story (in which no crime takes place) seems rather trivial, especially in our contemporary context. In reality, "Scandal" contains deep overtones of social criticism. On the surface, Irene Adler is a mere adventuress: Watson describes her as "of dubious and questionable memory." Yet she emerges as a heroine, not only of just this tale but of the entire Holmes canon. To Holmes, you must remember, she is always *the* woman, who "eclipses and predominates the whole of her sex."

In this classic example of the Type A structure, the story begins with Watson's comments on Holmes's unromantic nature and intolerance for "the softer passions." Watson also contrasts his own domestic happiness (he is now married to the former Mary Morstan, from *The Sign of the Four*) with Holmes's "bohemian soul." We also hear of some of Holmes's recent cases, in which Watson had no part—"of his summons to Odessa in the case of the Trepoff murder, of his clearing up of the singular tragedy of the Atkinson brothers at Trincomalee, and finally of the mission which he had accomplished so delicately and successfully for the reigning family of Holland."

The action of the story begins when Watson, while driving through Baker Street one night, was "seized with a keen desire to see Holmes again." Noting that the apartment was lit up, and seeing Holmes pacing back and forth, the doctor rang the bell and was shown upstairs into his own former home. After some further conversation about Watson's weight gain and ignorance of the number of steps leading to the second floor (seventeen), Holmes shows his friend the letter that came by the last post—the note from (as it turns out) the king of Bohemia, announcing that he will visit Holmes that same evening. After deducing from the paper that the writer of the note was wealthy and a German, Holmes looks from the window and sees a 300-guinea pair of horses with a carriage. He remarks, "There is money in this case, Watson, if there is nothing else." Watson offers to leave, but Holmes asks him to remain: "I am lost without my Boswell ... I may need your help, and so may he."

The man who enters is described in detail: physically huge, wildly overdressed, marked with the characteristic Habsburg lip, and grotesquely masked. Holmes, of course, is not fooled: "Your Majesty had not spoken before I was aware that I was addressing

Wilhelm Gottsreich Sigismond von Ormstein, Grand Duke of Cassel-Felstein and hereditary king of Bohemia."

The king's problem, as it turns out, involves Ms. Adler, the retired (at age thirty!) operatic contralto who has obviously been his mistress. He was foolish enough to allow himself to be photographed with her, and now fears for his upcoming marriage to the daughter of the king of Scandinavia. It seems that Irene has threatened to send the photograph to the royal family into which the king intends to marry: he is sure that nothing will stop Irene from breaking up his engagement out of revenge. "Rather than I should marry another woman, there are no lengths to which she would not go," he says. "I know that she will do it. You do not know her, but she has a soul of steel. She has the face of the most beautiful of women, and the mind of the most resolute of men."

The interview concludes with the king giving Holmes a blank check to spend in getting the photograph, plus a thousand pounds "for current expenses." As Holmes says, "There is money in this case, if there is nothing else." Indeed, that phrase might be said to describe the king himself. In this second section of the story, he shows himself to be both foppish and foolish. He is physically unattractive, his personality is unappealing, and he seems to have no sense of humor or wit. Both here and in his later remarks he is clearly enthralled by his exalted station in life (which, of course, has come about by the pure chance of birth). Holmes is cool towards him at the beginning, and grows progressively colder, to the point that he refuses to shake His Majesty's hand at the end.

If the King is the central figure at the beginning of "A Scandal," the middle of the tale belongs to Holmes. Here he makes his preliminary investigation of Ms. Adler by dressing up as a drunken groom and hanging out with the stablemen. By chance he observes Godfrey Norton's visit to Briony Lodge, and the hurried departure of first Norton and then Irene for the Church of St. Monica. Following in a cab, he is just in time to witness their marriage. Holmes then plans and arranges the staged scene by means of which he contrives to get himself into the house, where he observes the lady go to the hiding place of the photo: he actually catches a quick glimpse of it before Irene, learning that there is really no fire, puts it back.

Confident of getting the photograph the next morning, Holmes returns to Baker Street with Watson, only to hear someone wish him a good night. Holmes realizes that he has heard that voice before, but can't figure out whose it was. We should also note that Watson is much impressed by Ms. Adler—to the point that he contemplates refusing to carry out his role in Holmes's plot.

The concluding section of the story is short: the next morning the king calls and takes Holmes and Watson to Briony Lodge, where they are met by a maid who informs them that Mr. and Mrs. Norton have fled to the Continent. In the secret hiding place they find Irene Adler's own account of her triumph. The king says again that Irene would have made a great queen, if only her social status matched his own. Holmes remarks coldly, "She seems, indeed, to be on a very different level to Your Majesty," and asks for the photograph of herself that Irene had left in place of the one the king was after. In the last paragraph, Watson tells us that Holmes no longer makes fun of the cleverness of women, and always refers to Irene and her picture with the term, "*the* woman."

The King is now free to marry his princess, Irene leaves the stage with her new husband, and Holmes is left with a lesson in humility and a greater respect for women. In short, everybody gets exactly what they deserve. This, I suggest, is the mark of a classic comedy, which is precisely what "A Scandal in Bohemia" really is. Moreover, comedy is often associated with satire and irony, both of which are present here.

For a full understanding of what Conan Doyle put into this story, it is necessary first to define these terms. The word "satire" is frequently tossed around as if it had no specific meaning. It is, in fact, the art of making an attack on some person, thing, or idea by means of indirection. The author sets up a straw man, and then attacks this character. If the reader is perceptive, he will recognize the true target of the attack, the impact of which is amplified because the reader is himself involved in it. Irony, on the other hand, is the frustration of what is expected; frequently it works through a twist at the end of the story.

I have mentioned the characteristics of the king of Bohemia in this story. He is, of course, a fictional character—but it must have been difficult for anyone in England to miss the fact that "von Ormstein" looks and acts very much like the man who in 1891 was still the prince of Wales, heir to the throne of Great Britain. The prince was known for his card playing, gambling, good eating, and womanizing. As the son of Victoria and her husband, the German nobleman Prince Albert, he was half-German himself, and spoke English with a guttural accent all his life. Like the king in the story, he was not considered very smart. And when I remembered that he married a daughter of the king of Denmark (read: "the king of Scandinavia"), the identification was even more obvious.

Note: Queen Victoria took a dislike to her first son virtually from the time of his birth. She did not think he looked noble, and apparently considered him mentally slow. Growing up in a loveless household, which he eventually had to share with eight siblings, and cloistered away from the English public, it is not hard to see why the prince turned out the way he did. His mother appears to have deliberately refused to retire so as to keep her least-favorite offspring from reaching the throne at all: she remained queen for sixty-four years, the longest reign of any British monarch except for Elizabeth II.

I am happy to report, however, that when he finally did become King Edward VII—after the death of his mother in 1901—to the surprise of everybody, the much-vilified prince of Wales turned out to be quite a good king. Indeed, if Edward had lived past 1910, his influence might have tamed his nephew, Kaiser Wilhelm II, and World War I might never have occurred. Edward VII was much like Shakespeare's Prince Hal—the young wastrel who becomes a great monarch after reaching the throne.

There is irony, too, in "A Scandal in Bohemia." Consider this:

in the first two Holmes novels, *A Study in Scarlet* and *The Sign of the Four*, Conan Doyle created Holmes as an intellectual superman with (especially in *Scarlet*) few endearing characteristics. Now, in writing his first Holmes short story for magazine publication, and perhaps a larger and more inclusive readership, the good doctor had a brilliant inspiration: he had his Nietzschean superman taken down a peg or two by a woman. And to be capable of besting the great Sherlock Holmes, she had to be made a very unusual, special woman indeed. To produce the irony of Holmes being outwitted by a female, Doyle created Irene Adler—perhaps the most remarkable woman in all of Victorian fiction.

Here's another irony: Irene would have been an outcast among the upper-class ladies of her own day. She was an adventuress— she had to be, if she were to become embroiled with the king of Bohemia. While of course there is no mention of the nature of their relationship, it could only have been a sexual affair. Thus, ladies of the day would have refused to talk with her in the street. They would have shunned her at any social gathering, and never have invited her to anything. After all, this woman was being kept—she was little better than a whore! She could hardly have found the king attractive physically or a match for her intelligence, nor could she ever count on marriage to him. There were just two things that could have attracted her to him—his wealth and regal status. This, I submit, is why Watson refers to her as being "of dubious and questionable memory." As the king is a thoroughly unlikable character, so Victorian readers would never have approved of Irene's behavior. In short, neither of the two main characters in "A Scandal" would have been very attractive in the Britain of 1891.

There is yet another irony here, however. While Irene Adler would have been a social outcast among any but artists, writers, and musicians, her paramour—the foppish, foolish king—would simply by virtue of his position as a hereditary monarch have enjoyed the highest possible social standing. The self-same ladies who would have turned their faces away from Irene Adler would have fallen on their knees to kiss the hand of Wilhelm Gottsreich Sigismond von Ormstein.

What is to be said about a society such as this, where a mere title creates a fawning, adoring public, while a woman who protects herself from a paramour by maneuvering him into having his photograph taken with her is shunned, despised, and ignored? Certainly Irene Adler violates all the rules which circumscribe the behavior of the upper-class women of her time—but the message is that those standards are hypocritical and wrong, not necessarily the female who violates them.

What Doyle essentially did in this story was to create in Irene Adler the prototype for today's liberated woman. By making her the irresistible person she is, he performs the remarkable tour de force of turning "the bad girl" into the heroine—not just of this story but of the whole canon. (More on this as we get to other stories.) No wonder Holmes always refers to her as *the* woman.

Nor is that all. If indeed Sherlock Holmes reflects the feelings and opinions of his creator, this story demonstrates that Doctor Doyle thought and felt deeply about the suffocating mores of Victorian England. Without making an obvious attack on the world of his time and place, he yet conveys a highly critical attitude about both fawning adoration of royalty and rigid restrictions on the lives of women. There is in this story an undercurrent we will find in many other Holmes stories—a strong hint of social criticism which is easily missed by superficial or unthinking readers.

Before leaving the fascinating Ms. Adler, there are a few additional points I wish to make. The first concerns her name. "Irene" is of Greek origin, and while I, like Shakespeare, know no Greek, I have been informed that the name means "peace." "Adler," meanwhile, is the German word for "eagle"—a bird of prey which (especially in the United States, where it is the national symbol) is associated with strength, independence, and a sense of nobility.* One

---

* In this context, it is worth noting that Irene—born in New Jersey in 1858—was an American.

can therefore conclude that the name "Irene Adler" means "peaceful eagle." Did Dr. Doyle give her that name haphazardly, or without knowledge its meaning? Possibly. But as we read on in the canon, we will find that he had fondness for the use of what I call "aptonyms"— names particularly appropriate to the characters who bear them. As the prototype of "the new woman," Irene Adler could very well be described as a "peaceful eagle"—a pioneer who challenges established rules of conduct, but only when justified—by making the lives of members of her sex less restrictive and more gratifying. We will encounter many other aptonyms in the canon, which makes the use of "Irene Adler" less likely to have been fortuitous. I am reasonably sure that in using this name for this particular character, Dr. Doyle knew precisely what he was doing.

Apropos of the name, I have heard that the British pronunciation of "Irene" differs from the American. In this country we say "eye-reen." Across the Atlantic, I understand, they say "eye- reenie." However one pronounces it, the meaning is not changed.

There is still more to bring up about Ms. Adler. We are told that she is an operatic singer—a contralto, possessing the lowest, deepest female voice. We also know that she is quite familiar with and comfortable in men's clothes. In opera, there are many so-called "trouser roles," in which a male character is portrayed and sung by a woman: Ms. Adler would surely have performed some these on stage. But she also wears pants on the street, saying, "Male costume is nothing new to me. I often take advantage of the freedom it gives ... I ran upstairs, got into my walking clothes, as I call them, and then came down just as you departed." How many upper-class women do you suppose would have dressed like that on the street in the London of 1891? How many would have taken a lover like the king, aware that he was using her, and responded by using and manipulating *him*? (Who do you suppose was paying the rent at Briony Lodge?) Who convinced him to pose for a photograph with her, giving her a powerful hold over him to be used perhaps for protection from him, or possibly for blackmail should he try to cut her off financially?

Getting that photograph taken was her master stroke. He sought to explain away his foolishness on the ground that he was young and inexperienced—but no royal personage in Europe in that day and age would ever be so completely unaware as to allow himself to fall into the power of a clearly venal mistress who was obviously on the make. One wonders what his parents and courtiers must have said—and what they must have thought!

The king did learn something from his experience—that Irene was not to be trifled with. He expressed his feeling about her when he told Holmes, "She has the face of the most beautiful of women and the mind of the most resolute of men."

Now, let us consider that remark in the context of the other things we know about Irene—her low-register voice, her fondness for cross-dressing, her "soul of steel," and her willingness to challenge the restrictions on conduct so vexing to women of her type. Given these facts about her, it is easy to see Irene Adler as a sort of prototype for a very real twentieth-century chanteuse—the late Marlene Dietrich. Of course, Dr. Doyle could not have known anything of her when he created Irene in 1891, but he could well have imagined or known of some other similar women in his own time. What I am suggesting, of course, is the possibility that Doyle may have conceived of Irene Adler as bisexual. If indeed he did envision her as a brilliant, sexually and socially liberated "new woman," it becomes easy to explain both Watson's reference to her as "of dubious and questionable memory" and Holmes's own belief that "she eclipses and predominates the whole of her sex." No wonder Irene Adler was to Holmes always and forever "*the* woman."

This brings us back to a word Watson uses to describe his roommate in the second paragraph of this story—a word which, given the title of the tale, immediately catches one's attention. Watson first describes his own domestic happiness, and then contrasts it with his partner: "Holmes," he writes, "loathed every form of society with his whole bohemian soul." Of course, Holmes was not from central Europe: the term "bohemian" as used in this context clearly refers to

Holmes as one of those artistic, creative people who shun bourgeois respectability in favor of a freer, more personally satisfying lifestyle.

Now, given that Sherlock and Irene are both bohemians in this sense, where is the "Scandal in Bohemia"? Not, I would suggest, in what is now part of the Czech Republic. Von Ormstein may have been king of that Bohemia, but Sherlock Holmes is clearly king of the international realm of the counterculture. The real "Scandal in Bohemia," as seen in this context, is Irene Adler's marriage to the pedestrian Godfrey Norton. Her true soulmate, obviously, was meant to be the man she outwitted—Sherlock Holmes. Just as Irene's defiance of social standards would have been considered scandalous by the bourgeoisie, so her abandonment of her true nature to marry Norton would have been a scandal to the bohemian world of which she had been a part. Holmes must have realized in an instant who his life partner should have been, and her hurried decision to marry another man—with her destined partner as a witness, no less—clearly hurt him to the quick. He never forgot her.

So, the very first Holmes short story appears, upon close reading and with a little imagination, to be not the trivial tale it may appear on the surface, but a complicated story of social criticism, true passion, and betrayal. It is, I believe, a 7,000-word masterpiece.

A final comment. It is impossible to get into Doyle's mind today, but I wonder if perhaps the genesis of this story could have been the dual meanings of the word "bohemian." After all, why else should he have made the king come from that region? (The fact that the prince of Wales had a German father and spoke with a guttural accent in this context was simply a happy coincidence.) Why else did he create Irene as a singer who broke all the rules of feminine conduct, making her a bohemian in the cultural sense? And above all, why did he specifically use the adjective form of the word "bohemian" in reference to Sherlock Holmes? I cannot believe that all this was accidental. What almost certainly was a coincidence is the fact that five years later, in 1896, Giacomo Puccini's opera about life among the Parisian counterculture, based on the book by Henri Murger, was first produced at Turin, Italy. Its title could well have been used for Doyle's story—it was La Boheme (in English, The Bohemian Girl.)

"THE RED-HEADED LEAGUE"

> *First publication: The Strand,* August 1891
> *Structural type:* A (four-part structure)
> *Crime:* Attempted robbery
> *Evildoers:* John Clay; "Archie"
> *Official police:* "Peter Jones" (Athelney?)
> *Length:* Approximately 7,000 words

"The Red-Headed League" was the third Holmes short story written, and it was originally intended to be the third published. But *The Strand* was still a new magazine, and its editor, Herbert Greenhough Smith, felt "League" was much superior to "A Case of Identity," the story written immediately before it. Wishing to make a maximum impact, he changed the order of publication, so that "League" became the second story to see print, while "Identity" was held over until the September issue.

This created a small problem, for in the opening section of this Type A story one finds a reference to "the very simple problem presented by Miss Mary Sutherland." Her case is to be found in the next story, "Identity"—thus the mention of it here becomes meaningless to the reader.

"League" is widely considered one of the better Holmes shorts. When it was published, the basic plot idea—getting a character out of the way so that a criminal enterprise could be conducted—was original. Doyle, however, reused the same idea at least twice more—in "The Stockbroker's Clerk" from *The Memories*, and again in "The Three Garridebs," from *The Case-Book*. However, "League" is still notable for Holmes's investigation, and for its villain, the unforgettable noble rogue, John Clay, who clearly believes that the royal blood in his veins gives him license to lie, cheat, and steal.

"A CASE OF IDENTITY"

First publication: The Strand, September 1891
Structural type: A
Crime: None (?)
Evildoer: James Windibank, aka "Hosmer Angel"
Official police: None
Length: Approximately 6,000 words

This story is precisely what "A Scandal" was not: trivial. If it is worth mentioning at all, it is probably for its depiction of the giddy and none-too-intelligent Mary Sutherland and her Duchess of Devonshire hat. Note also the irony of Windibank's alias: it's an anti-aptonym—for whatever the man may be, he is anything but an "angel."

"THE BOSCOMBE VALLEY MYSTERY"

First publication: The Strand, October 1891
Structural type: A
Crime: Murder
Evildoer: John Turner (?)
Official police: Lestrade (first appearance in a short story)
Length: Approximately 8,000 words

Murder in a beautiful bucolic setting, leading to (of all things) a happy ending. Holmes succeeds in clearing an innocent man with some neat detective work. Lestrade is at his worst in this story, but Holmes one-ups him at the end.

Pleasant reading!

"THE FIVE ORANGE PIPS"

First publication: The Strand, November 1891
Structural type: A
Crime: Murder

> *Evildoers:* **Captain James Calhoun and his two mates on the bark**
> **"Lone Star"**
> *Official police:* **None**
> *Length:* **Approximately 6,500 words**

Holmes's young client, John Openshaw, is killed on his way home after consulting the detective. Taking this as a personal affront, Holmes turns all his powers to tracking down the killers. The American background helps make this story particularly relevant on this side of the pond. There's a wonderful atmosphere of storms, nicely integrated into the resolution of the story. A good one!

Historical note: The Ku Klux Klan was founded by some bored ex-Confederate soldiers in December 1865. At first it was a sort of joke to ride around the Tennessee countryside at night dressed in white sheets and pretending to be ghosts. But they soon found that the former slaves could be terrorized by what they saw, and the joke turned serious. The Klan movement spread rapidly through the South and soon organized under the leadership of the ex-slave trader and Rebel cavalry general, Nathan Bedford Forrest. By 1869, common criminals took to dressing in Klan costumes and things got out of control. Grand Dragon Forrest announced the dissolution of the Klan that year. No mention of Elias Openshaw ...

The contemporary Klan has no direct connection to the original group.

"THE MAN WITH THE TWISTED LIP"

> *First publication: The Strand,* **December 1891**
> *Structural type:* **Variation of A—there are four parts, but the story**
> **begins with Kate Whitney visiting Mary Watson to ask for help**
> **in finding her husband, instead of at Baker Street**
> *Crime:* **None (?) Opium smoking? begging?**
> *Evildoer:* **None**
> *Official police:* **Inspector Bradstreet**

| *Length:* Approximately 7,800 words

A refreshing departure from the norm, this offbeat story begins ominously, but ends in comedy. But note the implicit social criticism: a man can make more money by dressing up and acting as a beggar than he can at a regular job.

"THE BLUE CARBUNCLE"

| *First publication: The Strand,* January 1892 (First story of the
| second series)
| *Structural type:* A
| *Crime:* Jewel theft and false testimony
| *Evildoer:* James Ryder
| *Official police:* None
| *Length:* Approximately 7,000 words

A jewel of a story (pun intended)! This is that rare thing—a Christmas story without sentimentality, and exactly in keeping with the feeling of the season. Its villain is saved from a probable criminal future by Holmes's forgiveness. So well-written that the reader feels the market closing, and the frustration of Ryder at finding that his goose has been sold by his sister. And the story ends in the best possible way as Holmes and Watson sit down to their Christmas dinner—a goose.

Note: The way Holmes gets information from Breckinridge the gambler is classic psychology. I can think of few Christmas stories as good as this.

"THE SPECKLED BAND"

| *First publication: The Strand,* February 1892
| *Structural type:* Variation of A—four sections but with an action
| beginning at the start of section two.

Crime: murder
Evildoer: Dr. Grimesby Roylott Official Police: None
Length: Approximately 8,400 words—the longest story in The
   Adventures

"A real creeper!"—as Doyle later said of *The Hound*. He once called this his own favorite story. It is the most atmospheric of the early Holmes short stories and unforgettable after even a single reading. And while there are at least two technical flaws in it—snakes do not like milk, and it seems unlikely that the broken-down walls of the Roylott estate could keep the cheetah and the baboon from taking off—Dr. Doyle was unconcerned about these little matters. Chances are few of his readers care either.

The more important thing about *Band* is that it introduces for the first time in the Holmes canon the concept of "guilt by inheritance." The despicable Dr. Roylott was hardly the first member of his family to leave the straight and narrow path, though he was certainly the last. Helen Stoner, in her first statement of the case to Holmes, recounts the steady decline of the Roylotts through "four successive heirs ... of a dissolute and wasteful disposition" during the eighteenth century, and of completion of the family's ruin by a gambler during the days of the Regency (in the first part of the nineteenth.) From one of the richest landed families in England, the Roylotts became the owners of nothing but a heavily mortgaged house and a few acres of ground. The present squire, Dr. Grimesby Roylott, took a medical degree and went out to India, but his career there was ended when, in a fit of anger, "he beat his native butler to death and narrowly escaped a capital sentence." Miss Stoner goes on, a paragraph or two later, to tell us that "violence of temper approaching to mania has been hereditary in the men of the family," and she ends by remarking how her stepfather had become the terror of the village, with his great strength and absolutely uncontrollable anger. The concept of evil in the blood, coming down from one generation to another, will be seen on several occasions in the Holmes canon, ending with the author's greatest work—*The Hound of the Basker-villes*. It must have been on Dr. Doyle's mind for several years, and it is one of the principal themes in his detective stories.

It should also be noted that Dr. Roylett's motive for murder of his stepdaughter Julia has been borrowed from "A Case of Identity," where it appears in a trivial context. This time there is nothing trivial about the motives or the crime. We need go no further than Shakespeare to see how the same material may be used as the stuff of both comedy and tragedy, according to the author's purpose.

"THE ENGINEER'S THUMB"

First publication: The Strand, March 1892
Structural type: A (four sections)
Crime: Counterfeiting, attempted murder, assault and battery
Evildoers: "Lysander Stark," "Dr. Ferguson" (aka "Dr. Becher")
Official police: Inspector Bradstreet (n.b. "Twisted Lip")
Length: Approximately 7,000 words

Like its immediate predecessor, "The Speckled Band," in its evocation of midnight horrors. Also like "The Man with the Twisted Lip"—not only because Inspector Bradstreet appears in both stories, but also because Watson initiates the action (or helps to do so) in both. Notable also for its use of "the enigmatic clue"—in which direction from the station was the house? Holmes answers this poser with a brilliant deduction.

This is the only detective story I can think of in which a character loses a thumb—a unique and memorable plot device. Also unique, at least in the Holmes canon, is the ending—the criminals get away scot-free. Also at the end, the victim, Victor Hatherly, remarks, ruefully, "I have lost my thumb, and a fifty-guinea fee, and what have I gained?" Holmes answers him with a laugh: "Experience," he says. This reply is hardly in good taste—but the same question will be asked in other stories, where the answers are not jocular as this one is intended to be.

"THE NOBLE BACHELOR"

> *First publication: The Strand*, April 1892
> *Structural type:* A, with a very short first section (one paragraph)
> *Crime:* None
> *Evildoer:* None (but the Noble Bachelor does not act very nobly)
> *Official police:* Lestrade
> *Length:* Approximately 7,000 words

Interesting, in that the affronted party (Lord St. Simon) becomes "the bad guy" at the end. While he does nothing illegal, his overweening pride and attitude towards those of lower social standing is intolerable, and he emerges as the most unpleasant person in an otherwise appealing cast of characters. Lestrade, too—as in other early stories—comes off as a jerk. The story is most notable for its original plot, and for the final banqueting scene in which Holmes foresees a union of the United States and Great Britain.

"THE BERYL CORONET"

> *First publication: The Strand*, May 1892
> *Structural type:* B
> *Crime:* Robbery
> *Evildoers:* Sir George Burnwell, Mary Holder
> *Official police:* none
> *Length:* Approximately 8,000 words

This story is unique in the canon; it may be thought of as Doyle's riff on Bunyan's Pilgrim's Progress. As in that work, each of the characters in this story has been given an aptonym—the author's most extensive use of this device in the entire Holmes canon. (See my essay on names in the part of this book which follows the short story catalogue.)

"THE COPPER BEECHES"

> *First publication: The Strand,* June 1892
> *Structural type:* A, with an extended opening section—the exact
>   reverse of the form used in "The Noble Bachelor"
> *Crime:* False imprisonment
> *Evildoer:* Jephro Rucastle
> *Official police:* None
> *Length:* Approximately 8,000 words

If "The Beryl Coronet" recalls Bunyan, this story is Doyle's take
on a conventional "Damsel in Distress" tale. Here we have all the
elements: a lonely house; a mysterious locked attic room; a weird,
threatening master; a dangerous dog; glum if not grim servants—
the works. Notable for the use of malicious laughter to signal evil
and create fear. Also, for the third time in *The Adventures,* we find
the motive of "stepdaughter's money," as in "A Case of Identity" and
"The Speckled Band."

In this story, Dr. Doyle out-Dickens Dickens in coming up with
the name "Jephro Rucastle" for the villain. (See again the essay on
names in the Holmes canon, which appears after my thoughts on the
short stories.) Here also we meet Carlo, the mastiff—a true ancestor
of the Hound of the Baskervilles: "as large as a calf, tawny-tinted,
with hanging jowl, black muzzle, and huge projecting bones." Dr.
Doyle could create every sort of emotional response—including
horror—in his readers.

With this story, we conclude our look at the first two sets of
Holmes short stories.

Personally, I think that "A Scandal in Bohemia" is the best of
the lot, followed by "The Five Orange Pips," "The Speckled Band,"
"The Blue Carbuncle," "The Red-Headed League," and "The Man
with the Twisted Lip"—not necessarily in that order.

CHAPTER 3

The Memoirs of Sherlock Holmes

THIS COLLECTION WAS FIRST PUBLISHED IN BOOK FORM BY NEWNES IN 1893.

"SILVER BLAZE"

First publication: The Strand, December 1892
Structural type: B (Three sections)
Crime: Fraud
Evildoers: John Straker (aka William Darbyshire); Silas Brown
Official police: Inspector Gregory
Length: Approximately 8,500 words

One of the two Holmes short stories with a horse racing background (the other is "Shoscombe Old Place," from *The Case-Book*). It has an original plot, including a credible red herring, some fine reasoning by Holmes, and a nicely handled relationship between the detective and the skeptical Colonel Ross.

However, this story will always be recalled for its classic "Sherlockismus," so-called. Colonel Ross asks, "Is there any other point to which you would wish to draw my attention?" Holmes replies, "To the curious incident of the dog in the nighttime." Ross says, "The dog did nothing in the nighttime." "That was the curious incident," remarks Holmes. Whatever you choose to call this conversation, it is great writing. The solution of the mystery, explained after the race has been won, is both surprising and deftly handled. "Silver Blaze" earns a place among the better stories in the canon.

"THE YELLOW FACE"

> *First publication: The Strand,* February 1893
> *Structural type:* A
> *Crime:* None
> *Evildoer:* None
> *Official police:* None
> *Length:* Approximately 6,300 words

Notice that a month-long gap appears between the first publication dates of "Silver Blaze" and "The Yellow Face." In fact there was a Holmes short story in *The Strand* issue for January 1893—"The Cardboard Box." But when Newnes compiled the stories for the book, *The Memoirs of Sherlock Holmes,* Conan Doyle withheld that tale: this is why *The Memoirs* consists of only eleven stories rather than the full twelve which had run in the magazine. It is said that the author felt queasy about "Box" because it includes a woman making a pass at a married man. Whatever the reason, "The Cardboard Box" did not appear in book form until it was attached to seven other stories and printed in *His Last Bow,* twenty-four years after its composition.

"The Yellow Face" is a slight story in which Holmes does practically no detection. Moreover, his theories about the case turn out to be completely wrong. Doyle may have written this tale to take some of the gloss off his detective: Holmes says to Watson at the end, "If it should ever strike you that I am getting a little over-confident in my powers, or giving less pains to a case than it deserves, kindly whisper

'Norbury' in my ear, and I shall be infinitely obliged to you." Ironically, it was Dr. Doyle himself who seems to have been guilty of a lack of care in the writing of this tale. The genetic premise on which it is based is flat-out impossible. Whether the author should have known that when the story was written in 1892, I cannot say—but he could and should have been more careful about using it if he was uncertain.

In any case, neither Holmes nor his creator shines in "The Yellow Face," which must be counted among the poorer stories in the canon.

"THE STOCKBROKER'S CLERK"

> *First publication: The Strand,* March 1893
> *Structural type:* A
> *Crime:* Robbery and murder
> *Evildoers:* The Beddington brothers, aka Arthur and Harry Pinner
> *Official police:* Sergeant Tuson (City Police); Constable Pollock
> *Length:* Approximately 6,000 words

Another reworking of the plot idea first seen in "The Red-Headed League"—i.e., getting someone out of the way so that a criminal enterprise could be carried out. The device of having one man portray two brothers is interesting, and so is Holmes's client, the young Cockney. The end of the tale, with the attempted suicide of the murderer's brother, points up the fact that blood can be thicker than water—even among criminals. All in all, a workman-like job, but by no means among the best stories.

"THE GLORIA SCOTT"

> *First publication: The Strand,* April 1893
> *Structural type:* Atypical—the entire story consists of Holmes's narrative to Watson, containing reported events and conversations, plus the written account of old J.P. Trevor (James Armitage)
> *Crimes:* Mutiny and murder

Evildoers: Jack Prendergast and company; Hudson? Beddoes?
Official police: None
Length: Approximately 6,000 words

This story and the one which follows it, "The Musgrave Ritual," form a pair recounting the story of the young Sherlock Holmes.

Hardly any writers can equal Conan Doyle in telling action / adventure stories, which is the genre to which "The Gloria Scott" truly belongs. It is a Sherlock Holmes story only in the fact that it recounts an incident from his university years, which gave him the idea that a profession might be made from what had been merely a hobby. If you took the first half of the tale away, you would have in the remaining narrative of James Armitage a rip-roaring account of mutiny aboard a convict ship—an account that simply aches to be made into a movie. It illustrates something that may be true in several tales in the canon: it features Sherlock Holmes, but it is not about him, beyond the few observations and deductions he makes about the elder Trevor. Robert Louis Stevenson might well have been the author: this is a story right down his alley. A great read, but not a great Holmes case.

"THE MUSGRAVE RITUAL"

First publication: The Strand, May 1893
Structural type: Again, atypical. There is a section one opening scene, but the rest of the story is entirely Holmes narrating his solution to the mystery of "the Ritual" to Watson. Because everything about the case happened years ago, the technique works in this story—the reader can follow the detective's thinking without compromising the solution of the case before the end.
Crime: Homicide? (perhaps accidental)
Evildoers: None? Perhaps Rachel Howells, perhaps Brunton
Official police: None
Length: Approximately 6,300 words

If "The Gloria Scott" story first gave Holmes the idea of becoming a detective, "The Musgrave Ritual" is the earliest account we have of him as an active investigator. We learn that this was his third case. The idea of "the Ritual" is original and perhaps unique, and the solution and the object found in the bag are brilliant. This is a tale that never grows old: it is one of my personal favorites.

"THE REIGATE SQUIRES" (OR "THE REIGATE PUZZLE")

First publication: The Strand, June 1893
Structural type: A
Crime: Murder
Evildoer: Alec Cunningham, "Old Mr. Cunningham"
Official police: Inspector Forrester
Length: Approximately 6,300 words

Another story in which heredity is a factor. This time, the criminals are a vicious son and his aged father: the relationship is said to be evidenced by their handwriting. I have no idea whether this analysis would be considered valid today. Likewise, the dominance of one writer over the other is attributed to the handwriting. Holmes, while recovering from a serious illness, is still strong enough mentally and physically to deal with the young Alec Cunningham, who is depicted as a completely evil man. But his victim, the coachman William Kirwan, is hardly an innocent victim: it seems clear that he, young Alec, and Annie Morrison formed an "eternal triangle," and that William was threatening to blackmail his employer. He seems to have miscalculated Alec Cunningham's reaction, and paid for his mistake with his life.

Note: The Cunninghams's neighbor is named "Mr. Acton." It is virtually impossible for an informed person to see or hear the name "Acton" without recalling Lord Acton and his famous comment: "Power corrupts, and absolute power corrupts absolutely." Could this not apply to young Mr. Cunningham?

"THE CROOKED MAN"

> *First publication: The Strand*, July 1893
> *Structural type:* A, with an extended first section
> *Crime:* Apparent murder
> *Evildoer:* Colonel James Barclay
> *Official police:* None
> *Length:* Approximately 5,100 words

A story of treachery and cruelty, with a plot whose origins go back nearly 3,000 years. Names are important in this story: the husband's name was James, and another man was Henry—but Mrs. Barclay was overheard by the maid to say, twice, "David," during an argument with her spouse shortly before his death. There is also the mysterious "Teddy," who adds a touch of the outré to tale.

Consider the title of this story for a moment. Conan Doyle uses a peculiar adjective here. It would have been just as graphic if the title had been something like "The Twisted Man" (n.b., "The Man with the Twisted Lip"), or "The Hunchback," or "The Crippled Man." Yet the author employs the word "crooked." Why? I suggest that Doyle was asking the reader to pose this question: just who in the story is "The Crooked Man?" Of course, the surface answer is obvious—Mr. Henry Wood, with his bent back and crouched posture. But then why not call the story "The Crippled Man?" Doyle uses the word "crippled" when recounting the statement of Miss Morrison, who witnessed the meeting of this individual with Mrs. Barclay.

So we are asked to think, "Who else in this story might be called crooked?" Thus we come to the dead man, Colonel Barclay—the officer who in order to clear his way to the hand of Miss Nancy Devoy, Deliberately ordered his underling into a trap. James Barclay was crooked indeed—morally crooked to the core. What is more, the author gives us clues to the moral state of the Colonel. Major Murphy tells Holmes of some peculiarities in the conduct of this "dashing, jovial old soldier." First, he was "acutely uneasy if he were absent from his wife for a day." Second, on occasions he showed himself "capable of considerable violence and vindictiveness." Third, "a singular sort of depression came upon him at times ... the smile had often been struck from his mouth, as if by some invisible hand ... For days on end, when the mood was on him, he had been sunk in the deepest gloom." His colleagues had noticed "a certain degree of superstition" which "took the form of a dislike to be left alone, especially after dark." It "had often given rise to comment and conjecture."

Are these not the signs of a guilty conscience? Compare Colonel Barclay's condition with that of another soldier with a dark stain in his past—Shakespeare's Macbeth, who, like Colonel Barclay, was afflicted "while joining in the gaieties and chaff of the mess table." (See the banqueting scene in the play, at which Macbeth is struck by a vision of the murdered Banquo.) This brings us to the central problem of the story: if neither Henry Wood nor Mrs. Barclay killed Colonel Barclay, who did? Wood gives the answer: "It was a just Providence that killed him." David was not punished for sending Uriah to his death in order to win Bathsheba—but three thousand years later James Barclay died for the same crime. Was this Doyle's way of saying that while justice may be long delayed, eventually God will punish the evil man? In short, this strange story may in fact be an affirmation of belief in the concept of moral justice. If this were not his intended message, why was the story written at all?

"THE RESIDENT PATIENT"

> *First publication: The Strand*, August 1893
> *Structural type:* A
> *Crime:* Murder
> *Evildoers:* Biddle, Hayward, and Moffat—the Worthington Bank Gang
> *Official police:* Inspector Lanner
> *Length:* Approximately 6,000 words

This case offers as good a picture of Sherlock Holmes at work as you will find in any of the short stories. He listens to Dr. Trevelyan's statement, goes immediately to Brook Street—where Blessington gives the party a less-than-friendly greeting—and after a short conversation, goes off, telling Blessington to tell the truth. The next morning Holmes receives a note from Dr. Trevelyan, and hurrying to the Brook Street house finds Blessington dead and the police on the scene. From the cigar ends and footprints, he deduces murder and recognizes a confederate in the house, suggesting that Lanner arrest the page. By four in the afternoon he has ascertained the identity of the three intruders, and the case is neatly solved within twenty-four hours after Holmes was first called in. The Greeks would be pleased!

As might be expected, Dr. Doyle writes frequently about physicians—good, bad, and nondescript. Dr. Trevelyan falls into the last category. Note too that Doyle once had a resident patient: he married the man's sister!

"THE GREEK INTERPRETER"

> *First publication: The Strand,* September 1893
> *Structural type:* A
> *Crime:* False imprisonment; murder
> *Evildoers:* Harold Latimer, Wilson Kemp
> *Official police:* Gregson (first short story appearance)
> *Length:* Approximately 6,300 words

The criminal elements in this story are commonplace, yet "The Greek Interpreter" must be given a place among the best of the Holmes shorts for two related reasons. First, it continues with the theme of inheritance of characteristics, and in so doing introduces us to one of literature's greatest characters—Sherlock's older and smarter brother, the amazing Mycroft Holmes. The "inheritance" theme leads us to meet Mycroft: in the first section of the story Sherlock and Watson are conversing when the subject turns to "atavism and hereditary aptitudes: How far is any singular gift in an individual due to ancestry and how far to his own early training?" Or to put the matter more succinctly, does the talent come from nature or nurture? Watson suggests that nurture is the key; Holmes agrees "to some extent." His own ancestors were country squires—nothing very distinguished there. But then he mentions his grandmother, speculating that he may have inherited his own talent from her. She was a sister of the French artist, Vernet. Holmes says, "Art in the blood is liable to take the strangest forms." (Here Dr. Doyle could speak from personal experience—his father's family was noted for drawing and cartooning, but he himself found a talent for writing.) "But how do you know it is hereditary?" Watson asks, and Holmes comes back with "Because my brother Mycroft possesses it in a larger degree than I do." And from here they are off for the Diogenes Club, and Watson's first encounter with Mycroft. What follows is one of the most wonderful scenes in the entire canon: Sherlock and Mycroft stand at the window, rivaling each other with brilliant streams of observation and deduction. In the end, Mycroft goes one-up on Sherlock by noting that the widower across the street has more than one child. This rapid-fire dialogue is the best thing in the story, and unmatched anywhere else in the canon.

We learn little more about Mycroft in this story, but later, in "The Bruce Partington Plans" (from *His Last Bow*) we hear more about Mycroft's true role in life. For now, I will only say that had Dr. Doyle wished to do so, he could have created in Mycroft Holmes the first and undoubtedly the greatest of all the armchair detectives in literature. Not Baroness Orczy's "The Old Man in the Corner," not Nero Wolfe (whom Rex Stout may well have based on Mycroft), nor any of the other detectives who solve crimes without moving about could ever have outdone Mycroft. And the concept of having two different detective brothers, vying with each other in works by the same author could have been a terrific monetary success.

"The Greek Interpreter" closes with the criminals found stabbed to death in Budapest. We never learn more than this: one wonders how Sophie Kratides managed it. Perhaps some new mystery writer will solve this conundrum someday.

"THE NAVAL TREATY"

> *First publication: The Strand,* October and November 1893
> *Structural type:* A, with elongated first and third sections
> *Crime:* Espionage
> *Evildoer:* Joseph Harrison
> *Official police:* Inspector Forbes
> *Length:* Approximately 11,000 words

This, the longest of the fifty-six Holmes short stories, employs a riff on the theme common to "The Red-Headed League" and "The Stockbroker's Clerk." In those stories, the challenge for the criminal is to keep someone away from the place where a crime is planned. Here, Holmes must keep a room occupied to prevent a planned crime from taking place.

Of the four Holmes stories dealing with espionage, this one is clearly the weakest. Aside from Lord Holdhurst, who, Watson says, "seemed to represent that not too common type—a nobleman who is truly noble," none of the other characters are particularly interesting. This is especially true of Joseph Harrison: far, far from the James Bond or Sidney Reilly model, he is just a selfish man who by pure chance gets an opportunity to steal a valuable document which he sees as a means of recouping his stock market losses—his sister's happiness or his future brother-in-law's reputation be damned. No dashing spy, he—just an ordinary commonplace villain.

"THE FINAL PROBLEM"

> *First publication: The Strand,* December 1893
> *Structural type:* Atypical. The hounds are the prey here!

Crime: **Attempted murder of Sherlock Holmes, by both Professor Moriarty and A. Conan Doyle**

Evildoers: **Professor Moriarty, Colonel Sebastian Moran (?)**

Official police: **Inspector Patterson (?) (not an active participant)**

Length: **Approximately 6,000 words**

Remarkable for its introduction of the master criminal, Professor James Moriarty, and for two brilliantly written scenes: the confrontation between Holmes and the Professor at Baker Street, and Watson's description of the Reichenbach Falls.

When Conan Doyle decided to kill off his great detective, he was practically forced to create "The Napoleon of Crime." No ordinary criminal or accidental death would suffice: only a criminal with the stature of a King of Crime could bring about the death of the King of Detection in a convincing manner. Also, this man could not be a conventional crook: he had to be an educated man with standing in society. And so the genius, Professor James Moriarty, the author of *The Dynamics of an Asteroid*, came into being.

But if Dr. Doyle really thought he was done with Holmes, he made the biggest miscalculation of his life. The legions of Sherlock fans simply would not stand for the loss of their favorite character. For six years, the pressure on Doyle to bring back Holmes grew ever heavier, and at last he gave in. His masterpiece, *The Hound of the Baskervilles*, was apparently begun in 1899, and appeared in serial form beginning in August 1901. Still, Doyle left himself a bit of wiggle room by dating the events in that novel in 1889, while Holmes was still alive. His final capitulation did not come until October 1903, when "The Empty House" was published containing a living Sherlock Holmes.

Note on the Reichenbach Falls Passage: When I was an undergraduate at the University of Chicago fifty years ago, I was lucky enough to take a course in Shakespeare from Professor Norman Maclean, a great teacher and later the author of *A River Runs Through It*, which became a popular movie. Dr. Maclean was discussing *Othello* one day, and he pointed out how the playwright did not merely *describe* the storm scene, when Othello's vessel struggles to reach safety at Cypress: he used language to *create* the storm. This is precisely what Conan Doyle does with the Reichenbach.

He begins like this: "It is indeed a fearful place." Then follows a stream of words which by their sight and sound generate that fear in the reader, emulating the sound of falling, rushing water: "torrent," "plunges," "abyss," "spray," and "smoke." Consider "shaft," with its hard *ft* sound; "hurls," "chasm," "glistening coal black rock," repeating the *s* sound of hissing water combined with the hard sound of those two *k*s; then "narrowing, creaming, and boiling," "pit," "roaring, flicking, and hissing," followed by "giddy," "whirl," and "clamor"— words which make one feel dizzy. Then come, in the last sentence of the paragraph, "peering," "breaking," and "black rocks"—again combining the "ing" sound with the hard *k* sounds, concluding with "listening," "half-human shout" and "booming out of the abyss."

I dare you, ladies and gentlemen, to read this passage aloud and not feel something of the power and danger of the waterfall being described. This is magnificent writing, far beyond the level of Dickens and his mawkish sentimentality. Conrad said that good writing should make you *see*: I go one step further and say that it should make you *feel*. That is what Conan Doyle does throughout this last story in *The Memoirs*. No wonder readers refused to accept the end of Sherlock Holmes!

CHAPTER 4

The Return of Sherlock Holmes

THIS COLLECTION WAS FIRST PUBLISHED IN BOOK FORM BY NEWNES, IN December 1905.

"THE EMPTY HOUSE"

First publication: The Strand Magazine, October 1903
Structural type: A (four sections) but with parts one and three
    expanded
Crime: Murder, attempted murder
Evildoer: Colonel Sebastian Moran—"the second most dangerous
    man in London"
Official police: Lestrade, now much more civil towards Holmes
                   Length: Approximately 7,200 words

STILL ANOTHER "INHERITANCE" STORY. LIKE HIS LATE employer, Moriarty, Moran had a tendency towards corruption, which began to evidence itself while he was still in India. This is important, in the way Dr. Doyle explains how Holmes remained alive after his encounter with

Moriarty at the Reichenbach Falls, and how he reappeared before Dr. Watson—who, for the first and only time in his life, fainted dead away. But the story is perhaps most interesting in the way the author permeates it with the imagery of the tiger hunt—note how often that animal is mentioned in this tale. After all, in "The Final Problem," Holmes was the hunted. Now, Moran still thinks of Holmes as the game—but in fact it is Holmes who entraps the man who believes he is the stalker, while he is actually the prey. At one point, Moran is described with "savage eyes and bristling mustache," and "wonderfully like a tiger himself." As with all the best Holmes stories, "The Empty House" is exceptionally well-written and completely unforgettable. It is indeed a triumphant return for Sherlock Holmes as well as for his creator, who once again began writing some of the best mystery fiction ever put on paper.

And yet, nobody is perfect. It is rare to catch Dr. Doyle out on a matter of grammar or syntax, but there is a glaring little mistake in the original text of the "The Empty House." While recounting his adventures after the death of Moriarty, Sherlock tells Watson that he "traveled for two years in Tibet therefore, and amused myself by visiting Lhassa and spending some days with the head Llama." Of course, he meant the foremost religious leader of Tibetan Buddhism—but the way he misspelled it, Doyle had Holmes paying a visit to the head South American pack animal. "Llama"—correctly pronounced "yama," as in Spanish—is not what the author meant at all. But this error survives uncorrected in *The Complete Sherlock Holmes Short Stories*, which was reprinted from the original text. It does not appear, however, in my one-volume *Complete Sherlock Holmes*.

"THE NORWOOD BUILDER"

> *First publication: The Strand*, November 1903
> *Structural type:* A
> *Crime:* Attempted fraud; bearing false witness

Evildoer: Jonas Oldacre
Official police: Lestrade

This is another story in which the author reuses a plot element which we have seen before. Holmes discovers the hiding place of the odious Oldacre by doing what Bartholomew Sholto did to find the treasure room in *The Sign of the Four*, thirteen years earlier. Still, this is a beautifully executed story, with Homes besting his old rival, Lestrade, who has been tweaking him throughout the tale. Holmes's deductions from the holograph will are truly fine, but the greatest thing about "The Norwood Builder" is the little piece of artistic philosophy it contains. Holmes remarks of Oldacre that "he had not that supreme gift of the artist, the knowledge of when to stop. He wished to improve that which was already perfect ... and so he ruined all." So far as I am aware, that "supreme gift" belonged to Doyle, and I have tried to be governed by it during my own career as a TV and radio personality, teacher, and writer.

"THE DANCING MEN"

First publication: The Strand, December 1903
Structural type: A
Crime: Manslaughter
Evildoer: Abe Slaney, "The Most Dangerous Crook in Chicago"
Official police: Inspector Martin, Sussex Constabulary
Length: Approximately 8,500 words

This story forms the first part of a trilogy which also includes the two tales which follow it: "The Solitary Cyclist" and "The Priory School." All three have a common underlying theme—the relationship between love and selfishness.

Also, "Dancing Men" is another example of a story where the crime is committed in England, but the backstory which leads to it comes from America. *A Study in Scarlet* and "The Five Orange Pips" share this same trait. So does "The Yellow Face," and we will find it again in full panoply when we come to *The Valley of Fear.*

The opening section of "Dancing Men" is a classic example of the same trick Dupin used on his nameless companion, and which Holmes denigrated in *Scarlet*—that is, breaking into his friend's thoughts with a pertinent comment. In this case, Holmes stuns his Boswell by saying, "So, Watson, you do not propose to invest in South African securities?" Watson is indeed taken aback. Holmes then explains his own thought process, and Watson responds, just as Holmes predicted—"How absurdly simple!" Then enters the client, Mr. Hilton Cubitt, bringing with him the first drawings of the dancing men. As more drawings appear, Holmes recognizes them as bearing messages, and again like Poe in "The Gold Bug," solves the mystery. To the reader in 1903, it may have seemed a great and almost magical accomplishment, but in truth the "Dancing Men" form the simplest sort of substitution cipher, taking no great intellect to decode.

Indeed, the story is most notable for its depiction of the tragic heroine, Elsie Patrick, and her luckless husband. Elsie is truly tragic, in that her own ruin and that of her husband stems from a flaw in her character—her inability to be open about her past and her unwillingness to trust her husband. This surely stems at least partly from the wide gulf which separates them: he, the scion of an old Norfolk family in England, she a girl from the rough-and-tumble young city of Chicago in far-off, wild America. Had she only been able to trust him, no shooting would have occurred. This same pattern has been encountered in "The Yellow Face," but the outcome in that story was far more pleasant than what happens here. That, however, is one thing that makes this the far better, deeper story—if the reader only sees beyond the little puzzle of the cipher to observe the much more serious problem between the Cubbits—which even Holmes can do nothing about.

Elsie loves Hilton, but her selfishness—her fear of losing him if she opens up to him—ruins both their lives.

"THE SOLITARY CYCLIST"

First publication: The Strand, January 1904

Structural type: A

Crime: Attempted forced marriage; abduction and assault; attempted murder or manslaughter

Evildoers: Williamson, "Roaring Jack" Woodley, Carruthers

Official police: None

Length: Approximately 6,500 words

At the beginning of this story, Watson writes that this case "did not permit any striking illustration of those powers for which my friend was famous," and he is surely correct. Holmes does very little detecting here: he sends Watson down to Charlington, berates him for not finding anything useful, goes to the scene himself, and comes back without much more data, but with a cut lip and a bump on his head, courtesy of Mr. Woodley—whom he sent home in a cart. About the only interesting thing in "Cyclist" is Carruthers's love (if it is really love) for his employee, Miss Violet Smith. Watson tells Carruthers to his face that what he sees as love, the doctor calls self-ishness: Carruthers admits that he could not tell Miss Smith of her danger because she would have left him if he did. Carruthers's reply is the essence of the story: "Maybe the two (love and selfishness) go together." Here we find the link between the previous story and this one, as well as its connection to "The Priory School," which follows. Unfortunately, while "The Solitary Cyclist" may link the three stories together, it suffers greatly by its placement between the tragedy of the Cubits, in which the possessive Abe Slaney cannot accept that Elsie now loves another and better man while she in turn cannot trust her husband and so brings on disaster, and the great tale of the Duke of Holderness, which follows. I regret having to say so, but not only is this story the weakest link in the love and selfishness trilogy, but one of the two poorest tales in *The Return* as a whole.

"THE PRIORY SCHOOL"

> *First publication: The Strand*, February 1904
> *Structural type:* B—action opening, and three sections corre-
>   sponding to the traditional three acts of a play (exposition,
>   development, resolution)
> *Crime:* Murder, kidnapping (?)
> *Evildoer:* James Wilder, Reuben Hayes, Duke of Holdernesse
> *Official police:* none
> *Length:* Approximately 10,500 words (among the longest stories)

Surely this is one of the most memorable and most important of all
the Holmes short stories. It opens with the dramatic entrance of the
marvelously named school headmaster, Dr. Thorneycroft Huxtable:
could anyone find a more perfect moniker for a pompous, self-im-
portant pedagogue?

But immediately afterward we readers get a shock: Dr. Huxtable
tells Holmes that His Grace, the Duke of Holdernesse, has offered a
reward of £6,000 for information about the whereabouts of his kidnapped young son and the man or men who have taken him. Up to
this moment, Holmes has always claimed that money was no importance to him and that his work was its own reward. Yet, he now
astounds us. "It is a princely offer," he says. "Watson, I think that we
shall accompany Dr. Huxtable back to the North of England."

This a stunner: before he knows anything at all about the case,
other than that the duke is involved, he drops everything—the Fer-
rers Documents and the Abergavenny murder which is about to
come to trial—and heeds the siren song of big money. Question: is
this out of character, as our previous acquaintanceship with Holmes
would suggest? Or is it in fact his true character, which he has taken
pains to keep hidden? "I never get your limits, Watson," the great
detective has said. Now Watson must be thinking of what is buried
deep in Holmes's personality. Perhaps we can theorize that Holmes
had had some previous experience with this great Duke which has

led him to dislike the man, to the point where he is obviously anxious to get his hands on that reward. But we have no data: we can only surmise. However, it is clear from the beginning that Holmes has little respect or feeling for this nobleman.

Again in this story we find the theme of love and selfishness at the heart of the plot. The Duke of Holdernesse may be a great statesman, but he is a terrible husband and father. Because his elder son, James Wilder, reminds him of his former mistress (who was Wilder's mother) he puts his younger son and legitimate heir in dire peril at the hands of Wilder and his brutal associate, Reuben Hayes. Lord Saltire is lured away from the school by a phony communication from his mother, the Duchess, who lives in France apart from her husband. The German teacher, Heidegger, sees him leaving in the company of a man on horseback and pursues on his bicycle, only to meet his death at the hands of Hayes. The duke's selfish behavior in giving in to anything James wants thus leads to murder as well as kidnapping.

But there is another dimension to "The Priory School" which we have not yet discussed. By first pursuing and then collecting the reward which the duke has offered for discovering the whereabouts of young Lord Saltire and the identity of those who are keeping him, Sherlock Holmes puts himself in the position for all practical purposes of blackmailing the duke to keep the nobleman's complicity quiet. For the first time we see Holmes on the wrong side of the law—but it will not be the last time. What is more, he also implicates Watson in the crime: the Duke has offered £6,000 reward, but writes a check for £12,000: presumably because both Holmes and his friend will be expected to keep the Duke's participation in covering up the crime out of the papers. Watson writes nothing more about the incident, but it is unlikely that he rejected the reward.

This will not be the last time Holmes induces his Boswell to commit a crime, either. One wonders if Doyle was influenced in turning Holmes into a lawbreaker by his brother-in-law, E.W. Hornung, who in 1898 had created his own series of stories featuring Raffles, the gentleman crook who uses his cricket playing to act as cover for his criminal career. Hornung in fact dedicated the first Raffles stories to Doyle. Was turning Holmes into a blackmailer Doyle's salute to his brother-in-law? Just a thought.

Whatever else one says about it, "The Priory School" is a terrific read. From the first page to the last, it captures the reader's attention and never lets go until Holmes pockets the Duke's check at the end with the line, "I am a poor man." Every character in the story— from the ignoble duke (and the ignoble Holmes!) down to Herr Heidegger; his surly killer, Wilder's accomplice, Hayes; and Wilder himself—is so vividly depicted that we seem to have met them in person. Holmes's observation of the cattle tracks in the morass is positively brilliant, and his accusation of the Duke to his face makes a great climax. "The Priory School" is, to me, among the foremost Holmes short stories.

"BLACK PETER"

> *First publication: The Strand,* March 1904
> *Structural type:* Classic A (four sections)
> *Crime:* Murder; manslaughter?
> *Evildoers:* Patrick Cairns, Peter Carey
> *Official police:* Stanley Hopkins (his first appearance)
> *Length:* Approximately 7,000 words

After the intensity and complexity of "Priory," we might have expected a letdown in the story which follows it. In fact, we get nothing of the sort. "Black Peter" is a classic example of Sherlock Holmes at the top of his form as a detective. It is also remarkable for its unique murder weapon, and finally for introducing a young Scotland Yard inspector named Stanley Hopkins, of whom more will be said later. He appears in three Holmes shorts (the other two are also from *The Return*: "The Golden Pince-Nez" and "The Abbey Grange.") We are told early in the story that he was "a young man for whose future Holmes had high hopes, while he in turn professed the admiration and respect of a pupil for the scientific methods of the famous amateur." On the basis of what he does and does not do in this case, however, one wonders if Holmes's fondness for Hopkins may be based more on Hopkins's admiration and respect for the master than on his own talents as a detective. In none of the three cases in which he appears does he show any more ability than Lestrade, or Gregson, or any of the other Scotland Yarders who populate the canon.

"Black Peter" is probably the only detective story ever written in which the murder weapon is a harpoon. But then, Conan Doyle is almost certainly the only detective story writer who actually served on a whaling ship and had a personal acquaintance with that instrument. In 1880, he was a surgeon on the whaler *Hope* for eight months, so he knew just what strength and skill was required to drive a harpoon clean through a man's body and deep into the wooden wall behind. Incidentally, the *Hope* operated out of the port of Peterhead, which may have influenced the author when he chose a first name for Captain Carey.

If there is anything to regret in "Black Peter" it is that we do not get to witness the scene of Sherlock Holmes in the back of the butcher shop, trying futilely to transfix the carcass of a pig with a huge harpoon. He succeeded only in satisfying himself that by no exertion of his strength could he pin the pig to the wall by a single blow. When asked if he would like to try, Watson demurs: "Not for the world," he replies. (I am confident that he speaks for every reader of the story over the past century-plus, unless there happened to be a real nineteenth-century harpooner among that crowd.) At this juncture, the young Inspector Hopkins interrupts their conversation. It appears that he had no inkling that harpooning a man to a wall was a task far beyond the capability of an ordinary man. When his prime suspect, young Neligan, was found trying to break into the cabin on the next night, he proved to be a frail, timid landsman as incapable of this killing as a newborn babe—yet Hopkins still refused to give up his theory of the case. No wonder that I suspect the extent of Hopkins's supposed talent for detection.

Actually, the case turns on two sets of initials—the "P.C." on the tobacco pouch found at the crime scene, and the "J.H.N." and "C.P.R." from the notebook. Hopkins gets off the track right at the beginning of his investigation because he simply assumes that the initials "P.C." stand for "Peter Carey"—even though Black Peter had no pipe and Hopkins already knew that he smoked very little. Hopkins never even explored the possibility that the "P.C." who owned the tobacco pouch was someone other than the victim. Is this good detection? Holmes says that he is disappointed in Hopkins, as well he has a right to be.

"Black Peter" succeeds as a story mostly because of Doyle's great skill as a storyteller and master of the English language. But it does succeed—a first-class tale reeking with the smell of the sea, which holds its own among the other wonderful stories in *The Return*.

"CHARLES AUGUSTUS MILVERTON"

> *First publication: The Strand Magazine,* April 1904
> *Structural type:* A, with a very short first section—one paragraph
> *Crime:* Blackmail, murder, burglary
> *Evildoers:* Milverton; Holmes, and Watson (!); an unidentified lady
> *Official police:* Lestrade (only after the fact)
> *Length:* Approximately 5,700 words

Another winner! This story has everything—a malicious villain, an unnamed but brave heroine, and knightly behavior in the tradition of chivalry by a couple of burglars who, fortunately for them, are not caught. It has one of the many midnight vigils which occur in the canon, except that this one has the added complication that Holmes and Watson are themselves in peril. No better-written story exists or could exist: the emotional content, the intensity, and the danger make the reader feel as if he or she is behind that curtain in Milverton's study.

Milverton himself is a masterpiece of characterization—"an evil Pickwick," he is probably the creepiest villain in the whole canon. Consider the following description: "His voice was as smooth and suave as his countenance, as he advanced with a plump little hand extended, murmuring his regret for having missed us at his first." The "smooth and suave" voice and countenance as described make one just feel the oil and the falseness of the man. Also those two adjectives—"a plump little hand"—make one's skin crawl over the man's total insincerity. Then there is his smile, for which the author found perfect adjectives—"frozen," and later, "insufferable." One truly despises Charles Augustus Milverton, perhaps more deeply than any other villain in the canon including Professor Moriarty, for to evil Milverton adds the additional sin of total and patent insincerity. This writing deserves the highest praise, for it makes you *feel*.

One other thing about "Milverton": in "The Priory School," Holmes may commit blackmail, but in this story of blackmail, both he and Watson clearly and unequivocally commit the crime of burglary. Certainly, their motive is pure enough, but had they been caught, that would not have spared them the most serious legal consequences.

"THE SIX NAPOLEONS"

> *First publication: The Strand*, May 1904
> *Structural type:* B—three sections, opening with Lestrade's visit to Baker Street
> *Crimes:* Burglary, murder
> *Evildoer:* "Beppo" (second name unknown)
> *Official police:* Lestrade
> *Length:* Approximately 7,200 words

Another well-written story, although this time the plot is not original: aside from the murder, it is a reworking of "The Blue Carbuncle." The criminal must find a way to get away with a stolen jewel: in "Carbuncle," he uses a live goose; in this story, it's a plaster bust of

Napoleon. The details are different, but in each case, it is Holmes who finds and secures the gem.

"Napoleons" is particularly interesting for its glimpse of the Italian section of London. Inspector Hill is never seen, but his knowledge of the Saffron Hill Italian colony is a key to the solution of the case. The characters are vividly drawn, and include: Pietro Venucci; Horace Harker, the frustrated newspaper man who cannot get a scoop on a story which takes place at his own front door; "the big, blond German" manager at Gelder and Company; Mr. Sandeford of Reading, who doesn't want to take advantage of Holmes, who has promised to pay ten pounds for a bust that cost Sandeford just fifteen shillings; and Lestrade, now much more a colleague of Holmes than the sneering rival he was formerly. Holmes's key contribution to the solution is that the busts were broken only in places where there was light to see by, leading to the conclusion that the thief was looking for something when he smashed them. Altogether, still another excellent story—well-imagined and, as usual in *The Return*, flawlessly executed.

"THE THREE STUDENTS"

> *First publication: The Strand*, June 1904
> *Structural type:* A
> *Crime:* None, although academic cheating is attempted
> *Evildoer:* None, although Gilchrist might have become one
> *Official police:* None
> *Length:* Approximately 5,700 words

Mixed into this series of fine stories we find this trivial one. It was as if Conan Doyle was getting his breath after four strenuous efforts; this and the two stories which immediately follow it are relatively pedestrian. In the "The Three Students" there is virtually no action and not much detecting by Holmes. The characters are less brilliantly portrayed, and by the end the reader may well feel cheated—"Is that all there is?" Almost certainly the weakest story in *The Return*.

"THE GOLDEN PINCE-NEZ"

First publication: The Strand, July 1904
Structural type: Classic A
Crime: Homicide
Evildoer: "Professor Coram," aka Sergius; "Anna"
Official police: Stanley Hopkins
Length: Approximately 7,800 words

In this, the second Stanley Hopkins case, the young detective shows hardly any more talent for the profession than he did in "Black Peter." He is amazed and astonished at the deductions Holmes makes from the pince-nez glasses found in the dead man's hand ("To think that I had all that evidence in my hand and never knew it!"). Hopkins also misses the significance of the coconut matting in the corridors, and he is baffled by an enigmatic clue contained in the victim's last words: "The professor, it was she."

If Hopkins is in something less than top form in this story, so is Conan Doyle. It has several weaknesses, one of which is that we are given no explanation of how and why that convenient priest's hole, so important to the plot, just happened to be behind the bookcase in the professor's bedroom. For that matter, how did he know it was there? It's easy for the casual reader to simply skip over these questions, but the unexplained secret room does weaken the story. (Compare how the same author handles this problem so much more deftly in *The Valley of Fear*, twenty-one years later.)

This is also one of the many Holmes tales in which the action is set in England, but the backstory which supplies the motive is set in some other far-off country. Often that country is the US. He also employed India, South Africa, and Australia in this context, and in this story, he uses Russia. Dr. Doyle may have been the first detective-story writer to employ this device, but he was certainly not the last.

"THE MISSING THREE QUARTER"

> *First publication: The Strand*, August 1904
> *Structural type:* B Action opening (Overton's telegram)
> *Crime:* None
> *Evildoer:* None, although Lord Mt. James is nasty enough
> *Official police:* None
> *Length:* Approximately 7,500 words

Not so much a detective story as a tale of human tragedy, but with comic overtones: both Cyril Overton and Lord Mount-James are exaggerations of widely recognized types, and thus satiric and comic portraits. Yet the story ends in tragedy for two young people who should not be so burdened. Like Puccini's opera *La Bohème*, which was first performed two years later, this is a comedy with a tragic ending. An unusual if not unique combination in detective fiction!

"THE ABBEY GRANGE"

> *First publication: The Strand*, September 1904
> *Structural type:* Classic B, with the most famous opening lines in the
>   canon: "Come, Watson, come! The game is afoot. Not a word!
>   Into your clothes and come!"
> *Crime:* Apparent murder, which turns out to be homicide
> *Evildoers:* Sir Eustace, Jack Crocker (?)
> *Official police:* Stanley Hopkins
> *Length:* Approximately 8,000 words

This is certainly one of the best Holmes stories Dr. Doyle ever wrote. It has the most dramatic and unforgettable opening—the scene of the detective and the doctor riding through the silent streets on the way to Charing Cross at four in the morning on a bitter winter day is simply superior writing. It has a beautiful setting marred by domestic unhappiness. Every character is brilliantly portrayed: Sir Eustace is a drunken brute; Lady Brackenstall, an Australian commoner, is truly a noble woman; her maid, Theresa Wright, is more like a mother than a servant to Mary; and Captain Crocker is Prince Charming come to life. The story begins with Holmes on the wrong track, and it ends with another great scene: the "trial" and acquittal of the suspect.*

Holmes has his own struggle over what to do with his prime suspect in this case, and while we are told that Sir Eustace was killed while in a fair fight with the captain (who freely admits to it), Holmes realizes that if the police ever caught Crocker, "nothing on earth would save him." Holmes goes on to say, "Once or twice in my career I feel that I have done more real harm by my discovery of the criminal than ever he had done by his crimes. I have learned caution now, and I had rather play tricks with the law of England than with my own conscience."

Holmes never explains *how* he "learned caution," but if we read *The Return* carefully and consider its stories not merely as unconnected tales but in relation to each other, it is not hard to see what happened. In "The Priory School," Holmes in effect commits the crime of blackmailing the Duke. In "Charles Augustus Milverton,"

---

* I had just written the last sentence of the first paragraph—"The story begins with Holmes on the wrong track, and it ends with another great scene: the 'trial' and acquittal of the suspect"—when a bolt of lightning hit me. When Sherlock suddenly hustled Watson off the London-bound train because he was dissatisfied by his investigation at the Abbey Grange, I realized that this was a literal illustration of the phrase. Holmes and Watson wait at the station for a train going back to the Abbey—of course on the other track! Holmes returns to the scene of the crime, reopens his investigation and solves the mystery.

Since Dr. Doyle did not use the phrase "the wrong track" I cannot know whether this use of the railway phrase was intentional—but this may be the first, last, or only literal usage of the words "the wrong track" in all of literature.

he and Watson commit burglary to prevent the Lady Eva Blackwell from having her marriage to the Earl of Dovercourt wrecked by the blackmailer, Milverton. In short, Holmes has now himself been on both sides of the law: he has stood in Captain Crocker's shoes, having done a criminal act for a morally valid reason. It could have been Holmes himself who faced the serious charges of burglary had the results of his evening at Appledore Towers been different. At last, we meet for the first time the fully mature Sherlock Holmes, who has now learned the difference between the law and justice. How different is this Holmes from the somewhat egotistical young man of *A Study in Scarlet*! It has taken thirty-five appearances and seventeen years, but at the end of "The Abbey Grange," Sherlock Holmes has finally grown up.

As to Hopkins, he has, like the Bourbons, "learned nothing and forgotten nothing." In this, his last appearance, he completely ignores Holmes's hint about the missing silver, and walks out of the canon.

"The Abbey Grange" is the twelfth story in *The Return*, and it seems likely that when he wrote it, Dr. Doyle felt that having brought his character to full maturity, he was now done with Sherlock Holmes for good. This is a great story—but within a couple of months Conan Doyle apparently changed his mind, for he wrote a thirteenth story to conclude *The Return*—a story so remarkable that it surpasses even "The Abbey Grange" as the intended coda to the Sherlock Holmes series.

"THE SECOND STAIN"

First publication: The Strand, December 1904
Structural type: A: four sections with Watsonian introduction
Crime: Espionage, murder
Evildoers: Eduardo Lucas, Mme. Henri Fournaye, Lady Hilda Tre-
    lawney Hope
Official police: Lestrade
Length: Approximately 8,400 words

It appears that Dr. Watson, in his opening section of this story, is writing what Conan Doyle himself wished to tell his public: that there were to be no more Holmes stories. It is almost certain that Doyle had intended "The Abbey Grange" to be his finishing stroke, but nothing in that story specifically communicates that to the reader. Now, with the announcement that Holmes has retired to his beekeeping, Watson tells us that this story of espionage will be Holmes's last appearance in print. Of course, we know today that it was not—but Conan Doyle almost certainly meant it to be.

"The Second Strain" is the second story of espionage in the canon, following "The Naval Treaty" from *The Memoirs*: still to come were "The Bruce-Partington Plans" and the ultimate Holmes spy story, "His Last Bow," in which "Mr. Altamont" is the agent. "Stain" and "Treaty" are similar in that in both stories an important document, which could lead to war if it reaches the wrong hands, is stolen—and then seems to have disappeared. No great international catastrophe occurs, because in neither case does the document reach the market. The questions Holmes must answer in both cases are, "Why has the missing document not shown up? Who has it, and where is it?"

Despite the plot similarities, however, "Stain" is a far better story. Not only was the security in "Treaty" incredibly lax, making the tale impossibly unconvincing to present-day readers; not only were the characters in the story mere stick figures (excepting only Lord Holdhurst, the nobleman too poor to buy new boots): but also, the story lacks the excitement and tension that a spy tale ought to have. In "Stain" none of these criticisms apply.

There is, however, another reason why this final story of *The Return* is infinitely better than Doyle's earlier ventures into the espionage field. Let us take a closer look.

The action begins with the visit to Baker Street by Lord Bellinger, the Prime Minister, and his Secretary for European Affairs, Mr. Trelawney Hope. They tell of how the document was received—it was a letter from "a foreign potentate"; from his description, doubtless

Kaiser Wilhelm of Germany—and how it disappeared. Immediately after their departure, Holmes tells Watson how he plans to recover the missing document, and names the three most important foreign spies in London—the only three, he says, "capable of playing so bold a game." They are Oberstein (whom Holmes will encounter again later in the canon), La Rothiere, and Eduardo Lucas. "I will see each of them." But Watson, who has been reading the morning newspaper, informs his friend that Lucas was murdered the night before. Holmes says, "Well Watson, what do you make of this?" Watson's answer is, "It is an amazing coincidence."

Remember that comment—I believe that it is of vital importance in understanding the story. Holmes has hardly replied that "the odds are enormous against it being a coincidence," when Lady Hilda Trelawney Hope arrives—"the most lovely woman in London." She implores Holmes to tell her what was in the stolen paper. Of course, he cannot tell her, but he does go so far as to say, in answer to her question, that her husband's political career may suffer if the incident is not set right. Then she leaves, and Holmes wonders "What did she really want?" He then leaves the house asking Watson to remain on guard there in case more visitors show up.

For the next three days Holmes says nothing about the case to Watson as he dashes in and out. Watson finds a few more facts about Lucas in the newspapers; the valet, Mitton, is first arrested and then, having an alibi, he is released. On the fourth day, news from Paris arrives, about the mad Mme. Fournaye, whose husband turns out to have been Eduardo Lucas under a false name. She was seen watching the London house on the night of Lucas's murder, and upon returning to France showed signs of mania. Holmes expresses his frustration with the case—and just then Lestrade sends a note to Holmes indicating that something has occurred. Holmes and Watson proceed to the Godolphin Street house to meet the Scotland Yarder, who tells them of the discovery of the turned carpet, indicated by the stains on the rug and the floor. Lestrade himself seizes on the importance of this. "Who shifted the carpet, and why?" he asks.

Holmes tells him to question the constable on duty at the house: "Ask him how he dare admit people and leave them alone in this room. Don't ask him if he has done it. Take it for granted. Tell him you *know* someone has been here. Press him … " Lestrade does so, and Constable MacPherson confesses that he did let a young woman into the room. But then she saw the stain on the carpet and fainted. He tried to revive her with water, but could not, so he went around the corner to the pub for some brandy; when he returned the young woman had left. While Lestrade was getting this story out of MacPherson at the back of the house, Holmes threw back the carpet and found the secret cavity beneath it—but the hiding place was empty.

Holmes learned from MacPherson that the woman was tall and very pretty. On the way out the door, Holmes showed MacPherson a photograph. "Good Lord, Sir!" said the policeman on seeing the photograph. Then Holmes announces that the mystery is solved, and that there will be no war. The last section of the story is set at the Hope house; in it, we hear the whole story of how Lucas blackmailed Lady Hilda into giving him the missing letter in exchange for her own foolish letter, written before her marriage. She also explains how she was in the room when Mme. Fournaye broke into it, and how she witnessed Lucas putting the document she had brought into the cavity under the floor. Then she tells how she eventually got it back, and Holmes restores it to the dispatch box where Trelawney Hope finds it.

I have presented this recapitulation of the story in detail in order to put to the reader this one vital question: Just what did Holmes do to solve this mystery? He did not discover anything useful either about the murder of Lucas or about the whereabouts of the letter. Indeed, if not for the completely coincidental appearance of Mme. Fournaye on the scene of the meeting between Lucas and Lady Hilda, the case would never have been solved at all. Holmes had argued that the death of Lucas at the very time when the letter disappeared could not have been a coincidence: the odds against it would be enormous; "No figures could express them." And yet, Holmes is completely wrong; the events of the disappearance of the letter and the murder of Lucas by his estranged, maddened wife *did occur by pure coincidence.* The only real clue to the fate of the letter was discovered not by Holmes, but by his old Scotland Yard adversary, Inspector Lestrade! Perhaps one could argue that the Scotland Yarder did not grasp the full significance of his discovery—yet the fact is that it was Lestrade who noticed that the stain on the carpet and the stain on the floor did not coincide, and it was Lestrade who realized that the carpet had been turned and wished to know who turned it and why. This is just the kind of detail that Lestrade, and Gregson, and the other Scotland Yard detectives used to ignore, before Holmes taught them all to appreciate details. Now, ironically, it is Lestrade, using what he has learned from Holmes, who deserves the most credit for solving the mystery.

So, then, what am I pointing out? Simply that in this case, billed as his greatest triumph, the only thing Holmes brought to the solution of the case was the photograph of Lady Hilda which he carried and showed to Constable MacPherson as he and Watson left the Godolphin Street house. This story is ironic in the extreme: the murder has nothing to do with the disappearing letter; Holmes has hardly anything to do with the solution; and Lestrade is the man who appreciates the clue of the second stain—Lestrade, who so often was the butt of the jokes.

I believe that in what he clearly meant to be the last Sherlock Holmes story, Conan Doyle parodied the entire genre of mystery fiction. In the last line of the tale, Holmes (or was it Doyle?) says, "We also have our diplomatic secrets," and the secret in this story is that the author is hoodwinking his readers and making them like it.

Now I ask you—isn't this in a nutshell the whole art of mystery fiction?

In what he intended to be the last Holmes short, Dr. Doyle completed the circle that began with *A Study in Scarlet* back in 1887 with an ironic gem of a story in which Holmes contributes hardly anything to a tale of pure coincidence in which his old rival, Lestrade, finds the pertinent clue and discloses it to Holmes, rather than the other way around. What better way could the author have found to end (as he intended) his career as a writer of detective stories than to debunk and make fun of the whole genre?

COMMENTS ON *THE RETURN OF SHERLOCK HOLMES*

When one reviews the thirteen tales which collectively make up *The Return*, one is struck by the generally superior level of creativity and the high standard of writing which is characteristic of Conan Doyle's work during this period. Perhaps more importantly, the author here broadened the scope of the Holmes stories to include the trilogy of tales which concern themselves with the relationship of love and self-ishness, and Holmes's first appearances on the criminal side of the law and as he comes to recognition of the gap which sometimes exists between what is legal and what is just. We also find in *The Return* the tragic consequences of a wife's inability to trust her husband and a father's failure to manage his family life. At last, having done all this within the detective story context, Dr. Doyle wrote a masterpiece of irony in which he ridicules that entire genre by showing that things may come about by coincidence and that the Great Detective can be completely off-base. Read as a loosely integrated book rather than as a random collection of short stories, *The Return of Sherlock Holmes* joins its immediate predecessor, *The Hound of the Baskervilles*, as an example of literary entertainment which explores much deeper levels of human experience.

CHAPTER 5

His Last Bow

THIS COLLECTION WAS FIRST PUBLISHED IN BOOK FORM BY JOHN MURRAY (London, 1917), and George H. Doran (New York, 1917).

For four years after the first publication of "The Second Stain," Conan Doyle wrote no more Holmes stories. During this period, he published *Sir Nigel*, first in serial and then as a book. He stood for Parliament as the Unionist candidate for Hawick District, but was defeated in the election. In 1906 his first wife, Louisa Hawkins, Lady Doyle, died of tuberculosis, leaving Doyle deeply affected. During the following year he was successful in clearing the name and reputation of George Edalji, who had been convicted of cattle maiming largely because he was a dark-skinned native of India. Later that year he married again: this time, his bride was Jean Leckie, with whom he spent the last twenty-four years of his life. She was to bear him two sons and a daughter during the next five years. In January 1908, Sir Arthur and his new wife, now the second Lady Doyle, took up residence at Windlesham, Crowborough, Sussex, where he spent the remaining twenty-two years of his life. And in the autumn of 1908, the first new Sherlock Holmes story since "The Second Stain" was published in *The Strand*. It first appeared under the title "The Singular Experience of John Scott Eccles," but was later renamed "Wisteria Lodge" with the original title becoming the name of the first part of the tale while the second part was called "The Tiger of San Pedro." A second new story, "The Bruce-Partington Plans," appeared in December of the same year (1908), also in *The Strand*: then Doyle was silent about Holmes for another two years.

For the December, 1910 issue of *The Strand*, Conan Doyle produced another Holmes story—"The Devil's Foot"—and three months later, he published another, "The Red Circle," which appeared in the March and April numbers of the magazine. One more Holmes story, "The Disappearance of Lady Frances Carfax," was published in December 1911. Dr. Doyle then wrote no more until two years later, when "The Dying Detective," ran in *The Strand*'s December number. So over a period of nine years (1904–1913) Doyle wrote and published just six Holmes stories. He made up for it by producing the fourth and final Holmes novel, *The Valley of Fear*, which saw serial publication in *The Strand* between September 1914 (just after the opening hostilities of "The Great War") and May 1915. Holmes reappeared in the September 1917 issue, when *The Strand* published the last espionage story in the canon, "His Last Bow," and the next month these seven stories, plus "The Cardboard Box" (printed in *The Strand Magazine* back in January, 1893, but omitted when *The Memoirs* came out in book form later that year) appeared as a book, *His Last Bow*, with John Murray as publisher.

The stories in this collection do not appear either in order of writing or of publication. The following chart shows both order of publication and placement in the book version of *His Last Bow*.

Order of Publication	Order in the Book
"The Cardboard Box"	"Wisteria Lodge"
"Wisteria Lodge"	"The Cardboard Box"
"The Bruce-Partington Plans"	"The Red Circle"
"The Devil's Foot"	"The Bruce-Partington Plans"
"The Red Circle"	"The Dying Detective"
"Disappearance of Lady Francis Carfax"	"Lady Frances Carfax"
"The Dying Detective"	"The Devil's Foot"
"His Last Bow"	"His Last Bow"

Just who was responsible for the changed order of stories—the publishers, Conan Doyle, or both—and why the order was changed, I do not know.

His Last Bow as it appears in the book form is, therefore, a sort of grab bag of Holmes stories written over a period of fourteen years, and as in *The Return*, there are some relationships between the individual tales. We shall discuss these stories in the order in which they appear in the book.

"WISTERIA LODGE"

First publication: In 1908—it was originally published under a different title, but this two-part story was soon put together under the "Wisteria Lodge" name, with each of its two parts having names of their own.

Structural type: A—four sections with Watson introduction. The first two sections comprise part 1 ("The Singular Experience of Mr. John Scott Eccles"). The third and fourth comprise part 2 ("The Tiger of San Pedro").

Crime: Murder, kidnapping

Evildoers: "Mr. Henderson," aka Don Juan Murillo; "Lucas," aka Lopez

> *Official police:* Baynes (Surrey Constabulary), Gregson
> *Length:* Approximately 9,500 words

The theme of this story is the meaning and implications of the word, "grotesque." Holmes raises the question on the very first page of the tale, and he ends the discussion in the very last paragraph. "It is but one step from the grotesque to the horrible." One is reminded of Sherwood Anderson's book, *Winesburg, Ohio*—the "book of the grotesques." Perhaps the most notable thing about this story is the character of Baynes, the Surrey detective. If Stanley Hopkins was a disappointment, Mr. Baynes is the real thing—a detective in the very model of Holmes. Indeed, in this story, Mr. Baynes does nearly all the detecting: it is from him that we learn the identity of the mysterious "Mr. Henderson." I'm somewhat surprised that Doyle never used Baynes as the central character in a series of his own. "Wisteria" is a good example of detective fiction—except that the best detective work in the story is not done by Sherlock Holmes.

"THE CARDBOARD BOX"

> *First publication: The Strand,* January 1893
> *Structural type:* Classical A
> *Crime:* Double murder
> *Evildoers:* Jim Browner, Sarah Cushing
> *Official police:* Lestrade
> *Length:* Approximately 7,000 words

Whoever placed this story immediately after "Wisteria Lodge" had perhaps an inspiration, for "Box" is a perfect example of the grotesque melding into the horrible. The first section includes Holmes doing another Dupin—following Watson's train of thought by observing his features, especially his eyes, and then breaking in with a pertinent comment: "You are right, Watson. It [war] does seem a most preposterous way of settling a dispute." The action of "Box" begins with a newspaper account of a strange package sent to "Miss Cushing" of Croydon: a box containing two severed human ears. Lestrade has asked Holmes for help, so off to Croydon go the pair. They step into a human tragedy which moves Holmes to become philosophical: "What object is served by this circle of misery and violence and fear? It must tend to some end, or our universe is ruled by chance, which is unthinkable. But what end? There is the great standing perennial problem to which human reason is as far from an answer as ever." As I interpret these words, Holmes is asking the central religious question of the twentieth century: "Where is God?"

To that puzzler, as Holmes says, we have yet no answer. At the time "The Cardboard Box" was written, Conan Doyle had not yet expressed this sort of philosophical questioning in a Holmes story, but in the later part of the canon it becomes increasingly evident. It is possible that Dr. Doyle withheld "Box" from the first book publication of *The Memoirs* because he may have felt that such concerns were inappropriate to a detective story and would not be well-received by his readers. In any case, "The Cardboard Box" is a much better fit in the context of late Holmes than it would have been fourteen years earlier. In *His Last Bow* it relates back to "Missing Three Quarter" in *The Return* and forward to "The Veiled Lodger" and other material in *The Case-Book*.

"THE RED CIRCLE"

> *First publication: The Strand,* March and April 1911
> *Structural type:* Classic B (three sections)
> *Crime:* Homicide (self-defense)
> *Evildoers:* "Black Gorgiano:" Gennaro Lucca (?)
> *Official police:* Gregson, Leverton (Pinkerton's)
> *Length:* Approximately 6,500 words

How brilliant and subtle a writer was Conan Doyle? Consider this passage from "The Red Circle" (emphasis mine): "In the middle of the floor of the empty room was huddled the figure of an enormous man, his clean-shaven, swarthy face grotesquely horrible in its contortion and his head *encircled* by a ghastly halo of blood, lying in a broad wet *circle* upon the white wood work."

"It's Black Georgiano himself," cries the American detective, Leverton. Visualize, if you will, the scene—the leader of "The Red Circle" society lies dead in the center of a red circle of his own blood—ironic retribution for his crimes!

This is one of my favorites among the later stories, partly because of the dark atmosphere it creates; partly because Holmes is at his best in detecting the switch in lodgers almost from the beginning; and partly because I find Signora Emilia Lucca perfectly irresistible. But the real theme here is education: Watson asks why Holmes goes further into the case, when he has little to gain from it. Holmes replies, why did you study cases when you would get no fee? Watson's answer: "For my education, Holmes." Then comes the message: "Education never ends, Watson. It is a series of lessons, with the greatest for the last." Here again Holmes turns philosophical, and one cannot but believe that he is speaking for his creator as well as in character. At the very end of the story, Gregson remarks, "What I can't make head or tail of, Mr. Holmes, is how on earth you got yourself mixed up in the matter."

"Education, Gregson, education. Still seeking knowledge at the old university." Then Holmes goes on with a comment that links this story with "Wisteria Lodge" directly, and indirectly with "The Cardboard Box" as well: "Watson, you have one more specimen of the tragic and grotesque to add to your collection." Perhaps whoever arranged these first three stories in *His Last Bow* in this order did so because he saw them as a trilogy of grotesques, just as we found the three "love and selfishness" stories in "The Return" placed together to suggest the common theme which they share. If indeed this was the case, my money is on Conan Doyle himself as the arranger.

"THE BRUCE-PARTINGTON PLANS"

> *First publication: The Strand*, December 1908 (*Note:* This story was
> written and published more than two years before "Circle,"
> which it follows in the book collection. Why, if not to allow the
> three previous stories to appear together?)
> *Structural type:* Modified B—there is no action at the beginning,
> but neither do we have the typical Watsonian introduction,
> and the action begins a few paragraphs into the story, with the
> arrival of Mycroft's telegram
> *Crimes:* Espionage, murder
> *Evildoers:* Colonel Walter; Hugo Oberstein
> *Official police:* Lestrade, in his tenth appearance
> *Length:* Approximately 9,600 words—one of the longer stories in the
> canon

Surely this is among the very best Holmes shorts. "You have never risen
to greater heights." says Watson after Holmes's truly brilliant inspiration about the body proves to be true, and Watson is probably correct.
Not only that, but we find the pair about to break the law again by
entering Oberstein's house at night. Mycroft's presence alone is enough
to lift this tale out of the ordinary, and the midnight trap and capture
of the traitor is nicely handled. One question: Holmes says, "This was
not the bird that I was looking for." Who, then, was he expecting? This
we never find out. One more note: the story demonstrates that sub-
marines were on Doyle's mind as early as 1908: "Danger," his warning
essay about the threat of U-boat war to England, did not appear until
July 1914—just days before war broke out.

Before leaving this story, I wish to make some remarks about
the remarkable figure of Mycroft Holmes. When we first met him,
in "The Greek Interpreter," we are told little. "He has an extraordinary faculty for figures, and audits the books in some of the
government departments. Mycroft lodges in Pall Mall, and he walks
around the corner into Whitehall every morning, and back every

evening. From year's end to year's end he takes no other exercise, and is seen nowhere else, except only in the Diogenes Club, which is just opposite his rooms." We have had to wait fifteen years and nineteen stories until he makes his second full-fledged appearance (he has a cameo as a carriage driver in "The Final Problem"). Only now do we hear "what Mycroft is"—"the most indispensable man in the country." In fact, "occasionally, he *is* the British government."

Holmes goes on: "Well, his position is unique. He has made it for himself. There has never been anything like it before, nor will be again. He has the tidiest and most orderly brain, with the greatest capacity for storing facts, of any man living ... The conclusions of every department are passed to him, and he is the balance. All other men are specialists, but his specialty is omniscience ... In that great brain of his, everything is pigeon-holed and can be handed out in an instant."

Think about it for a moment or two, and you will realize that in the person of Mycroft Holmes, Sir Author Conan Doyle created the prototype of the modern computer. Al Gore may not have invented the internet, but in this story, dating from 1908, Dr. Doyle imagined a human data processing machine which "can focus on bits of information and say off-hand how each factor would affect the other." Should Doyle not get some credit for devising, out of his own unassisted brain, the concept of the modern intelligence-analyzing machine?

"THE DYING DETECTIVE"

> *First publication: The Strand,* December 1913
> *Structural type:* Modified B, in three sections—Mrs. Hudson comes
>   to Watson, Watson visits Holmes and is sent to get Smith, Watson
>   returns and serves as witness as Smith visits Holmes
> *Crimes:* Murder; attempted murder (of Holmes)
> *Evildoer:* Culverton Smith
> *Official police:* Inspector Morton (Scotland Yard)
> *Length:* Approximately 7,000 words

I have never been particularly fond of this story, probably because it is the premier example in the canon of Holmes's willingness to use and manipulate even those closest to him regardless of their own feelings. We have seen this side of Holmes before—remember his engagement to Agatha, the maid, in "Charles Augustus Milverton"? He trifles with her affections on the excuse that he needed information and had a rival who would cut him out—but he never considers how the girl might feel.

In this story, first he convinces poor old Mrs. Hudson that he is dying, getting her to bring Watson to him. Then he uses Watson most cruelly (pretending he is going mad) to get his old friend and partner to bring Culverton Smith to him. Question: why did he need to bring Watson into the case at all? Mrs. Hudson might just as well have been sent to Smith, while Inspector Morton hid behind the head of the bed to act as witness to the dialogue between Smith and his would-be victim.

This story has virtually no action at all, so it depends almost entirely on the author's use of language and dialogue for its success. Fortunately, Doyle was a master at using both descriptive language and conversational dialogue. Consider his description of Mr. Culverton Smith: "I saw a great yellow face, coarse-grained and greasy with heavy double-chin, and two sullen, menacing grey eyes which glared at me from under tufted and sandy brows. A high bald head had a small velvet smoking-cap poised coquettishly on one side of its pink curves. The skull was of enormous capacity, and yet, as I looked down, I saw to my amazement that the figure of the man was small and frail, twisted in the shoulders and back like one who suffered from rickets in his childhood." From that passage, can there be any doubt that this man is evil to the core? The words he speaks only serve to reinforce the conclusion one derives from his appearance, and indeed Culverton Smith is certainly one of the nastiest, most despicable villains in the entire canon—and not just because his intended victim is Holmes.

In later stories, Doyle relies on descriptions of faces, eyes, and mouths to help create and define his characters, especially criminals. Not for nothing was he the nephew of one cartoonist and grandson of another, and the scion of a whole family of artists and illustrators. Holmes says (in "The Greek Interpreter") that "Art in the blood is liable to take the strangest forms." In the case of his creator, it took the form of a great writer.

One other aspect of "The Dying Detective" is worth noting: Culverton Smith's motive for the murder of his nephew, young Victor Savage. It was to profit from a reversion—the motive that brought Mr. Stapleton to recreate the Hound of the Baskervilles. As I have noted before, the theme of the past governing conduct in the present is quite familiar in the canon of Sherlock Holmes.

"THE DISAPPEARANCE OF LADY FRANCES CARFAX"

> *First publication: The Strand,* **December 1911**
> *Structural type:* **Modified A—four sections, but the usual Watsonian**
> **introduction is replaced by a dialogue between Holmes and**
> **Watson concerning Watson's boots and a Turkish bath**
> *Crime:* **Robbery, false imprisonment, and attempted murder**
> *Evildoers:* **"The Reverend Schlessinger" (aka "Holy" Peters), and his**
> **wife, Annie**
> *Official police:* **Lestrade, again**
> *Length:* **Approximately 6,600 words**

I keep rereading this story, hoping to discover why it has always seemed flat, dull, and lifeless to me. I have yet to figure out the reasons, yet my reaction to the tale of the Lady Frances has never changed since I first read about her when I was about twelve years old. The central problem here is the question of how to dispose of a body, and Doyle's idea must have been original back in 1911. All the other elements of a rip-roaring read are present here, including a race against time—and yet, at least for me, the story of Lady Frances simply refuses to come alive.

"THE DEVIL'S FOOT"

> *First publication: The Strand,* December 1910
> *Structural type:* Classic A
> *Crime:* Two murders and two men driven to madness
> *Evildoers:* Mortimer Tregennis; Dr. Leon Sterndale (?)
> *Official police:* None
> *Length:* Approximately 8,500 words

Holmes calls this "The strangest case I have handled," and it very well might be. First, there is the scene—the further extremity of the Cornish peninsula. Here is Poldhu Bay, called by Watson "an evil place" because so many vessels have been wrecked there. Then there are the moors, similar in character to the scene of *The Hound*: Watson mentions "the glamour and mystery of the place, with its sinister atmosphere of forgotten nations" (a reference to prehistoric man). Too, "The Devil's Foot" is simply full of references to the Prince of Darkness: Mortimer Tregennis suggests that the first crime is devilish," and "not of this world." "Something has come into that room which has dashed the light of reason from their [his brothers'] minds. What human contrivance could do that?" When the Vicar comes to see Holmes the next morning, with the news of Mortimer Tregennis's death, his first words are "We are devil-ridden, Mr. Holmes! My poor parish is devil-ridden! Satan himself is loose in it!" Later, Dr. Sterndale says to Holmes, "I believe you are the devil himself!" However, it was not the devil himself, but the Devil's Foot root which caused the trouble, when employed by human agents. One of the things that makes this story important is Conan Doyle's use of a clue involving the sense of smell. In 1910 this had probably never been done before, although it has certainly been used since. In fact, Dr. Doyle himself reused the idea in one of his last Holmes tales, "The Retired Colourman." Ellery Queen employed a smelling clue in his novel *The Tragedy of Y,* over twenty years after "Devil's Foot," and I imagine other writers have also put the idea to good use.

Yet while the invocation of Satan and the use of a clue based on the sense of smell are important components of this story, there is still another dimension which demands recognition. Behind the whole sequence of events in Cornwall is the thwarted love between Leon Sterndale and Brenda Tregennis.

In love with each other for years, these two people were trapped by the legal and social structures of the times. Marriage was impossible for them, because Dr. Sterndale already had a wife. By the existing laws of Great Britain, he could not divorce her. That this situation should appear in the Holmes canon more than once is no surprise, given that for ten years (1909 to 1919, a period during which this story was written and published) Sir Arthur was president of the Divorce Law Reform Union. Presumably, he took the opportunity of this story to publicize how the present laws on divorce could not only cause great unhappiness but could even be a motive for murder.

For her part, Brenda Tregennis could not, according to the social code of the times, either live openly with a man not her husband or run away with him. Bound by mores of Edwardian England, she would have had no option but to wait patiently in the hope that Mrs. Sterndale would die. Thus, she sacrificed her happiness and lived a frustrated life for years—released only by her murder. This story of unhappiness and tragedy is the real "Cornish Horror," as the case was known. No wonder Dr. Sterndale had no problem with taking his revenge on the killer of the woman he loved. No wonder that Holmes, now aware of the gulf between law and justice, has no problem of conscience in sending Dr. Sterndale back to Africa rather than turning him over to the police to be tried for his action. These hidden, or at least not readily apparent, depths surely make "The Devil's Foot" one of the better stories among the later Holmes adventures.

"HIS LAST BOW"

First publication: The Strand, September 1917
Structural type: Variation of Type B—three sections, each being a

conversation between two characters: first, Von Bork and Baron
Von Herling; second, Von Bork and "Mr. Altamont"; third,
Holmes and Watson, with some comments from Martha the
servant and Von Bork.
Crime: Espionage
Evildoers: Von Bork; Von Herling
Official police: None
Length: Approximately 5,500 words

Very well-written and interesting, but in the last analysis, a piece of
wartime propaganda. The fourth and last Holmes story dealing with
espionage, it turns the table on the other three: in them, Holmes
protects England from the work of spies (although, as I have already
pointed out, he doesn't do much at all in "The Second Stain"). Here,
Holmes himself, in the guise of Altamont, the Irish American, is the
agent, seemingly working for (but really against) the German head
spy, Von Bork. As in "The Dying Detective," we get to witness the
great detective as a great actor, and I'm not sure that his performances in that role aren't at least as good as his work in detection.
As Altamont, he is superb; his American slang rings true, and his
daring to suggest that his principal, Von Bork, may be giving away
his own agents is a psychological stroke of genius: it convinces Von
Bork of Altamont's worth and reliability. Baron Von Herling, Von
Bork's boss as Secretary of German legation, also rings true: his long
talk with his top agent about what Britain will or should do when
the German army marches through Belgium to attack France might
have been overheard by a spy, it is so realistic.

But at the end, "His Last Bow" collapses into melodrama with
Holmes's stagy speech to Watson about the east wind coming, and
the last sentence of the story recalls the avaricious Holmes of "The
Priory School." The story may be very good propaganda, but propaganda is not literature.

This fourth collection of Holmes short stories is by no means
completely inferior to its predecessors: it contains at least one jewel of

the first water ("The Bruce Partington Plans"), and "Wisteria Lodge," "The Red Circle," and "The Devil's Foot" are all very good indeed. The other three stories are, to me, less effective—"The Dying Detective" because it presents an unpleasant side of Holmes's character; "Lady Frances" because it just doesn't catch fire for me, and "His Last Bow" because it lowers the purpose of the story to the level of melodramatic propaganda. Still, even less than top-level Holmes is still Holmes, and we are lucky to have as much of him as we do.

CHAPTER 6

The Case-Book of Sherlock Holmes

AFTER THE PUBLICATION OF *HIS LAST BOW* IN 1917, A FULL DECADE WAS TO pass before the fifth and last collection of Sherlock Holmes short stories, entitled *The Case-Book*, appeared in print on both sides of the Atlantic, published by John Murry (London, 1927) and George H. Doran (New York, 1927). The twelve tales which comprise it were written intermittently between 1921 and 1927, and all appeared first in *The Strand Magazine*.

As was true of *His Last Bow*, the book editors did not simply arrange the stories in the order of publication. The chart on the next page will show both the order of magazine publication and the sequence of stories in the book.

All the stories in *The Case-Book* were written after the death of the author's eldest son (1918) and brother (1919), and all but one, "The Mazarin Stone," after the passing of his mother in 1921. The entire *Case-Book* postdates his announcement of his belief in spiritualism, "The New Revelation," which came in 1918.

The Case-Book reflects a change in Dr, Doyle's postwar thoughts and feeling. Of the twelve stories

Stories in Order of Magazine Publication	Stories in Order of Appearance in the Book
"The Mazarin Stone" (October 1921)	"The Illustrious Client"
"Thor Bridge" (February and March 1922)	"The Blanched Soldier"
"The Creeping Man" (March 1923)	"The Mazarin Stone"
"The Sussex Vampire" (January 1924)	"The Three Gables"
"The Three Garridebs" (January 1925)	"The Sussex Vampire"
"The Illustrious Client" (March 1925)	"The Three Garridebs"
"The Three Gables" (October 1926)	"Thor Bridge"
"The Blanched Soldier" (November 1926)	"The Creeping Man"
"The Lion's Mane" (December 1926)	"The Lion's Mane"
"The Retired Colourman" (January 1927)	"The Veiled Lodger"
"The Veiled Lodger" (February 1927)	"Shoscombe Old Place"
"Shoscombe Old Place" (April 1927)	"The Retired Colourman"

in this collection, only four have a crime in them, and only three have a true villain. Holmes is depicted now as far more humane: the emotionless, thinking machine of the early stories is gone, and replaced by caring individual who feels deeply. Indeed, when "Killer Evans" shoots Watson in "The Three Garridebs," Holmes shows real injury. "If you had killed Watson," he says, "you would not have got out of this room alive." In several of the tales in this volume, Holmes acts more like a counselor than a detective—especially in "The Veiled Lodger"—and he is philosophical in "The Three Gables," "The Lion's Mane" and "The Creeping Man." As we have been doing with all the previous Holmes short stories, we will take up the twelve tales in *The Case-Book* one by one, in the order in which they appear in the collection rather than in order of writing or date of original publication.

"THE ILLUSTRIOUS CLIENT"

First publication: The Strand, February and March 1925
Structural type: A, with an expanded third section
Crimes: Assault and battery; burglary; vitriol-throwing
Evildoers: Baron Gruner, Sherlock Holmes, Kitty Winter
Official police: None
Length: Approximately 8,500 words

In some of the later stories, Conan Doyle uses the device of irony, and this tale is simply full of it. The former criminal, Shinwell Johnson, and the prostitute, Kitty Winter, are on the side of virtue. The nobleman, Baron Gruner, is not only a wife-killer but also a Casanova who likes to write about his conquests in a "lust diary." The detective, Sherlock Holmes, commits burglary, but is never arrested or tried for his crime, owing to the influence of his "Illustrious Client." The putative heroine, Violet De Merville—whom that client is endeavoring to save from a dangerous marriage to the murderous Baron—wants nothing more than to be wed to the brute, and is finally dissuaded not by Holmes nor by Kitty Winter nor by any other outside agency, but by the Baron's own hand. This headstrong and stupid woman is moved by nothing except the Baron's lust diary, and this is the final and greatest irony of all. Except for "The Second Strain," which we have noted previously, "The Illustrious Client" is Conan Doyle's most completely ironic Holmes story.

Some further comments on Miss Violet De Merville: Sir James Damery refers to her in glowing terms: "young, rich, beautiful, accomplished, a wonder-woman in every way." Yet, when I think about her, I see another side: a woman so attached to the Victorian ideal of womanhood that she seems to *want* to be used and abused by the man she thinks she loves. She will hear nothing against him, even when she is told that he murdered his first wife. She sees herself as a heroine, willing to make any sacrifice for Baron Gruner—even to give up her life for him, in the name of love. One wonders how she feels about herself: she cannot possibly have had much self-esteem. Therefore, she adopts an inhuman, almost insane view of the proper place for members of her sex in the world—to give all for her man, however badly he may treat her. She sees this sort of selfless sacrifice as heroic, and casts herself as a heroine according to the mores of her time and class. Her most telling remark, however, is this one about Baron von Gruner: "If his noble nature has ever for an instant fallen, it may be that I have been specially sent to raise it to its true and lofty level." Here she grants the possibility that the Baron is a devil, but casts herself in the role of his savior. If this self-deceiving, fantasy-living, headstrong person is "a wonder-woman in every way," heaven help the world.

"THE BLANCHED SOLDIER"

First publication: The Strand, November 1926
Structural type: Atypical, because the story is narrated by Holmes in the first person. There are four sections, as in a Type A tale, except that instead of a Watsonian first section we get a Holmesian explanation of how he came to write the story, together with a telling comment on the demands of the form and a paean to Watson as "an ideal helpmate." Also, section four consists of Holmes retracing the steps by which he solved the mystery. But he then goes on to introduce Sir James Saunders, who acts as a sort of deus ex machina in announcing that Holmes's solution

is wrong; then he provides a happy ending to the story. What is more, it comes about through a coincidence—shades of "The Second Strain"!

Crime: None

Evildoer: None

Official police: None

Length: Approximately 7,000 words

This is perhaps the most unorthodox story in the entire canon: unfortunately, just being different does not make it very successful. Conan Doyle did not write this piece until he was sixty-seven years old, and he had already written and published fifty-one previous Holmes short stories. Perhaps he was simply getting bored with the tried and true formula of having Dr. Watson narrate the doings of Holmes: he had already deviated from it once before, in "The Mazarin Stone," where Watson appears as a character only.

This story was the first in which Holmes himself was assigned the role of narrator as well as detective, and I would argue that the most important thing about "Soldier" is how it points up the problems inherent in this technique.

Many if not most contemporary detective-story writers seem to use their detective characters as narrators as well, and while that may help the reader to identify more closely with the main character, it makes it difficult to conceal the outcome of the investigation until the end of the tale, where it can be used with maximum effect. The reader's attention is held throughout the episode because they want to know the outcome—and when the detective finally unmasks the guilty party and explains how he solved the mystery, the reader should feel something like, "Gee, why didn't I see that?" In short, the difficulty which plagues the detective-narrated story is the inherent conflict between what the detective has discovered during the investigation and the necessity of keeping such information from the reader until the conclusion of the story, where it will have the maximum impact. The first-person narrative by the detective would be perfectly appropriate if the object of the work was to explain and encourage the art of detection (which Holmes continually tells Watson that his stories should be). But if the object is to engross, puzzle, entertain, and finally satisfy the reader, what is in the detective's mind—his thought process—must be kept secret until the end. Holmes says precisely that in "The Blanched Soldier": "I am compelled to admit that, having taken my pen in my hand, I do begin to realize that the matter must be presented in such a way as may interest the reader." Arthur Conan Doyle seems to have realized this from the very beginning of his mystery-writing career, when he devised not just one but two ways of accomplishing it. The first was taking his cue from Poe and making Dr. Watson the narrator. Second, he created Holmes as a secretive man who, like Napoleon, keeps his thinking to himself until the moment of triumph, and also has an innate love for the theatrical—the dramatic disclosure, the surprise at the conclusion which we find so often in the Holmes stories. In other words, the author had very good reasons for imparting these traits to his master detective: they keep both Watson and the reader in the dark about what is in Holmes's mind until the end of the story. The genius in this is that readers take Holmes's personality for granted, and they do not see it as a device at all: thus, they never question Holmes's unwillingness to tell what he is thinking until the glorious end. Unable to employ the device of using Holmes's character traits to keep things secret from the reader in this story, the author was obligated to use an unconvincing dodge: he keeps Sir James's identity and profession a secret until the very end of the story, with no apparent good reason. This, I submit, is both awkward and unfair to the reader, who feels let down and vaguely unsatisfied at the ending. If indeed this was an experiment on Doyle's part, it cannot be called a success.

"THE MAZARIN STONE"

| *First publication: The Strand, October 1921*

> *Structural type:* A, with some variation. Each of the four sections is
>   delineated by the characters who appear in it.
> *Section 1:* Watson and Billy, the page
> *Section 2:* Holmes and Watson
> *Section 3-A:* Holmes and Count Sylvius, later joined by Sam: recovery
>   of the jewel
> *Section 4-B:* Happy ending—Holmes, Watson, and the discomfort of
>   Lord Cantlmere (a coda)
> *Crime:* Jewel robbery; possible attempted murder
> *Evildoers:* Count Negretto Sylvius, Sam Merton; unpleasant person:
>   Lord Cantlemere
> *Official police:* None (Youghal of the CID is mentioned but does not
>   actually appear)
> *Length:* Approximately 5,400 words

This story is clearly a transcription of the one-act play, "The Crown Diamond," which had toured England that year. Transforming his play into a short story must have been easy for Conan Doyle, but without actors to turn the words on the page into living characters the story version is uninspiring, to say the least. The wax dummy in the window, lifted from "The Empty House," was used far better in the earlier story; its companion idea—the air gun—is no longer as threatening now that Colonel Sebastian Moran is not at the trigger. Worst of all is the use of the gramophone to simulate Holmes playing his violin.

I suppose that in 1921 this may have been an original device, but since S.S. Van Dyne reused it in one of his Philo Vance novels of the twenties it has become trite and hackneyed. Of course, what others may have done with his idea is not Doyle's fault: nevertheless, I can't see any contemporary reader accepting it without a horse laugh.

Moreover, the story's origin in a one-set, one-act play contributes to the lack of life in this curiously dull tale. It may be okay for actors to be literally confined in a box set, but it makes for a story of stupefying lifelessness. Certainly, "The Mazarin Stone" is among the poorest Holmes short stories.

"THE THREE GABLES"

> *First publication: The Strand,* October 1926
> *Structural type:* B: three sections, with a dramatic entrance
> *Crime:* Burglary; previous assault and battery
> *Evildoers:* Isadora Klein; Barney and Susan Stockdale and the
>   Spencer John gang
> *Official police:* a nameless inspector from Scotland Yard
> *Length:* Approximately 5,500 words

Another story about a woman on the make—this time, it is Isadora Klein, an ambitious, aging, hot-blooded Spanish former beauty. Through her previous marriage to "Klein, the aged German sugar king," she acquired a fortune; now, with Herr Klein deceased and out of the way, she wants a title as well. Her target is the young Duke of Lomond—she is old enough to be his mother, but still has hopes if Douglas Maberly's book can be suppressed. One can only hope that the young man, or perhaps his mother, can see the danger posed by Isabella the Cougar and call off the wedding.

Holmes does not shine in this story. He does little detecting: most of what he learns comes from "Langdale Pike," a sort of early-day paparazzo who deals in society gossip. Then when he is in position to punish the ambitious and unscrupulous Mme. Klein, he backs off and takes her £5,000 sop to Mrs. Maberly, letting our lady cougar off with nothing more than a warning. The story begins with drama and ends with a let-down. We will see this same pattern in other stories from *The Case-Book.*

One can have a bit of fun with some of the names in this story: "Mortimer Maberly married his Mary, who then became Mary Maberly. Did Mary Maberly marry Mortimer Maberly merrily? Maybe!"

This whole tale reeks of nastiness, from Holmes's racist disrespect for Steve Dixie at the beginning through the work of "wicked Susan" in the middle and down to the schemes of Isabella toward the end. If it had never been written or published, we wouldn't have missed much: I can't imagine anybody getting much pleasure from reading this tale of ugliness.

"THE SUSSEX VAMPIRE"

First publication: The Strand, January 1924

Structural type: A, with an extended Holmes-Watson beginning and a short coda— Holmes's final note to the initiators of the case— at the end.

Crime: none, except discipline to a child

Evildoer: "Jacky"

Official police: None

Length: Approximately 5,500 words

While "The Sussex Vampire" may not be one of the best stories in the canon, it is notable for more than one reason. First, it is dead center in the tradition of detective / mystery fiction in that it takes a subject (in this case, vampirism) which is associated with the weird, the emotional, and the irrational, and explains it in perfectly sane and rational terms. Second, the story is related closely to other parts of the Holmes saga: the poisoning of the dog harks back immediately to "Silver Blaze" and the treacherous midnight surgery of John Straker. Also, its heroine shares a common background with several other women in the saga, a point which I will explain further in this essay. And finally, the "Vampire" echoes down the corridors of time as an ancestor of one of the great mystery stories of the twentieth century.

The Peruvian lady known in the tale only as "Mrs. Ferguson" is one of a surprising number of women from tropical areas who appear in the canon, especially in the later stories. In "The Three Gables" we met the Spanish Isadora Klein. Earlier, we found Emilia Lucca from Italy, the lodger in the "The Red Circle"; later in *The Case-Book* we will encounter Maria Pinto Gibson from Brazil. All are descendants of Dr. Doyle's prototypical "hot" girl from the tropics, Beryl Garcia of Costa Rica, alias "Mrs. Stapleton" in *The Hound of the Baskervilles.* The author appears to have been fascinated by the stereotypical passionate, beautiful, hot-blooded, jealous female from the torrid zones: "Mrs. Ferguson" is just another of this type. In her own way, however, she is a heroine, willing to sacrifice everything rather than tell her husband the truth for fear of hurting him.

I mentioned that a great mystery novel of the twentieth century recalls this Holmes short story. That book is *The Tragedy of Y*, originally published under the pseudonym of "Barnaby Ross" and later as by Ellery Queen (another pseudonym, for Frederic Dannay and Manfred B. Lee). *Y* is a truly great novel, with dimensions far beyond this Holmes short story, but nobody who has read both works can doubt the influence of "The Sussex Vampire" on the later book. For one thing, a central character in the short story shares several things with a similar person in the Queen novel. And while vampirism has no place in *Y*, a different sort of evil involving the blood certainly does. "Is it madness, Mr. Holmes? Is it something in the blood?" Any reader of *The Tragedy of Y* will immediately see the connection. I do not wish to write more about the Queen novel, other than to advise every reader who appreciates good books to get hold of a copy of it and waste no time in reading it. This book is a landmark in the history of American mystery fiction. Conan Doyle was dead and buried before it was written, but I cannot doubt that had he been alive to read it he would have liked the way it relates to his own story.

"THE THREE GARRIDEBS"

> *First publication: The Strand,* January 1925
> *Structural type:* Slightly modified B: there is no dramatic opening,
> but the story is in three sections defined by the location and time
> of the action depicted in each: section one is set in Baker Street;
> section two, in Nathan Garrideb's museum-like room; section
> three in the same room on the following day.
> *Crimes:* Counterfeiting; attempted murder

> *Evildoers:* "John Garrideb" (aka "Killer" Evans, aka James Winter),
>   Rodger Prescott (aka "Waldron")
> *Official police:* None (though Lestrade is mentioned as a source of
>   information)
> *Length:* Approximately 5,500 words

This is surely one of the better stories in *The Case-Book*, although the basic plot idea is not original: in fact, it goes all the way back to the second Holmes short to see print—"The Red-Headed League" from *The Adventures*, which first appeared in August 1891, over thirty-three years earlier. Moreover, the same idea was reused in a slightly different way in "The Stockbroker's Clerk" from1893. Yet the story succeeds, partly because it is rich with characters. The villain is among the most interesting "bad guys" in the canon: he is described as "chubby and rather childlike, so that one received the impression of quite a young man [he was really forty-four] with a broad, set smile on his face." So far, he recalls Charles Augustus Milverton, the "evil Mr. Pickwick" of *The Return*. But Watson goes on: "His eyes, however, were arresting. Seldom in any human face have I seen a pair which bespoke a more intense inward life, so bright were they, so alert, so responsive to every change of thought." Here is another Chicago crook, but a far more interesting man than Abe Slaney of "The Dancing Men." "Killer" Evans is semi-comic figure, and it's hard not to like him even when he shoots Watson. He is proof that even at the age of sixty-six, Conan Doyle could still create a complex character and make the reader like even a violent villain.

Likewise, in the person of Nathan Garrideb—with his "cadaverous face" and "dull dead skin"—Doyle created another wonderful type. He is described as amiable, and as he talks with Holmes at their first meeting, he is "polishing a coin." Considering the profession of the previous tenant of the house in Little Ryder Street, this is a brilliant touch! The man is much like his collection and the room in which he keeps it: Holmes calls him "an old fossil," which describes him perfectly.

If it had nothing more to offer, "The Three Garridebs" would be worth reading for its characters alone. But it does offer something more—the reaction Holmes displays to the slight wound suffered by his friend and partner at the hands of "Killer" Evans. Holmes throws his "wiry arms" around his Boswell, saying "You're not hurt, Watson? For God's sake, say that you are not hurt!" For the first and only time, Watson realizes the "depth of loyalty and love which lay behind that cold mask. The clear, hard eyes were dimmed for a moment, and the firm lips were shaking. For the one and only time I caught a glimpse of a great heart as well as of a great brain." This is a far, far different Holmes from the character whom we first met in *A Study in Scarlet* back in 1887. Even yet we have not discussed every aspect of this tale, for this story is where we learn that Holmes refused a knighthood. This is something his creator claimed that he wished to do too—but when the time came, he reluctantly accepted the honor from King Edward VII. Perhaps Doyle felt better about becoming a knight when he had Holmes refuse the title.

Lastly, the author seems to have been experimenting again with the idea of a comic (or at least semi-comic) Holmes story. He had played with the idea before, in "Three Quarter Missing"—and there, as here, he used exaggerated caricatures of two people to add the comic dimension to a story which in the end turns out to be unrelieved tragedy.

So, even if "The Three Garridebs" cannot be considered a true top-level story, it cannot be called a failure, either.

"THOR BRIDGE"

First publication: The Strand, February and March 1922
Structural type: Classic A. The Watsonian opening section is among the best—with its reference to James Philimore and his vanishing act, the cutter "Alicia" and her vanishing, and "Isadora" (sic) Persano and his remarkable worm. The following three sections can be delineated by location: Bates and Gibson

> visit Baker Street; Holmes and Watson conduct investigations
> in Hampshire and at Winchester in section three; and the final
> episode is set at Thor Bridge, where Dr. Watson's revolver plays
> its starring role.
>
> *Crime:* Apparent murder
> *Evildoer:* Maria Pinto Gibson
> *Official police:* Sergeant Coventry (local police)
> *Length:* Approximately 8,500 words

"Thor Bridge" is the outstanding story in *The Case-Book*. It has everything: an original plot—one of Conan Doyle's best—and the same exceptional gift for characterization we found in "The Three Garridebs": consider the description of Neil Gibson, "the Gold King," as "an Abraham Lincoln keyed to base uses instead of high ones." Other outstanding points about the story: Mrs. Gibson, the ultimate picture of "the hot-blooded woman of the Tropics," driven by her intense love for her husband to do a despicable thing; Mr. Marlow Bates and his misdirection at the beginning of the story, and the characteristic late-story feature of a person changing their life for the better under the beneficent influence of another. In "Thor Bridge," all these elements come together (as they frequently don't in other late-Holmes stories) to produce the best Holmes tale Doyle ever wrote after the Great War.

"THE CREEPING MAN"

> *First publication: The Strand,* March 1923
> *Structural type:* A, with four sections, although the first—Watson's
>   introduction—is ruthlessly shortened to a single paragraph.
> *Crime:* none in the legal sense, but a great fault in the moral realm
> *Evildoers:* Professor Presbury?; Dorak; Lowenstein of Prague
> *Official police:* None
> *Length:* Approximately 7,000 words

Clearly, this is not a conventional detective story. In fact, it is really a fable which carries an important moral message: when a man tries to overcome the settled order of the universe, what comes of his effort?

The answer is always tragedy. Here an older man seeks to change himself into a young one: he only succeeds in turning himself into something subhuman. The interesting question is why Conan Doyle wrote this morality tale at the time he did. I do not know—but I am aware of a case in America which might have influenced him. It involved a millionaire socialite, named Harold McCormick—a member of the McCormick family whose ancestor Cyrus McCormick invented the mechanical reaper. Mr. McCormick was in his senior period of life, when he developed a passion for a much younger woman. She was an operatic soprano named Ganna Walska, and Mr. McCormick was absolutely stricken with her. He spent some of his fortune promoting her career, and she did get singing engagements even if nobody would have confused her with the great Rosa Ponselle.

But Harold McCormick was not content to be her guiding spirit: he wanted an amorous relationship, but he felt that his age stood in the way. How could an older man win a young woman? By making himself younger, of course. This is what Professor Presbury tries to do in the story, and what Harold McCormick attempted in Chicago. He heard of a scientist who was experimenting with monkey glands, hoping to discover a fountain of youth.

In the story, Professor Presbury does turn himself into a vigorous young ... ape. In real life, Harold McCormick turned himself into nothing more than a laughingstock. In time, Ganna Walska faded from his life and from the operatic stage.

But the juicy story of the old man and the monkey glands did not fade away: I heard it from my mother (who was a teenager when it was the talk of the town). The question now is, did Conan Doyle hear about it and use it as the inspiration for "The Creeping Man?" Wouldn't you like to know? Wouldn't I?

"THE LION'S MANE"

> *First publication: The Strand*, December 1926
> *Structural type:* A, but with the Watsonian introduction in the first
>   section replaced by a Holmesian account of his life in retirement,
>   and how the case came to him.
> *Crime:* Apparent murder
> *Evildoer:* Cyanea Capillata (A giant jellyfish—but doesn't it sound
>   like the name of an Italian woman?)
> *Official police:* Anderson (Sussex Constabulary), Inspector Bardle
> *Length:* Approximately 6,500 words

Conan Doyle's third and final attempt to write a Sherlock Holmes
short story without Dr. Watson as the narrator. For the second time,
he has Holmes himself tell the story in the first person. One can
only report that the experiment was no more successful on this
occasion than it was with "The Mazarin Stone" or "The Blanched
Soldier." The solution turns on having Sherlock suddenly and for
no good reason recall "the thing for which I had so eagerly and
vainly grasped." That, of course, was the meaning of the enigmatic
clue that Fitzroy McPherson uttered just before his death: "The
lion's mane." If there had been some stimulus which helped recall
the phrase to Holmes's mind, it might have made the story at least
a little more convincing. As it is, Holmes's sudden recollection of
where he heard the three words of the title reduces the solution to
pure chance.

Even worse, when the reader learns that Cyanea was the killer,
it's a letdown. If the criminal cannot think or plot, the whole premise
of the detective story—that what one person can do, another can
explain if only they are smart enough and work hard enough to
penetrate the original thought process—is vitiated. Why Dr. Doyle
even wrote this story as it stands, I cannot fathom. Perhaps he was
trying to break all the rules of the genre: if so, he proved that there

is a good reason why those rules have governed the world of detective fiction since 1841.

As a final note, one may argue that Poe, who started the whole business, had an ape as the killer in his first detective story. The retort must be that the ape was only emulating the human behavior which he had observed, and the brutal murders he committed could have just as well had been done by a human intelligence. The "Rue Morgue" story, at its philosophical base, is really telling us that we are no better than orangutans.

"THE VEILED LODGER"

First publication: The Strand, **February 1927**
Structural type: **A, slightly modified so that the fourth and last section takes place two days after the story has apparently ended, and becomes a coda.**
Crime: **Attempted murder**
Evildoers: **Ronder, Leonardo the Strong Man, Mrs. Ronder**
Official police: **Edmunds (Berkshire Constabulary)**
Length: **Approximately 4,000 words—the shortest story in the canon**

Another tale of tragedy with a moral lesson at its end. A plotted crime miscarries, ending in the death of an unpleasant man and the tragic disfigurement of a once-beautiful woman. It is in the last analysis an assertion that our lives are not our own to end, and that the example of patient suffering is worthwhile. "The ways of Fate are indeed hard to understand," says Holmes to Mrs. Ronder. "If there is not some compensation hereafter, then the world is a cruel jest." The second-to-last Holmes short story to be published, and probably the next-to-last composed, this somber tale is probably the best of all the "philosophical" Holmes stories, and it is wonderfully written. But it is hardly fun to read, however beneficial its lesson.

"SHOSCOMBE OLD PLACE"

First publication: The Strand, April 1927—the very last Holmes
   short story to be written and published
Structural type: A (four parts)
Crime: Fraud
Evildoer: Sir Robert Norburton (?)
Official police: None
Length: Approximately 5,700 words

Doyle's last six Holmes stories all ran in *The Strand* between October
1926 and the following April (no story was published in March). Save
only "The Veiled Lodger," none of the other five last tales is very
satisfactory: surely this one is not. Still, it starts with promise and the
elements of a crackling good adventure. Sir Robert is nearly bankrupt and dependent on his sister for everything; on the property is
the ancient, moldering crypt and a furnace just ready for disposing
a body or two. Then there is the strange behavior of Lady Beatrice
Falder's spaniel when it meets a carriage on the road one day.

Yet at the end, all this collapses into a trite account of how Sir
Robert gets better than he deserves and the reader much less. Perhaps even worse, there is not a crackling moment in the entire piece.
While the elements of a good mystery story are present, there is no
excitement to speak of. In my estimation, this is one of the worst
stories in the canon.

"THE RETIRED COLOURMAN"

First publication: The Strand, January 1927
Structural type: A (four sections)
Crime: Murder
Evildoers: Josiah Amberly, Sherlock Holmes
Official police: Inspector MacKinnon (Scotland Yard)
Length: Approximately 4,800 words

I have never really liked this story, although in rereading it several times before writing about it I must admit that it is better than I had thought. One problem with it is that three of its important components had been used by Conan Doyle before. The "smell" clue is to be found in both "The Norwood Builder" and especially in "The Devil's Foot." The device of using a ruse to get a person out of the way goes all the way back to "The Red-Headed League," and had been used in "The Three Garridebs" not long before. There is a twist to it in this story, however: this time, it is used not by the criminal but by Holmes himself. Also, Holmes appears as a lawbreaker again: having sent Amberly and Watson on their wild-goose chase to Little Purlington, he burgles Amberly's house and finds important evidence. By this time, Holmes seems to revel in his "alternative profession," and boasts that he has no doubt that he should have come to the front of the class as a housebreaker. Also, the device of the interrupted written clue, while probably original with Conan Doyle, has been used many times since, most notably by Ellery Queen.

Still, none of these things are the primary reason this tale fails to grip me. The biggest trouble with "Colourman" is its lack of verve. Beginning with "Lady Frances Carfax" in 1911, several late Holmes stories suffer from this problem: it seems as if the author was having less and less fun writing them. "The Creeping Man," "The Lion's Mane," "The Three Gables," and "Shoscombe Old Place" all suffer from this problem. Perhaps as he approached seventy, Dr. Doyle was simply tired of writing detective stories, and continued to do so just for the money, which went to promote his last passion, spiritualism. In any case, with the book publication of "The Retired Colourman," the Sherlock Holmes saga comes to its end.

CHAPTER 7

Essays on the Short Stories

THEMES IN THE SHORT STORIES: UNRECOGNIZED BUT IMPORTANT

Having read through and studied the fifty-six Holmes short stories in some detail, my attention was drawn to several themes which seem to come up frequently. The fact that the first two stories in *The Adventures* feature ignoble characters from the ranks of the titled caught my eye: the king of Bohemia, Von Ormstein, is depicted as vain, stupid, and generally unappealing. John Clay, in "The Red-Headed League," is a murderer, thief, smasher, and forger. His grandfather may have been a royal duke, and he himself a student at Eton and Oxford, but he is just a common criminal in the eyes of the law.

I wondered how often Conan Doyle ascribed shameful behavior to the nobility. So I went looking through the canon, and indeed a surprising number of the stories contain royal rogues, ignoble nobles, nasty patricians, scions of great families who themselves become lawbreakers, and rich and powerful people who may be untitled (because they are American) but whose actions are questionable or worse. I call this collection "The Holmes Gallery of

Bad Guys," and I imagine that you will be surprised at how many members it has. In the fifty-six stories, I counted no less than fourteen titled personages who are either outright criminals or notoriously nasty people—and that's not counting the two members of the German nobility who appear in *His Last Bow*.

First place on my list of baddies belongs—by virtue of his appearance in the first of the short stories, "A Scandal of Bohemia," and also because he is the king of the ignoble nobles—to Wilhelm Gottsreich Sigismond von Ormstein (or was it really the future Edward VII?). In any event, I have already said everything I have to say about him in my discussion of that story, so we pass on to Mr. John Clay.

Clay may lack a title of his own, but his feelings about himself are made perfectly clear in his little talk with Inspector Jones during his arrest. In "The Red-Headed League," he says, "I beg that you will not touch me with your filthy hands. You may not be aware that I have royal blood in my veins. Have the goodness also when you address me always to say 'sir' and 'please.'" Jones accommodates him with a wonderfully appropriate (if ironic) retort. "Well, would you please, sir, march upstairs, where we can get a cab to carry your highness to the police station?" And Clay keeps up the charade: "That is better," he says, serenely. Then he makes a sweeping bow and exits the scene in the custody of the police detective.

Clay is clearly a supremely arrogant man who sees himself as superior to ordinary people regardless of his criminal career. He obviously believes that by virtue of his birth he has no responsibility to act according to the law. As the scion of a noble family, he considers himself a superior creature however badly he behaves, and his comments to the inspector disclose all too clearly how he thinks about himself. His remarkable ingenuity in creating the Red-Headed League demonstrates how bright and capable he is, but his selfish purpose in doing so shows him to be a classic example of good birth and superior education gone completely to seed. We shall encounter other examples of this same condition as we explore the Holmes canon further.

John Clay is not a duke himself, only the grandson of one. But there is indeed a duke in the canon—the Duke of Holdernesse, in "The Priory School," whose complicity in the kidnapping of his own son and legitimate heir is anything but noble. He may be a great statesman and a very wealthy man, but he is an abject failure both as a husband and as a father. Moreover, his conduct in this case is surely criminal, and he pays handsomely to keep his part in the affair a secret.

The duke's badly flawed character is reflected in that of his elder, illegitimate son, known as James Wilder, who also belongs on the roster of high-placed bad people. In his case, the problem is his jealousy of his younger brother, and his ability to manipulate his father because of his facial resemblance to his mother, the woman the duke truly loved. That he attempts to take advantage of his father's inability to dismiss him, say "no" to him, or discipline him for his association with the brutal Reuben Hayes marks him as unworthy of his ancestry. James Wilder, like John Clay, may come from royalty, but he is hardly noble.

In fact, the Holmes canon is simply riddled with tales of titled, highly or merely rich people who are legal or moral miscreants, or just plain nasty. The Duke of Holdernesse is not alone in breaking the law: consider, if you will, two other noblemen—Count Negretto Sylvius, in "The Mazarin Stone," and Baron Gruner in "The Illustrious Client."

The baron, we are told, murdered his wife and only escaped punishment because of a technical point of the law and "the suspicious death of a witness." Miss Kitty Winter, one of his former girlfriends, says she also knows of another murder or two, and Baron Gruner thinks nothing of having detectives who are looking into his life beaten up. Count Sylvius, who owes his life title to his half-Italian birth, trumps even the baron.* His criminal career adds, to multiple murders and jewel theft, forgery and train robbing. Either or both

---

* There is no title of "count" in the ranks of British nobility. The equivalent in

would not hesitate to kill again, especially if the victim were to be Sherlock Holmes: Baron Gruner actually has Holmes attacked, and Count Sylvius has him in the sights of an air gun.* "The Mazarin Stone," in which Count Sylvius is the leading villain, is unique in that it also contains two other characters who we find on the "badman" list. One of these, Old Baron Dowson, does not appear as a character, but is referred to by Holmes. The count remarks about the "agents" of Holmes who had been following him for the last two days. Holmes replies, "Really, sir. You compliment me. Old Baron Dowson said the night before he was hanged that in my case what the law had gained the stage had lost. And now you give my little impersonations your kindly praise!" The point here is not the capabilities of Holmes as an actor: rather, it is the man who complimented him on the night before his own execution. We have no data on what crime or crimes Old Baron Dowson may have committed, but clearly he was guilty of something pretty serious. Another titled criminal for our collection!

Yet there is still a third figure in this story who belongs in the gallery of upper-crust rascals. I am writing here of Lord Cantlemere, whom Holmes describes as "an excellent and loyal person, but rather of the old regime." Billy the page puts it more directly: "I can't stand his lordship. Neither can Mr. Holmes." He goes on to indicate that Lord Cantlemere wanted Holmes to fail. Holmes artfully gives Lord Cantlemere a little lesson in humility and civility, and the story ends on an upbeat note. But his lordship belongs on the list of ignobles all the same.

Lord Cantlemere is surely a cousin of Lord Mount-James, the

---

the United Kingdom is "earl," and to my knowledge there are no "ignobles" of that station in the Holmes canon. So, the Italian Count will have to suffice.

* When we first heard of the air gun (in "The Empty House," the first story in *The Return*) Holmes tells us that it was "an admirable and unique weapon … noiseless and of tremendous power. I knew Von Herder, the blind German mechanic, who constructed it to the order of the late Professor Moriarty." Now we hear that the maker is another German, Straubenzee, who works in London. Whether anybody ever built an air gun in real life, I do not know.

miserly uncle of Godfrey Staunton. Lord Mount-James is said to be among the richest men in England. One reason why is that "he never allowed Godfrey a shilling in his life," even though the young man—who is the missing three-quarter in the story by that name, from *The Return*—is his only heir. When we meet this crabby and totally disagreeable man, halfway through the tale, we find him to be just as nasty and money mad as Cyril Overton, Godfrey's rugby team captain at Cambridge, said he would be.

Conan Doyle's depiction of the old man is a masterpiece of focused characterization. He appears in less than two pages of print and in just twenty-nine lines of dialogue, yet we know him thoroughly and dislike him immediately—with good reason. Lord Mount-James is the closest thing to an outright villain in this story. Note how his attitude towards Holmes changes when it is pointed out to him that Godfrey may have been kidnapped as a means of getting at his uncle and his uncle's money. Nothing could disclose the man's ugly character more clearly.

Lord Cantlemere and Lord Mount-James are old men, but the much younger Lord Robert St. Simon, "The Noble Bachelor" from *The Adventures*, is well on his way to becoming just like them. As the second son of the Duke of Balmoral, he has the noble pedigree, all right—but his attitude and his conduct reveal a pompous, cold, and unnecessarily unpleasant personality. Lord Robert is forty-one years old—"ripe for marriage," as Holmes points out—when he escorts Miss Hattie Doran, daughter of a San Francisco millionaire, to the altar. But she disappears at the wedding breakfast, and foul play is suspected. We soon learn that Lord Robert has been using the actress and dancer Flora Millar as a plaything for some time: now, when he dismisses her, she tries to make a scene at the wedding, and afterwards approaches the new bride in the park and is seen conversing with her. How I'd like to know what Miss Millar had to say to the woman Lord Robert chose to marry! I suspect that his later coldness and hostility towards Hattie and her husband would be nothing compared to what Flora had to say about him to her successor in his affections. Considering that the "noble" bachelor undoubtedly wooed Miss Doran for her dowry—which would had been very large indeed—he comes off in the end as hardly noble. In fact, he is nothing more than a greedy, egotistical prig. If this is nobility, of what earthly good is it? How does it deserve the deference and respect that it so often receives from the British public?

Then there is the Marquess of Montalva, alias Juan Murillo, alias "Mr. Henderson," alias "The Tiger of San Pedro." "He had made his name as the most lewd and bloodthirsty tyrant that had ever governed any country with a pretense to civilization." Don Murillo's misdeeds probably out-evil those of any of the other people in my catalogue of ignoble nobles: he may be the worst of the worst. Yet he holds the status of an exalted personage.

Nor does the list end here. Among the lesser nobility we find unknightly knights and bad news baronets such as Sir George Burnwell in "The Beryl Coronet." Far from being chivalrous, Sir George is, in Holmes's words, "one of the most dangerous men in England—a ruined gambler, an absolutely desperate villain: a man without heart or conscience." The knights of King Arthur's Round Table would be appalled, especially at his seduction of Mary Holder, whom Sir George used to gain the opportunity of stealing the valuable coronet (it was worth a hundred thousand pounds). Sir George alone is enough to give knighthood a bad reputation; no wonder Holmes refused to accept it.

Sir Eustace Brackenstall of "The Abbey Grange" is another completely unchivalrous knight. A dangerous drunkard, he threw a decanter at the maid, set his wife's dog on fire, and contrary to every idea of chivalry, not only called her "the vilest name that a man could use to a woman" ("whore"? "bitch"?), but also stabbed her with a hat pin and beat her. Sir Eustace met his death at the hands of a commoner, who exhibited far more chivalrous behavior than the knight he dispatched.

Sir Robert Norberton, a baronet living at Shoscombe Old Place with his widowed sister, Lady Beatrice Falder, is our next candidate for the Gallery of Bad Guys. Forget that he once horse-whipped a man on Newmarket Heath and nearly killed him; Watson describes Sir Robert as "a devil of a fellow," and in the story he is deeply in debt and has just one hope—for his horse, Shoscombe Prince, to win the derby. "Everything he could raise or borrow is on the horse, and at fine odds, too," says the head trainer, John Mason. Sir Robert has hoodwinked the public and kept the odds on the Prince at forty-to-one by running the colt's half-brother, who looks just like the Prince but cannot run nearly as fast, in practices. Not only is he not above trickery, but Sir Robert, it appears, is having an affair with his sister's maid. On top of that, he gave Lady Beatrice's dog away to the local innkeeper. So Sir Robert is a desperate man: he conceals the death of his sister for three weeks before the big race, for fear that his creditors might seize the stables and the horse if they knew that she was dead. When Holmes learns the whole story from Sir Robert himself, he makes two comments: "Your conduct seems to be inexcusable, Sir Robert," and later, "This matter must, of course, be referred to the police ... As to the morality or decency of your own conduct, it is not for me to express an opinion" (which of course he has already done). Sir Robert may not be another Don Murillo, but neither can his behavior be said to be in any way in keeping with the idea of nobility.

Still we have not yet exhausted the roster of less-than-exalted conduct by those in high places. There is Dr. Grimesby Roylott, who, we are told, was descended from "one of the oldest Saxon families in England." We learn that "The family was at one time among the richest in England, and the estate extended over the borders into Berkshire on the north and Hampshire on the west." But Dr. Roylott, the scion of that distinguished family, is himself "a morose and disappointed man." He is more than that—a murderer, and "the terror of the village." So much for the distinguished family of the past: the man of the present is angry, bitter, and determined to have what he wants—control of his stepdaughters' inheritance. As another son of the upper crust who turned evil, he belongs to the "Gallery of Bad Guys."

So too does Colonel Sebastian Moran, son of Sir Augustus Moran, CB, once British Minister to Persia. Educated at Eton and Oxford (like John Clay: given the difference in their ages, Clay's grandfather and Moran's father may well have been contemporaries and known to each other). Colonel Moran is another example of a man whose early career was meritorious, but who later turned to crime. As Professor Moriarty's right-hand man, the colonel, though not titled himself, surely belongs on the list of upper-crust bad boys.

So too does the great explorer, lion hunter, and very lion-like Dr. Leon Sterndale, the villain—or hero—from "The Devil's Foot." His position is equivocal: yes, he murdered Mortimer Tregennis, but only after Tregennis murdered his lady, Brenda. As Holmes says to Watson, "You would not denounce the man?" And Watson's reply would probably have been my own, and yours: "Certainly not." Yet however understandable his conduct, Dr. Sterndale, a man of high position and accomplishment, is at least a candidate for the Gallery of Bad Guys.

Nor is Neil Gibson, "the Gold King," possessed of a title of nobility, but for a different reason: he is an American. Were he to have been a British subject, there is little doubt that he would have been created a knight if not a peer. If Dr. Sterndale's position is equivocal, so is that of Mr. Gibson. Watson describes him as, "an Abraham Lincoln keyed to base uses instead of high ones," and remarks on his "tall, gaunt, craggy figure," which "had a suggestion of hunger and rapacity." His estate manager, Mr. Marlow Bates, does not hesitate to call him "a villain—an infernal villain." Sherlock Holmes lectures him bluntly: "Some of you rich men have to be taught that all the world cannot be bribed into condoning your offenses." Based on these points, Mr. Gibson seems a worthy candidate for the Gallery of Bad Guys. *However*—under the influence of Miss Grace Dunbar, the Gold King appears to have experienced a change in his thinking and his attitude towards other people.

Miss Dunbar told this hardened business tycoon that, "a fortune for one man that was more than he needed should not be built on ten thousand ruined men who were left without the means of life." So Mr. Gibson may not deserve a place bedside the Juan Murillos and Count Sylviuses and Colonel Morans after all. His appears to be a special case, and he may deserve the benefit of the doubt.

There are still two other titled figures who may or may not belong on the list of ignoble nobles: Baron von Herling of the German embassy and his top spy, von Bork, who we meet in "His Last Bow." They are, after all, not working for themselves but for their government, and I am inclined to exempt them from membership in the Gallery on this account.

So our roster includes a king, a duke, three lords, a count, a marquess, two barons, three knights / baronets, two distinguished doctors, and several scions of noble or distinguished families who careers are unworthy of their ancestry. The total comes to at least seventeen individuals, not counting Neil Gibson or the two Germans. In the fifty-six short stories, that averages out to better than a quarter of the bad guys in the canon.

The question we must now ask is, "Why did Conan Doyle create so many such characters?" Such a high percentage of morally and ethically bankrupt members of the upper-class demands that we consider the possibility that the author was deliberately, if subtly, attacking the class structure and the dominance of wealth characteristic of his time.

By the second half of the nineteenth century the feudal supremacy of the landed gentry was rapidly breaking down, not only in Britain but across the continent as well. The rise of new wealth generated by the industrial revolution, the French Revolution and its ideals, the destruction of the old ways by the rise of Napoleon, and the appearance of a new and growing colossus across the Atlantic all contributed to the challenge to the feudal order and its institutions. Doyle, an acute student of history and society, was surely aware of the monumental changes going on, and the idea that in his Holmes stories he was attacking what he saw as an unjust and unwarranted deference toward social status and / or wealth cannot be dismissed out of hand. In short, I suggest that these stories, in addition to their wonderful value as entertainment, contain a serious degree of intentional social criticism that ought not to be ignored. The lesson hidden beneath these criminal, humorous, intellectually stimulating, and thoroughly enjoyable tales is that the titled, the rich, and the powerful are not always above abuse of their positions, and that unthinking kowtowing before them is unhealthy and unwise.

If indeed this is the case—and I think there is ample evidence that it is, especially in Doyle's own life aside from his writing—we must reconsider our entire attitude towards the Holmes canon.* Christopher Morley was wrong when he wrote, "Holmes is pure anesthesia." Certainly the anesthesia is there—thank goodness— but it is by no means all there is. We should read these stories with

---

* Conan Doyle's concern with social issues is well-documented: he participated in the Edalji and Slater cases, and he won justice for both. His ten years as president of an organization seeking reform of the very restrictive English divorce laws and his U-turn on the issue of Irish home rule are proof of his concern for other social and political issues. Christopher Morley, who was so wrong in calling the Holmes stories "pure anesthesia," was so right when in the same essay (his introduction to the complete one-volume edition of Holmes material) he pointed out that "Doyle was always also the 'fracianino-phile,' the helper of the underdog."

What is more, we have Dr. Doyle's own letters, in which he writes that he "had never approved of the titles," and that he had made up his mind not to accept the knighthood he was to be offered in 1902 until his mother insisted that to refuse would be an insult to the king—Edward VII, whom the author had satirized so deftly in "A Scandal in Bohemia" more than a decade earlier. "The title I value most is that of doctor," he wrote, and after having finally accepted the "Sir" before his name, he remarked that he felt "like a newly married girl who isn't sure of her own name." (These quotes come from Carr's *Life of Sir Arthur Conan Doyle.*)

While Doyle did finally accept the knighthood, he had Sherlock Holmes refuse it at the same honors list. Ironically, some years later, Sir Arthur was approached about a peerage by a representative of King George V—but he never got it because by then he had become a confirmed Spiritualist, a position which was intolerable to the Church of England of which the reigning monarch is the head.

an eye for the deeper implications they contain. We must, in other words, think of Conan Doyle as he thought of himself—as a writer of substance. Ironically, he realized that the very popularity of the Holmes stories might take away from his reputation as a serious artist, as indeed it has. But there is a second irony to be brought out—that the Holmes stories themselves contain more than ample evidence of their author's depth of thought and concern for social matters, and of his great skill as a master of English prose as well as a peerless storyteller.

When we contemplate all this material, the balance of probability suggests that Conan Doyle was indeed indicting the British (and continental) class system, as well as the American fawning over wealth and power, in tales generally considered to have no significance deeper than their value as entertainment. If this is true of the five collections of Holmes short stories, it ought to alert us to look out for similar content in the four Holmes novels—two of which, remember, were written before any of the stories we have been examining. Of course, not all the short stories are equally pregnant with deeper meaning—but to ignore social criticism where it does appear is unjust to both the author and the reader.

Moreover, there are other themes in these stories which should be pointed out when assessing the value of Doyle's work. One of these is the other side of the coin: if the upper strata of society come in for extensive if subtle reproach, how do the stories treat the less fortunate?

THE OTHER SIDE OF THE COIN: THE UNDERCLASS IN THE HOLMES CANON

If, as I have argued, the Holmes short stories contain an indictment of the upper crust, how then do they treat those who are at the bottom of the social heap? Do they show sympathy for the poor and powerless? The answer, I think, is more yes than no.

The canon does not describe many instances of lower-class people calling upon Sherlock Holmes for help—unsurprisingly, since few of them would expect to be able to pay for his services—but we know from Watson's observations in *A Study in Scarlet* that among the detective's clients in the early days were "an elderly slipshod woman, a railway porter in his velveteen uniform, and a seedy old man looking like a ... peddler." We meet few such individuals in the later stories—although Mrs. Warren, the none-too-well-off landlady of the mysterious lodger in "The Red Circle," not only comes to Holmes but argues him into looking into her case. However, she seems to be the exception who proves the rule: as Holmes's fame rises, so does the status of his clients.

There is, however, at least one segment of the lower classes with which Holmes interacts from the very beginning. I mean of course, that gaggle of young urchins he calls "my Baker Street boys," but who are better known today as "the Baker Street Irregulars." They appear first in the original Holmes story, *A Study in Scarlet*, and we meet them again in *The Sign of the Four*. As far as I can tell, they are mentioned just once in the fifty-six short stories (in "The Crooked Man" from *The Memoirs*) when Holmes hires one of them, a boy named Simpson, to keep in close contact with Henry Wood. I bring them up here because, although they would really belong in an essay on the novels, the subject we are now discussing—Holmes and the lower classes—dictates that I write about them now.

"What on earth is this?" asks Dr. Watson, when in chapter 6 of *Scarlet* "there came the pattering of many feet on the steps in the hall and on the stairs, accompanied by audible expressions of disgust upon the part of our landlady." Holmes replies gravely, "It's the Baker Street division of the detective police force," as six of the dirtiest and most ragged boys rush into the room. They stay just long enough to report no success, collect their wages—a shilling a day for each boy—and then they are off again in search of Jefferson Hope's Hansom. They "scampered away downstairs like so many rats and we heard their shrill voices next moment in the street."

Watson is no kinder in describing these boys than is Mrs. Hudson, who is exasperated at their invasion of her premises. He refers to them as "scoundrels" in addition to comparing them to rats as they scurry off.

But Sherlock Holmes exhibits a different attitude. "There's more work to be got out of one of those little beggars than out of a dozen of the force," he remarks. "The sight of an official-looking person seals men's lips. These youngsters, however, go everywhere and hear everything. They are sharp as needles, too; all they want is organization." Unlike Mrs. Hudson or Watson—or, I daresay, most people at that time—he neither swears nor sneers at them. Instead, he appreciates their intelligence, uneducated as they are, and is not so class-conscious as to ignore their talents or refuse to make use of them. Moreover, he pays them—and a shilling a day for those boys is not only the first and maybe the only money they have ever earned, but it must seem a small fortune to them. In time they do find not only the cab, but also its driver. If not for the keen work of these despised street kids, the capture of Jefferson Hope might not have been so easily accomplished.

Holmes (and by extension, Conan Doyle) deserves much credit for recognizing the potential of these youngsters—dirty, unlettered, unremarked, and undisciplined as they are. He is entitled to even more credit for employing them (how many London gentleman or ladies of 1887 do you think would do so?) and for treating them with dignity by paying them wages.

Holmes would have been quite out of the ordinary in seeing them as useful human beings deserving of his attention. Of course, they are a great help to him at minimal cost—but consider how they must have regarded him!

The Irregulars turn up again in *The Sign of the Four*, this time in search of the steam launch *Aurora*. This time, however, we see a difference in them. There are not just six, now, but an even dozen, and they have a leader (Wiggins, the tallest and probably eldest of the group.) Watson comments that, "There was some show of discipline among them, despite their tumultuous entry, for they instantly drew up in line and stood facing us with expectant faces." Wiggins reports to Holmes, who tells them what he wants them to look for. He pays Wiggins the money for the tickets they used to come to Baker Street, and then pays each boy a shilling in advance, and promises a bonus of "a guinea to the boy who finds the boat!"* A guinea was twenty-one shillings—more than a pound—and almost certainly more money than any of these kids had ever seen, let alone possessed. The money isn't the only important thing, however—maybe not even the most important part of the relationship. It is more than likely that none of these street boys had ever been appreciated by a gentleman before, nor given any respect or even any notice. This man Mr. Holmes—well, they're delighted to work for him and to call him "guvner."

Holmes's treatment of the Baker Street boys may not be evidence enough to prove that Arthur Conan Doyle had a better, more respectful attitude towards the lower classes than most of his contemporaries, but it does at least suggest that he saw in these despised youngsters a spark of humanity and a potential that many if not most others at that time and in that place ignored.

In addition to the Irregulars, the closest contact Holmes appears to have with the downtrodden is to be found in "The Illustrious Client," the first story in *The Case-Book*. While this tale is primarily concerned with members of the upper strata, it also introduces us to two notable people of the underclass, not to add the underworld: Shinwell Johnson and Kitty Winter. Watson first acquaints us with Johnson by apologizing for not having mentioned him before: that was because few of his accounts came from the later part of Holmes's career, when Johnson became a loose associate. Now we learn that Johnson is an ex-con whose two convictions and prison terms give

---

* This sentence implies a deeper arrangement between Holmes and the head Irregular, young Mister Wiggins. How did he have the cash in hand to bring his crew to Baker Street before Holmes repaid his "three bob and a tanner?" Also, how did Holmes send his message to Wiggins to bring his crew to 221B? Apparently, Holmes had set up not only a channel of communication with Wiggins, but also supplied him with money to pay for transport.

him easy entree into the criminal society of London. Having gone straight, he becomes a valuable source of information about the city's darker side. He is credited with the gift of "quick observation and an active brain," and it is Johnson who brings Kitty Winter into the case. She has been one of Baron Gruner's conquests, and while her status is never described, it is clear from what she says and how she hates her former lover that it was he who turned her out and made her become a prostitute. Accordingly, she lives now only "to pull him into the pit where he has pushed so many," clearly including herself. Eventually, she does revenge herself on "dear Adelbert" in a most dramatic and unpleasant manner. An ex-convict and an angry prostitute must surely be counted among the lowly.

The most remarkable thing about this story is how the author turns these two derided characters into the good people of the tale, while the titled and wealthy baron emerges as the villain, and the titled, wealthy "wonder woman," Violet de Merville, is in the end exposed as a shallow, overly romantic, fantasizing dupe.

We have seen Dr. Doyle perform a similar transformation before—in "A Scandal in Bohemia," where he makes Irene Adler, a social outcast who breaks all the rules of feminine conduct, into the heroine not only of one story but of the whole Holmes saga. Now he repeats his legerdemain with the ex-criminal Johnson and the degraded, vitriol-throwing Kitty Winter. The author may not glorify these members of the lower caste, but he does humanize them and show them sympathy and respect. The same is true of Eugenia Ronder, who helped to plan and attempt the murder of her husband in "The Veiled Lodger." She was "a poor circus girl, brought up on the sawdust, and doing springs through the hoop before I was ten."

In conclusion, I suggest that on the evidence of the canon, both Sherlock Holmes and his creator deserve commendation for their attitude toward and interaction with members of the lower classes in a too class-conscious society: Victorian and Edwardian Britain.

THE CROOKED HOLMES: SHERLOCK HOLMES, LAWBREAKER

In "The Bruce-Partington Plans," Sherlock Homes and Dr. Watson, equipped with a jimmy, a dark lantern, a chisel, and a revolver, break into Hugo Oberstein's West End house in search of evidence. The crime of burglary is defined as "entering into the dwelling place of another in the nighttime, with intent to commit a felony inside." Their action exactly constitutes a serious violation of criminal law, and when Holmes tells Inspector Lestrade about the expedition the next morning, the Scotland Yarder can only shake his head. "We can't do these things in the force, Mr. Holmes. No wonder you get results that are beyond us. But some of these days you'll go too far, and you'll find you and your friend in trouble."

That never happens—but Lestrade is right. How right he does not suspect, for Holmes clearly commits burglary not just in this case, but also in "Charles Augustus Milverton," "The Illustrious Client," and "The Retired Colorman." In "Lady Frances Carfax" he twice enters the Peters house. The first time, he leaves when asked to do so by a respectful policeman; but on the second occasion he brandishes a pistol to prevent the coffin from being moved away. This is certainly criminal in some way. In addition, Holmes may well have committed blackmail in "The Priory School," and his conduct in "The Three Gables" might fall into the same category of crime. True, he does not shake down Isadora Klein for his own account, but he does demand money from her for his client, Mary Maberly. "I suppose I shall have to compound a felony as usual," he remarks, as he collects a check for five thousand pounds from Mrs. Klein to send Mrs. Maberly on a round-the-world tour rather than expose Isadora's guilt in the beating of Douglas, her former lover.

Nor is that the full extent of Sherlock Holmes's extra-legal activities. In at least four other cases, he subverts the law by arranging that a man who has clearly broken it goes free (see "The Abbey Grange," "The Blue Carbuncle," "The Lion's Mane," and "The Beryl Coronet"). That makes at least nine occasions on which Holmes may have or clearly has broken the law himself, or that he helped another person to escape legal proceedings.

In the "Bruce Partington" case, Holmes really runs no risk of arrest or conviction—not with Mycroft (aka the British Government) to protect him. His theft of Baron Gruner's lust diary is never prosecuted owing to the "Illustrious Client," whose identity we never learn. As Watson puts it, "when an object is good and a client is sufficiently illustrious, even the rigid British law becomes humane and elastic."

Indeed, this brings us to the question of *why* Holmes is so often on the wrong side of the law. The answer, I think, can be found in the detective's growing realization that law and justice are not the same. His commitment to the latter leads him away from total obedience to the former. This almost certainly reflects a change in the attitude of Conan Doyle, as we will see when we get to *The Valley of Fear*. Many of the later short stories also indicate an increasing concern for the feelings and emotions of others which was absent in the early Holmes. One example is the detective's show of concern, even of love, when Watson is shot by Killer Evans in "The Three Garridebs." Indeed, if there is a theme running through the whole gamut of short stories, it is the slow but progressive growth in the character of Sherlock Holmes—from a somewhat self-centered thinking automaton (as Doyle originally created him) to a full-blooded and humane adult who no longer distrusts any emotions and claims to have none of his own.

Thus, when the cause is a good one, the later Holmes is more interested in the attainment of truly just solutions to vexing problems, rather than inadequate statutory remedies that merely conform to the letter of the law. There is, in short, method to Holmes's madness: he commits crimes and frustrates the working of the law in a personal search for true justice.

DOYLE, HOLMES, AND GENETICS: THE INHERITANCE THEME

Today there is considerable discussion of whether genetic inheritance may influence behavior, and if so how. The subject remains controversial, and there is no consensus about the answers. It's the age-old question—nature or nurture?

I suppose that we should not be surprised to find this theme in the Sherlock Holmes canon, although I have never come across any discussion of it. But Conan Doyle was a physician by profession, before he became a metaphysician as well. What is surprising is the extent to which the theme of inheritance of behavior permeates so much of the Holmes saga, especially in the part of it written before the First World War. It appears in two forms: "art in the blood," and the influence of ancestry on criminal behavior.

In its first aspect, the "inheritance theme" is introduced in "The Greek Interpreter," the ninth story in the second collection of Holmes short stories, *The Memoirs of Sherlock Holmes.*

The occasion is a discussion between Holmes and Dr. Watson, which turns to "the question of atavism and hereditary aptitudes." The point under discussion is how far any singular gift in an individual was due to his ancestry and how far to his own early training. That is, "nature or nurture?"

"In your own case," Watson says, "from all that you have told me that your faculty of observation and your peculiar facility for deduction are due to your own systematic training."

Holmes replies, "To some extent. My ancestors were country squires, who appear to have led much the same life as is natural to their class. But, none the less my turn that way is in my veins, and may have come with my grandmother, who was the sister of Vernet, the French artist. Art in the blood is liable to take the strangest forms."*

"But how do you know that it is hereditary?" Watson asks.

"Because my brother Mycroft possesses it in a larger degree than I do."

---

* Dr. Doyle must have known this from his own family history: his grandfather and uncle were both well-known artists, and he came from a long line of illustrators and cartoonists. In his own case, however, the artistic heritage found its expression in literary rather than visual arts.

This conversation leaves no doubt about how Doyle must have regarded the debate. In the following pages, as we meet Mycroft for the first time, the two brothers face off in what can only be described as a dazzling display of observation and deduction in which Mycroft one-ups his younger brother.

This scene is vital to a full understanding of the Holmes stories. It is remarkable how little attention seems to have been paid to Conan Doyle's interest and apparent belief in the power of "atavism and hereditary aptitudes" to influence individual behavior. In the case of the Holmes brothers, these factors lead to two exceptional careers, each contributing mightily to the world of literature, and to the delight of millions of readers. But the "inheritance factor" also appears in another context in the Holmes canon—as an influence which helps drive individuals into lives of crime.

The first of these characters is the unforgettable Dr. Grimesby Roylott, who makes his dramatic appearance in "The Speckled Band," the eighth story in *The Adventures*. His stepdaughter, Helen Stoner, tells us how "Violence of temper approaching to mania has been hereditary in the men of the family," and Dr. Roylott surely exhibits that quality. While living in Calcutta, in a fit of anger over some robberies in the house, "he beat his native butler to death, and narrowly escaped a capital sentence." More recently, "he hurled the local blacksmith over a parapet into a stream." It seems unnecessary to say more: Dr. Doyle was stating unequivocally that Dr. Roylott's darker tendencies could be traced to his ancestry.

This first assertion of the idea that heredity influences behavior might be dismissed if it appeared in only this story. However, we will find it recurring again and again in the Holmes canon—a clear indication that the author was at the very least fascinated by the idea.

We come across it next in the last story in *The Adventures*: "The Copper Beeches." As a matter of fact, "The Speckled Band" and "The Copper Beeches" are surprisingly similar. In each, a stepfather who has the use of his stepdaughters' money is threatened with losing it if she marries. In both stories the stepfather resorts to desperate means to prevent any wedding and thus to maintain his control of the cash. And in both stories the stepfather comes to ruin when a dangerous animal which he has been using to further his aims suddenly turns on him.

In "Beeches," however, Conan Doyle turns an old adage— "like father, like son"—on its head. The six-year-old son of Jephro Rucastle is notable for his violent, spoiled behavior: from this, Holmes draws the conclusion that the boy's father has the same tendencies. "My dear Watson," he says, "you as a medical man are continuously gaining light as to the tendencies of a child by study of the parents. Don't you see that the converse is equally valid? ... This child's disposition is abnormally cruel, merely for cruelty's sake." From whichever way one looks at it, the underlying idea is the same: that evil tendencies may be passed from one generation to another. Doyle, like Watson a medical man, appears to have been convinced that nature, in addition to nurture, may explain an individual's anti-social or even criminal behavior.*

We see the inheritance theme in a different form in "The Yellow Face," the second story in *The Memoirs*. In this case, however, Dr. Doyle slipped. Little Lucy Hebron, the daughter of a Caucasian woman and a light-skinned African American father, is described as "far darker than ever her father was." Dr. Doyle may not have realized it, but we know today that this is genetically impossible. In this instance the idea of a throwback makes good literature—but it is bad science. Still, this story illustrates again Doyle's belief that genetic inheritance can affect an individual: it just cannot affect skin color in the way the author uses it here.

In "The Reigate Squires," later in *The Memoirs*, the inheritance

---

* One wonders what became of young Edward when he grew up. Did his gleeful cruelty eventually express itself in crime? The author never tells us, but he might have written another story about young Edward Rucastle as an adult. Perhaps he might have come to the attention of Mr. Sherlock Holmes again, in a different context, twenty years or so after "The Copper Beeches." That would have been a clinching argument in favor of the inheritance theme.

theme appears in still another guise. This time, Holmes asserts that analysis of the handwriting of two men can show them to be blood relatives. I do not know whether contemporary science would validate this proposition, and I suspect that Dr. Doyle may again be on shaky ground. But even if he got his facts wrong for a second time, the story reiterates his belief in the influence of genetic inheritance.

This theme appears again in at least two other short stories: "The Final Problem" and "The Empty House." "The Final Problem" introduces us to Holmes's arch-antagonist, Professor James Moriarty. Holmes tells us about the professor's career, beginning with his "good birth and excellent education," and his "phenomenal mathematical faculty." He goes on: "At the age of twenty-one he wrote a treatise on the Binomial Theorem, which has had a European vogue. On the strength of it, he won the Mathematical Chair at one of our smaller universities, and had, to all appearances, a most brilliant career before him. But the man had hereditary tendencies of the most diabolical kind. A criminal strain ran in his blood ... dark rumors gathered about him."

We learn no more about the professor's diabolical hereditary tendencies, or about the "criminal strain" which "ran in his blood." But once again, the mere mention of these things is sufficient to show the author's interest and belief in the influence of genetic inheritance on criminal behavior.*

If Moriarty began with a promising academic career but later succumbed to the lure of crime because of a genetic predilection, then it is no surprise that he should have chosen to employ Colonel

---

* In the footnote here, I suggest the confusion over the names of the three brothers is easily resolved—the true family name was "James Moriarty." Double last names are hardly unknown in Great Britain; the author of the deathless opening line, "It was a dark and stormy night" was Bulwer-Lytton, and not too long ago the prime minister was Douglas-Home. That the James Moriarty family we are discussing did not use the hyphen may have been their own choice—or perhaps it was dropped by some careless printer and the family simply let it go.

Sebastian Moran as his chief of staff. For in "The Empty House," we learn that Moran, too, began his career with an excellent education and great promise as an honorable soldier. But he, too, turned to evil. Holmes (speaking for Conan Doyle?) offers this explanation of how this came about: "I have a theory that the individual represents in his development the whole procession of his ancestors, and that such a sudden turn to good or evil stands for some strong influence which came into the line of his pedigree. The person becomes, as it were, the epitome of the history of his own family." Watson's reply is brief and practical: "It is surely rather fanciful." Holmes replies, "Well, I don't insist upon it." This theory—that phylogeny recapitulates ontogeny—is discredited today. But as Holmes says, "Whatever the cause, Colonel Moran began to go wrong."* The mere mention of this theory is suggestive: it implies that not only was Conan Doyle interested in genetic inheritance as a cause of behavior, but in this even more radical idea of human development.

The inheritance theme is so prominent in *The Adventures*, and especially in *The Memoirs*, that it comes as quite a surprise to see it seem to disappear after "The Empty House." When we recall, however, that eight years passed between the composition of the second story collection and the writing of the third (*The Return*) we may consider that Conan Doyle's concerns in the later stories had probably changed. There may also be another reason why he seems to have lost interest in the inheritance theme after the turn of the century: Dr. Doyle had, between the second and third story collections, created his greatest exposition of the idea in the third Holmes novel, *The Hound of the Baskervilles*. I will conclude this study of the Holmes saga with an in-depth discussion of that great book, beyond any doubt the

---

* Not only do Moriarty and Moran have similar career profiles, but we ought to note the similarities between Moran's life and that of Dr. Grimesby Roylott. Both men went out to India in good standing and achieved great things there—but then both went into criminal activity. Dr. Roylott was imprisoned. Colonel Moran "made India too hot to hold him" and returned to England, where he continued his criminal career and was eventually hired by the professor.

finest work in the canon. For the moment, it is enough to point out how prominent the theme is in the first two volumes of short stories: to recognize its importance there alerts the reader to its presence, in preparation for its ultimate transfiguration in the novel.

THE MEANING AND MAGIC OF NAMES

Among the most striking devices employed by Conan Doyle in his Holmes stories, both short and long, is his use of names.

Of course, the English writer who used names most memorably prior to Doyle was Charles Dickens. No one at all familiar with English literature can ever forget his marvelously colorful character names: Uriah Heap, Mr. Pickwick, Oliver Twist, Bill Sykes, Fagin, Peggoty, Little Nell—to name just a few. They simply ring with sound and feeling. Doyle was aware of how Dickens had used the sounds and looks of proper names to help create characters and emotional responses to them, and he did not hesitate to employ the same tactic. A catalogue of colorful names from the Holmes canon might include such personal names as Athelney Jones, Jephro Rucastle, Dr. Grimesby Roylott, Reginald Musgrave, Abe Slaney, Jonas Oldacre, and Dr. Thorneycroft Huxtable—not to mention Sherlock and Mycroft Holmes. Doyle also excelled at creating marvelous place names. There is a house called High Gable, and its near neighbors are The Dingle, Oxshott Towers, Purdey Place, and Nether Walsing. We hear of other estates, such as the Abbey Grange, Fairbank, and Appledore Towers. Then there are towns like Abbas Parva, Tredannick Wollas, and Little Purlington. These names are glorious creations, just for the way they look on the page and sound to the ear. But they also create atmosphere and drama: I find myself entranced by them.

However, it took many years before I came to realize that Doyle had taken Dickens's use of proper names a step further: he employed what I call "aptonyms." An aptonym is a name particularly appropriate to a person, animal, place, or what-have-you. For example, consider a dentist who has the misfortune to be named "Payne." If his level of skill is somewhat below the norm, his name becomes a perfect aptonym. Another classic example—and a true one, I believe—was a former archbishop of the Roman Catholic Church: being the holder of a red hat, he was known as Cardinal Sin. We will find that Conan Doyle had a fondness for using aptonyms as a means of creating or presenting characters and places: they are found throughout the Holmes canon, in both the short stories and the novels. In so doing, he out-Dickensed Dickens.

Let us consider a few examples. The villain in the second Holmes story is, as we have noted before, the grandson of a royal duke whose name is "John Clay." Is it not true that he is literally a nobleman with feet of clay?

I had been reading and rereading the Holmes stories for forty or fifty years before I realized that they are peppered with aptonyms. What finally opened my eyes was "The Beryl Coronet," the eleventh story in the first collection of Holmes shorts, *The Adventures*. A brief retelling of this tale will demonstrate its unique characteristic—aptonyms for everybody!

The story concerns a banker, one Alexander Holder, and his family—his son, Arthur, and his niece, Mary. The latter is the daughter of his deceased brother, and she was adopted by Mr. Holder after her father's death. Approached by a highly placed person about a loan and impressed by the prospective client's lofty social position and undoubted wealth, Holder agrees to lend this gentleman fifty thousand pounds for a few days. As security, the client offers the Beryl Coronet, a crown worth double the amount of the loan. From the first, the banker knows that the coronet is not the personal property of his client, but belongs to the state—that is, the Crown. But swayed by the language as well as the social position of the borrower, he agrees to the deal. (The identity of this gentleman is never made clear, but it seems more than likely that it is the Prince of Wales himself.)

After the new client leaves with his fifty thousand pounds, banker

Holder begins to suffer doubts. Afraid of a robbery, he decides to take the coronet home with him and lock it up in his dressing room.

Mr. Holder then describes the people at Fairbank, as his house is called. He is disappointed with his son, Arthur, who has been living a high life among members of the wealthy aristocracy and always seems to be short of money. Arthur is somewhat influenced by his friend, Sir George Burnwell, who sometimes visits him at the house. Arthur is in love with his cousin Mary, to whom he has twice proposed—she rejected him on both occasions. Perhaps partly because of his feelings about his son, Mr. Holder has become very close to his niece: he calls her "a sunbeam in the house, sweet, loving, beautiful, a wonderful manager and housekeeper, yet as quiet and gentle as a woman could be. She is my right hand. I do not know what I could do without her."

After dinner on the night of the loan deal, Mr. Holder informs both Arthur and Mary about the coronet. Lucy Parr, a new serving maid, might have overheard this conversation.

Lucy has a boyfriend, Francis Prosper, a man with a wooden leg: he is a greengrocer who comes to the house to deliver produce and so communicates with Lucy over the back gate.

I need go no further into the story; for my purpose, it is enough to say that my law school background was piqued at the thought of the banker's family name, Holder. For in law, a banker is described as "a *holder* in due course." Was it mere coincidence that Conan Doyle gave his central character this name? Then I thought about the name of the house: Fairbank. It dawned on me that by taking the coronet home with him, Mr. Holder was using the house as a "fair bank" when he locked the coronet in his bureau. Thus, we have not just one, but two aptonyms. That set me thinking, and I realized (after many years) that *every* character in this story has a name especially appropriate to him or her. The suspected maid, Lucy Parr, is a stock character: she could be considered "par for the course." Her boyfriend Francis Prosper will do just that in the grocery business. Sir George Burnwell, Arthur's friend, turns out to be the villain of the piece: he seduced Mary, who told him about the coronet, and handed it to him through the window before running away with him. He will indeed "burn well" in Hell, according to Christian belief. Then there is the son, Arthur: he witnessed the theft and tried to take the coronet from Burnwell, but he got back only part of it. His father accused him of the theft, but he refused to defend himself because to do so would implicate his cousin, the woman he still loved. In short, young Arthur Holder acts according to the chivalrous example of his namesake, the legendary King Arthur of the Round Table.*

Also, do not forget that Arthur was the author's own first name!

Then there is Mary. In Christian tradition there are two outstanding women bearing that name. One, of course, is the Virgin Mother. The second is her contemporary, Mary Magdelene, a fallen woman and follower of Christ. Can we doubt that Mary Holder, who becomes a fallen woman herself in this story, owes her name to "the other Mary?"

"The Beryl Coronet" is unique in using aptonyms for all of its characters (as Bunyan did in *Pilgrim's Progress*) but many other Holmes stories employ aptonyms. Some examples:

---

* Holmes says of Arthur to his father, "You owe a very humble apology to that noble lad, your son, who has carried himself in this matter as I should be proud to see my own son do, should I ever chance to have one." Throughout the canon, the name Arthur is associated with men who act selflessly and chivalrously in the tradition of the ancient king, as recounted in Sir Thomas Malory's great book. In the very first Holmes story, we find Arthur Charpentier, who was accused of the murder of Enoch Drebber after his sister and mother disclosed to Inspector Gregson how the drunken American proposed that she run off with him and actually tried to pull her to the door when her brother entered the room and drove Drebber away. (*A Study in Scarlet*, chapter 6.) In "The Bruce-Partington Plans," Arthur Cadogan West defends his country and loses his life in the process. What more heroic and noble man could there be than this Arthur, who left his fiancé in the street to follow a man who might or might not be a traitor? At least three Arthurs in the canon are distinguished by their heroic, noble, and chivalrous action. Two of them attempt to protect women they love, and the third dies trying to protect his country.

One could hardly find a more appropriate first name for the aristocratic Musgrave (in "The Musgrave Ritual") than the one Doyle gave him: Reginald. For the name derives from the root "regis," meaning "king." (Consider the word "regicide," which means the killing of a sovereign.)

Abe Slaney, "The most dangerous crook in Chicago," contains a hidden aptonym: just spell it *Slain-y*. Slaney appears in "The Dancing Men."

Jonas Oldacre, the Norwood builder, is motivated to frame John Hector McFarlane by an "old ache"—his long-ago dismissal as a suitor by McFarlane's mother.

The formidable Dr. Grimesby Roylott's name is perilously close to "crimes by."

Another example: Jephro Rucastle of "The Copper Beeches," has a name which suggests several "apts." "Rucastle" suggests "rue," as in "you'll rue taking this position, Miss Hunter." It also suggests "ruin," the state the man will reach by the end of the story—and also, coupled with "castle," the condition of the family house. Too subtle, you say? Not intended by the author? Perhaps—but just the number of these aptonyms argues for the other point of view.

There are more examples from the short stories. The name of the Duke's older, jealous, and grasping illegitimate son in "The Priory School" is James Wilder: the case would be stronger if it was just James Wilde, but "wild" he surely is. "Susan" is a name frequently associated with female servants: consider our calling a food serving tray "a lazy Susan." Well, there are two maids in the canon named Susan—Susan Tarleton in "The Golden Pince-Nez" and Susan Stockdale in "The Three Gables" (whose mistress calls her "wicked Susan"). In "Silver Blaze," John Straker, the dishonest trainer, uses as his alias "William Darbyshire." If Holmes had really been on the ball, he would have immediately recognized the relationship of "Darbyshire" to "derby"—a horse race, pronounced "darby" in England—and realized that it was Straker who was using the name.

A strong case in favor of treating Doyle's use of aptonyms as conscious comes from "Thor Bridge," in which the prime suspect is called Grace Dunbar. She is arrested and jailed pending trial. Watson describes her in glowing terms, saying that "there was an innate nobility of character" in her face "which would make her influence always good." She refuses to say anything but the truth, even in her own defense against a charge of murder. She carries off the whole traumatic situation with calm and poise: what better name than Grace could there be for such a woman?

Still another aptonym is to be found in "The Devil's Foot," where we meet "the great lion hunter and explorer," Dr. Sterndale. He is a big man, with, as Watson puts it, "a craggy and deeply-seamed face with fierce eyes and a hawk-like nose, grizzled hair ... and a beard—golden at the fringes and white near the lips." He also has "a tremendous personality." This description suggests something lion-like—and his given name, Leon, means lion!*

In the same story, we find still another aptonym, although this one is less obvious. The person around whose actions the story revolves is Mortimer Tregennis. He is only one of several Mortimers in the canon, but possibly the most important one. The name derives from two French words: "mort," meaning dead or death, and "mer," ocean or sea. Together they mean, literally, "dead sea," and initially they described a place where there was still (or "dead") water. In time, the place name was applied to people who lived by such a body of water—it became a family name. Finally, the family name became a first name. It appears as both in the canon. Interestingly, when used as a man's first name, "Mortimer" is frequently shortened to "Mort," the original French root, meaning "death." No character in the Holmes saga is more closely associated with death than Mr.

---

*   In the following collection of short stories, we find one entitled "The Lion's Mane," and while there is no lion in it, one does appear in "The Veiled Lodger," and in *The Case-Book* as well. In his later years, Sir Arthur seems to have been somehow captivated by the king of beasts.

Tregennis, as any reader familiar with the story will realize: hence, we have another aptonym.

We even find in the canon what might be called an anti-aptonym: use of a name in an ironic manner to express the opposite of the possessor's true character. Think of "A Case of Identity," one of the earliest Holmes shorts, in which Mr. James Windibank uses as his pseudonym "Hosmer Angel." Readers of "Case" will immediately see that "Hosmer" is no "Angel."

At the risk of overwhelming the reader with aptonyms, I would like to point out at least three more, starting with a place name. In "The Dancing Men," the estate of the unfortunate Hilton Cubitt is called "Ridling Thorpe Manor," at least in English editions. (Some American editions render this name as "*Riding* Thorpe Manor.) The original is an aptonym, seeing that the estate is the scene of puzzling riddle—what do the dancing figures mean, and who put them there? The American version unfortunately ruins the aptonym.

While there may be many more aptonyms in the canon, there are just two more I wish to point out here. The first concerns the arch-villain of the Holmes saga—The Napoleon of Crime himself, Professor Moriarty. I had often wondered why Conan Doyle gave him this name: aptonymic thinking gave me an answer. The word root "Mor," means death. Combined with "arty" (art-like), it yields "Moriarty"—artist of death. I refuse to believe this is a mere coincidence. And to support the argument even further, Moriarty's chief deputy is Colonel Moran: there's that root "Mor" again.

Not long ago I came across a book titled *Baby Names Now*, written by Linda Rosencrantz and Pamela Redman Satran and published in 2001. My interest in names and their meanings would not let me put it down without reading at least some of it. I found that the authors had done a splendid job of research on the topic, and I began to look up some names that I had not known about. Completely by accident I discovered the male name Conan. Of course I read every word in the book about it, and I found that in Irish it means "intelligence" or "wisdom"! This amazed me: Dr. Doyle's first name, Arthur, is associated with heroic and noble conduct, and now I find that Conan connotes intelligence and wisdom. Talk about aptonyms—both his names are perfect aptonyms!

Enough about aptonyms: either I have convinced you, or I have not. But names function in other ways, and the one I am about to discuss may or may not have been a function of Conan Doyle's conscious mind. I refer to names which appear in different stories and in totally different contexts, but which may be a device to unify the collections. The great Irish author James Joyce did this in *Dubliners*, where it is clearly intentional and serves to interrelate the various stories. I am not convinced that Doyle deliberately used recurring names, or at least similar names, to interlock various stories: it may simply have been an example of his unconscious mind on the loose. In any case, here are a few examples.

In "The Boscombe Valley Mystery," the scene of the action is Hatherley Farm. Five stories later in *The Adventures* we encounter the young hydraulic engineer who loses his thumb to a meat cleaver: his name is Victor *Hatherley*. In "The Priory School," the fifth story in *The Return*, we learn that the Duke of Holdernesse married Edith, daughter of Sir *Charles Appledore*; her son is Arthur, Lord Saltire. Estranged from her husband, the duchess is living in the South of France. Two stories later in the same collection, we find *Charles* Augustus Milverton, king of the blackmailers, living at a house called *Appledore* Towers, which Holmes and Watson visit in the dark of the night with a surprising and tragic result.

A few other such correspondences: Sir Leslie Oakshott, the physician who treats Holmes after his beating in "The Illustrious Client," recalls James Ryder's sister, the goose-breeding Mrs. Oakshott of Brixton Road in "The Blue Carbuncle," and also Oxshott Towers, the home of Sir George Ffolliott (sic) in "Wisteria Lodge." Similarly, Colonel Lysander Stark—the thin, murderous Fuller's earth man from "The Engineer's Thumb"—has almost exactly the same name as Dr. Lysander Starr, the mythical Mayor of Topeka, Kansas, in "The Three Garridebs." The Bruce-Pinkerton Prize won by Dr. Percy Trevalyn in "The Resident Patient" is recalled by the Bruce-Partington Submarine, the plans of which are stolen in the story of the same name. Intentional or not, there are many more such correspondences in the canon.

In concluding this essay, I hope to have demonstrated beyond any doubt that Conan Doyle used proper names of people, places, and domiciles to deepen and make more effective his presentation of characters, emotions, and atmosphere in his Holmes stories. He follows Dickens's example in creating memorable names which by their appearance on the page and sound when read aloud contribute to the impact the author seeks to make on the reading public. But Dr. Doyle went even further down this road than his predecessor: by employing aptonyms he not only enhanced his delineation of character but also involved his readers in the process. For example, the name "Sir George Burnwell" is innocent enough on the surface, but when we discover what kind of man he is, our negative feelings about him are intensified—we recognize his fate in his very name.

So, what have we discovered in our study of the fifty-six short stories Dr. Conan Doyle wrote in which Sherlock Holmes appears as the leading character? Like any good attorney, let me sum up my case.

SOCIAL CRITICISM

While these stories have always been considered light entertainment, they contain a good deal of critical commentary on England in the Victorian and Edwardian periods—and some on America as well. First, they indicate that the author had a critical view of at least some of the titled and the wealthy, whom he felt did not always deserve the unquestioning respect and obedience they expected to receive, regardless of their behavior. The world was changing rapidly, and the value of the rigid class system is clearly questioned. This also applies to the American worship of money and the attitude of the very rich toward those they considered below them.

Second, the stories include a challenge to the rigid social

restrictions which constrained and confined women. Conan Doyle created Irene Adler, who becomes the heroine of her saga not only despite her violation of these restrictions, but because of it. At least three stories—especially "The Devil's Foot"—point out the inequity of the English divorce laws.

Third, these stories indicate that Holmes (and by extension, his creator) had at least some respect for the downtrodden. Compare, if you will, Holmes's attitude toward the street boys whom he employs with that of Mrs. Hudson and even that of Watson. Also, just as Doyle transforms Irene Adler from an object of derision, even by members of her own sex, into a heroine, so also he finds value in the ex-convict Shinwell Johnson and the prostitute Kitty Winter, both of whom are better people than the aristocrats with whom they are contrasted—the evil Baron Gruner and the hopelessly over-romantic and socially unaware Violet de Merville.

THE THEMES OF INHERITANCE AND ATAVISM

Again and again in the Holmes saga Conan Doyle raises the question of whether genetic inheritance influences behavior, and especially the proposition that it influences people to commit crimes. In this area, Dr. Doyle anticipates the current debate of these same questions—"nature or nurture"—and he seems to come down on the side of inheritance at least to an extent.

THE SKILL OF THE WRITER

Anyone who reads these stories seriously can hardly miss Doyle's mastery of the English language which they so clearly demonstrate. He proves himself to be a virtuoso in descriptive writing, and in the development of character, the creation of convincing dialogue, and the use of atmosphere. No writer that I know surpasses Doyle, and few approach him, in the use of names—including but not limited to his use of aptonyms to disclose or describe personality traits in his characters, or atmosphere in his settings. In every way, Conan Doyle must be regarded as a writer of the very highest rank.

Moreover, to his credit, he never stopped experimenting, seeking new ways to tell his stories and new stories to tell, and becoming more philosophical as he grew older. Sherlock Holmes became a much wiser, deeper, and more likable person as a result. In 1887, when Holmes made his debut in *A Study in Scarlet*, who could have foreseen that this brash, somewhat egocentric, and deliberately machine-like individual would in time develop feelings and become concerned with the meaning and purpose of human life?

THE GREAT IRONY

Above all, the Holmes short stories demonstrate something that Sir Arthur himself failed to recognize. He was so convinced that his Holmes stories would detract from his artistic reputation that he tried to kill off the series by murdering the hero he had created. He appears to have realized that great popularity with the public may come at the cost of not being taken seriously by the academic establishment. For further proof, see the parallel case of O. Henry.

What Sir Arthur apparently did not see or understand is that even in these detective stories, which he considered mere trifles, he demonstrated great depth of thought and analysis of the world in which he lived. Moreover, the Holmes saga exhibits the author's exceptional technical skill, and his unexcelled gift for storytelling. Even if all his other work were to be ignored, the Holmes short stories alone are enough to place their creator in the very highest rank of writers in the English language.

Alerted by these short tales to the true stature of Conan Doyle as a writer, we are now ready to tackle the four longer Holmes works— novels, novellas, or whatever else one may call them. We will find, I believe, that in these four tales, there is literary merit even beyond anything we have yet seen.

PART 2

The Four Sherlock Holmes Novels

CHAPTER 8

A Study in Scarlet

IT ALL BEGAN WITH THIS NOVELLA, WHICH DR. DOYLE WROTE IN 1886 AT the age of twenty-seven. At that time, he already had behind him two stints as a shipboard surgeon—the first on a whaler and the second on a passenger steamer. He had an unsuccessful medical partnership in Plymouth and a more rewarding general practice in Southsea. He had published his first stories and nonfiction. His marriage to Louisa Hawkins in 1885 can only have increased his efforts to supplement his income through writing.

Thus, he began a detective story strongly influenced by the work of Edgar Allan Poe, but longer and more elaborately worked out. He found a publisher—Ward, Lock, and Co.—but only on condition that the story would not appear for another year. He was paid £25 for the copyright, and in December 1887, the tale was published in *Beeton's Christmas Annual*.

It seems the vogue today to denigrate this first Holmes book as much inferior to those that came later, and certainly Dr. Doyle at this stage of his career was not yet the consummate literary master he was to become. However, *Scarlet* is a remarkably good book, especially when one considers that it was not only the author's maiden attempt at the form, but also only the third detective novel written in English. (Only Wilkie Collins's *The Moonstone* and Dickens's unfinished *Mystery of Edwin Drood* preceded it.) In this essay I hope to show why I consider this first Holmes story quite worthy of comparison with its creator's later work—it has a convincing plot, contains some excellent characterization and use of the language, and ideas quite on a par with those in Doyle's later Holmes work.

STRUCTURE

The apparent structure of this novella divides the story into two parts. The first is entitled "A Reprint from The Reminiscences of John H. Watson, MD, Late of the Army Medical Department," while the second is entitled "The Country of the Saints." Each part contains seven chapters. At first, the structure appears quite simple.

Not so, if you read the book with care. Indeed, the first half introduces the major characters and describes the crimes and successful capture of the perpetrator. But the second half, despite its title, contains only five chapters devoted to the lives of John and Lucy Ferrier in America, and ends with Jefferson Hope beginning his lifelong effort to revenge their deaths at the hands of young Drebber and Stangerson. The final two chapters are set in London after Hope's capture, and they contain his story (in chapter 6) and Holmes's account of how he solved the case (chapter 7). These two final chapters really constitute a third section of the novel.

Seen in this way, we find that the first and third parts are set in London in the "present," while the second part takes place twenty years earlier, and 7,000 miles away, across the Atlantic. Part 3 might have been called "A Continuation of the Reminiscences of John Watson, MD"—which indeed is the title Doyle gave to chapter 6, although it applies equally well to chapter 7.

One should also note how the sections of the second part are delineated not only by where and when they take place, but also the character of their narrators. The first and third parts are told by Watson, who is not only an eyewitness of their events, but also in a small way a participant. The second part—the American backstory—is narrated instead by an impersonal third person, presumably obtaining his information from Jefferson Hope himself. The fact that this narrator could have been Watson, who was present at Hope's post-capture interview with the three detectives and yet was not allowed by the author to tell the story himself, suggests that Dr. Doyle wished to set off this section of the saga from the parts that precede and follow it.

In fact, when one examines the structure of *Scarlet* closely, it becomes apparent that the novella conforms quite neatly to the traditional three-act form of storytelling employed in the theater: exposition, development, and resolution. The only difference is that the story is not presented in chronological order: the American background to the London crimes is reported in a flashback. Organizing his tale in this way was, I suggest, a stroke of genius on Doyle's part.

Moreover, just as the second part of the novella can be subdivided into two clearly different sections, so can the first. The author does not begin his tale with the first crime, as might be expected. Instead, the first two chapters form a subsection of the first part of the novel, which is devoted to introducing us to the two principal characters in the book—Dr. Watson, the physician who narrates the story and at the end promises to write a description of who really solved the mystery, and how; and Sherlock Holmes, the eccentric and occasionally exasperating genius who has a great impact on Watson. The interplay between these two allows us to see Holmes through Watson's eyes, so that the detective appears almost superhuman.

This formula was used by Poe in his Dupin stories, but Poe never fleshed out his nameless narrator or gave him a personality of his own. Doyle did exactly that in these first two chapters, and then again at the end of the book. Thus, I suggest that this is really Dr. Watson's story: it is about how meeting and observing Holmes affects the physician. In short, while Holmes is clearly the most remarkable character in the story, it is fundamentally not about him, but rather about his new friend and roommate. And to the extent that Watson represents and connects with the reader, it is also about how Holmes affects the reader. This, I think, is a major reason the Holmes saga has been so overwhelmingly popular for nearly a century and a half. Doyle's genius had him start his story not with the crimes, but with the man whose world is changed by his contact with the eccentric but fascinating detective. The reader is "in loco Watson," and his or her own life is transformed as well.

The second subsection of the first part (chapters 3–7) describes the investigation and the investigators—Gregson, Lestrade, and Sherlock Holmes. We meet the two rival Scotland Yarders at the scene of the first crime—the house at 3 Lauriston Gardens—and watch through Watson's eyes how Holmes approaches the case. At the end of the third chapter, Holmes delivers his Parthian shot about the meaning of the writing on the wall—the first of his many put-downs of "the Force" which are to be found throughout the canon. In the next two chapters Holmes and Watson monitor the work of the Scotland Yard men. By the sixth chapter, Holmes announces that he has nearly a complete case, shocking not only Gregson and Lestrade, but also Watson and the reader. In this chapter, each of the official detectives pursues a different lead, only to find themselves with incorrect solutions. At last, in the seventh chapter, Holmes learns from Lestrade of the discovery of the pills in their box. "The last link!" cries Holmes. "My case is complete." He follows this declaration with the experiment involving the old, sick terrier. This is soon followed by the entrance first of Wiggins—with the announcement that he has the cab downstairs—and then by the appearance of the cabman and the arrest. As far as I can tell, the murderer's name has never been mentioned until Holmes utters it here—a delightful trick for the baffled reader, for whom the information comes entirely out of the blue. Few detective story writers I know have been able to so construct their tales that the perpetrator's name remains hidden so completely until the moment of revelation. Doyle did it in his very first effort at detective fiction—a subtle but telling clue of his greatness as an author of works in this genre.

The first chapter of part 2 introduces us to old John Ferrier and "Little Lucy," and how they are saved from death on the great alkali plain by the immigrating Mormons.

Twelve years pass between the end of the first chapter and the beginning of the second. John Ferrier has become a wealthy man, and Lucy, now seventeen, is "the flower of Utah." In this chapter she first meets Jefferson Hope when he calms her frightened horse, and soon becomes her suitor. They agree to marry in two months, when he returns from his mine in Nevada.

Chapters 3, 4, and 5 comprise the second subsection of the second part: they describe the pressure on the Ferriers from the prophet (Brigham Young) and the elders; the return of Hope and the flight of the three from Utah; and finally the grim events which occur on the trail. This section concludes with Hope dedicating the rest of his life to revenge—including a short account of his dogged pursuit of his quarry across America and Europe until he runs them to earth in London.

This brings us to the last two chapters of the book, which I have called the third part. This includes Hope's own account of the murders, and it concludes with Holmes's explanation of how he solved the mystery. One might expect this information to be found at the end of the first part—but Doyle there withholds everything but the name of the accused, thus leading the reader into the backstory. By the time the reader reaches the closing lines, he or she is so impressed by the story that demand for more of Watson and Holmes becomes nearly inevitable. The author may or may not have foreseen the possibility of a sequel to his first detective novella, but he certainly arranged his material in such a way that he encourages demand for one. In short, the structure of this first Holmes story enhances the possibility of a second.

PART 1: WHAT DR. WATSON WROTE
Part 1, Subsection 1: Chapters 1–2

In studying *Scarlet*, it will be useful to look closely at each chapter individually. Detailed structural analysis reveals much about a book that may be missed by casual readers: I hope that a careful reading of this novella will convince people of the magnitude of Dr. Doyle's accomplishment here, which is all the more remarkable as his first venture not only into the detective story genre but also as his first attempt at fiction beyond the short story form.

We begin then with the first part of the book.

CHAPTER 1: MR. SHERLOCK HOLMES

Dr. John H. Watson begins his account of the Drebber-Stangerson-Hope case with some comments on his own history. We learn hardly anything about his background before the year 1878, when he was awarded his degree as Doctor of Medicine by the University of London.

Immediately afterward he apparently enlisted in the Army Medical Department, and after training at Netley, was attached to the Fifth Northumberland Fusiliers as assistant surgeon, and posted to India, where the second Afghan War had just broken out. His military career was both short and painful: wounded at the Battle of Maiwand, he was saved from capture by his courageous and devoted orderly, Murray, and sent to recover at the base hospital at Peshawar. While there, however, he suffered a case of enteric fever which came close to ending his life.

Sent back to England on a troop ship, he found himself alone in London. Having no relatives in the country, and apparently without any financial resources beyond his wound pension, he soon came to realize that he would have to economize. On the very day that he reached that disappointing decision, he was recognized by a former subordinate with whom he had worked at Saint Bartholomew's

Hospital. This man, whose name was Stamford, joined him for lunch, and over their meal they fell into conversation. Asked what he was doing at the present time, Dr. Watson replied that he was looking for comfortable lodgings at a reasonable price. By a happy chance Stamford had that morning met another young man in similar circumstances who had found a suitable apartment but needed a roommate to share the rent. So that afternoon Watson and Stamford drove down to the hospital, and there, in the chemical laboratory, they found the man they were looking for. Stamford then uttered the magic words of the introduction: "Dr. Watson, Mr. Sherlock Holmes." Holmes asked Watson how he was before noting, "You have been in Afghanistan, I perceive." For the first time (but certainly not the last) Holmes stuns both Dr. Watson and the reader: from this moment on, we are hooked.

This first chapter ends with Holmes's triumphal discovery of a reliable test for bloodstains, followed by a short conversation between the two prospective roommates, and at the very end, Watson's question to Stamford, "How the deuce did he know that I had come from Afghanistan?" "That's just his little peculiarity," Stamford replies. "Oh, a mystery!" Watson says, delighted. And the proper study of mankind being man, he determines to study his new acquaintance. Stamford replies, "I'll wager he learns more about you than you about him. Goodbye."

CHAPTER 2: THE SCIENCE OF DEDUCTION

After a couple of paragraphs describing their moving in and Watson's first observations of his new roommate's habits and behavior, we find Watson's first physical description of Sherlock Holmes: "In height he was rather over six feet, and so excessively lean that he seemed to be considerably taller. His eyes were sharp and piercing ... and his thin hawk-like nose gave his whole expression an air of alertness and decision. His chin, too, had the prominence and squareness which mark the man of determination. His hands were invariably blotted with ink and stained with chemicals, yet he was possessed of extraordinary delicacy of touch." It was during the first few weeks of their co-tenancy that Watson drew up his famous chart entitled, "Sherlock Holmes—his limits." I shall not bother to copy it here, but suffice it to say that this catalogue, in the tradition of Homer's catalogue of the Greek ships in *The Iliad*, was another brilliant idea of young Doyle. It contributes to the mystery about Holmes, befuddling Watson and the reader while introducing a note of humor into the story. It is central to the developing relationship between the two friends, which, as I have already suggested, is for me the heart of the entire Holmes saga.

The important part of chapter 2, however, is the article by Holmes called "The Book of Life," which Watson picks up at the breakfast table, and describes as "ineffable twaddle." Holmes reveals that he wrote it himself, and that he has "a trade of my own. I suppose I am the only one in the world. I'm a consulting detective, if you can understand what that is." He then goes on to explain to Watson how by observation and deduction he knew that the doctor had been in Afghanistan.

We know that Dr. Doyle had been much impressed by one of his teachers at Edinburgh—Dr. Joseph Bell, whose use of those twin faculties was key to his renowned skill at diagnosis, and who led the young author to create his famous detective character. It is also more than likely that Dr. Doyle came up with the idea of making Holmes "a consulting detective" under the influence of his medical background. It is common for a physician to turn to a specialist when aid is needed in handling a difficult case. Doyle must have reasoned that if doctors could consult with experts, why not detectives? He therefore endowed his character with acute powers of observation and deduction, making him also a walking encyclopedia of crime—the precise tools which his profession required. Instantly, Holmes was separated from all other detectives of fact or fiction, and he remains unique to this day.

Holmes also reveals something else in these paragraphs—his

youth and somewhat inflated ego. He puts down Dupin (after whom he was modeled) and Lecoq (whom he describes as "a miserable bungler"). Moreover, for the first time (but surely not for the last) he bewails the absence of crimes and criminals in his time. "What is the use of having brains in our profession? ... No man lives or has ever lived who has brought the same amount of study and of natural talent to the detection of crime which I have done. And what is the result? There is no crime to detect, or, at most, some bungling villainy with a motive so transparent that even a Scotland Yard official can see through it." All this material is by way of establishing Sherlock Holmes as a sort of Nietchzean superman, genus detective. Watson, irked by his new friend's egoism, resolves to test him. A "commissionaire" bearing a large blue envelope appears on the street, and Watson remarks "I wonder what that fellow is looking for?"

"You mean the retired sergeant of marines," Holmes replies. When the man has come upstairs and delivered his note to Holmes, Watson asks his trade and learns that he does commissions but does not have his uniform on, as it is being repaired. "And you were?" asks the doctor. "A sergeant, sir, Royal Marine Light Infantry, sir," the young man replies. Holmes has triumphed again.

At this point—the closing lines of chapter 2—the foundation has been laid not only for the story of *A Study in Scarlet*, but the entire Holmes canon. It is now time to move on to subsection 2 of part 1, in which the action of this first Holmes novella begins.

Part 1, Subsection 2: Chapters 3–6

CHAPTER 3: THE LAURISTON GARDEN MYSTERY

Immediately after the commissionaire has left, Holmes explains how he recognized the man as a retired sergeant of marines, and then tosses over to Watson the note their visitor has brought. It is from Tobias Gregson of Scotland Yard, requesting Holmes's aid in the investigation of the murder of Enoch J. Drebber, whose body was found in an empty house off the Brixton Road at about two o'clock that morning. Holmes decides to go, and on the spur of the moment invites his roommate to come along, "If you have nothing better to do." Off they go together in a hansom. Holmes talks of nothing but violins during the ride.

Now we get to watch Holmes conduct a scene-of-the-crime investigation for the first time. The detective orders the cab to stop a hundred yards from the house, and the two friends finish their journey on foot. As they approach the death house, Holmes looks over the ground, the sky, the houses on opposite side of the street, and the line of brick walls and wooden railings in front of the four houses (two unoccupied) which make up Lauriston Gardens.

When he finally does approach the house, Holmes is careful to stay off the muddy path, walking instead on the strip of grass beside it while keeping his eyes riveted to the soggy ground. "Twice he stopped," Watson says, "and once I saw his smile, and heard him utter an exclamation of satisfaction." The reader might be tempted to skip past these lines in his hurry to get into the house and see the corpse. Notice, however, how the author has subtly indicated that Holmes has seen something important in the muddy pathway. While Watson could see nothing in the marks there, he had already determined that Holmes "could see a great deal which was hidden from me."

Inspector Gregson greets Holmes and Watson at the door, remarking that he has left everything untouched pending their arrival. "Except that!" replies Holmes, indicating the path. Gregson's reply is telling: "I have had so much to do inside the house," he explains. "I have relied on my colleague, Mr. Lestrade, to look after this."

Holmes asks just one question before going inside: he gets Gregson's assurance that neither of the Scotland Yarders came to Lauriston Gardens in a cab. The alert reader now knows not only that Holmes has found an important clue on the path, but also that he has determined that a cab was at the scene of the crime, and that this fact has some bearing on the investigation. Gregson's "look of astonishment" tells us that he has either not seen or not recognized the importance of what Holmes has observed outside the house.

Watson's following description of the interior of the death house is a brilliant piece of atmospheric creation. Like the structure itself, everything is dark and empty. Words like "vulgar," "flaring," "mildew," "yellow," "imitation," "stump," "dirty," "hazy and uncertain," and "thick layer of dust" produce in the reader a profound feeling that this ugly, depressing, empty room is a perfect theatre for murder.

In the next paragraph, the stage is occupied by the body of the victim. Again the choice of words is masterly: Watson says that his "attention was centered on the single, grim, motionless figure which lay stretched upon the boards, with vacant, sightless eyes staring up at the discolored ceiling."* And then: "His hands were clenched and his arms thrown aboard, while his lower limbs were interlocked, as though his death struggle had been a grievous one. On his rigid face there stood an expression of horror, and, as it seemed to me, of hatred such as I have never seen upon human features. This malignant and terrible contortion, combined with the low forehead, blunt nose, and prognathous jaw, gave the dead man a singularly simious and ape-like appearance, which was increased by his writhing, unnatural posture. I have seen death in many forms, but never has it appeared to me in a more fearsome aspect than in that dark, grimy apartment." Even at the age of twenty-seven, Arthur Conan Doyle could write with chilling effect.

There is another aspect to the description of the body. The low forehead, apish countenance, and look of terror and hatred are calculated to dispel any feeling of sympathy the reader may have for this man. Here, we feel at once, is the corpse of an evil person who deserved whatever befell him. This attitude will become an

---

* At least since the time of Shakespeare, actors have called the stage "the boards." The use of those words here reinforces the theatrical imagery of this scene.

important factor in shaping our responses in the long narrative which is to follow.

Holmes makes two other moves before beginning to examine the death room. First he gives the body a quick examination, ending with the sniffing of the dead man's lips and a glance at the soles of his boots. Then the detective says, "You may take him to the mortuary now. There is nothing more to be learned." But as the body is lifted onto a stretcher to be carried out, a ring falls to the floor and rolls away. Lestrade grabs it and says, "There's been a woman here. It's a woman's wedding ring." Note that Lestrade puts his discovery backwards: instead of first identifying his find as a woman's wedding ring, he jumps to the conclusion that there has been a woman in the room. It's a small touch, but a remarkable illustration of the difference in the way the logical Holmes and the careless Lestrade observe and deduce.

The next step is to consider the contents of the dead man's pockets. Gregson has them laid out on one of the low steps: cards and the initials on a handkerchief suggest the identity of the victim— Enoch J. Drebber, of Cleveland, Ohio.

There is also a pocket edition of Boccaccio's *Decameron* (a decidedly racy classic) with the name "Joseph Stangerson" on the flyleaf, and two letters from a steamship line. One of these was addressed to Mr. Drebber and the other to Mr. Stangerson, care of American Exchange, to be left until called for. This appears to indicate that these two men were traveling together, and that they were about to return to the States. Gregson attempted to discover more about Stangerson, but had learned nothing. Again, we get a suggestion of a clue which Holmes has discovered in his pointed questions to Gregson about his telegraphic message to Cleveland, but neither Gregson nor the reader has any idea of what Holmes wanted to know from Ohio at this point.

Now Lestrade interrupts with news of his discovery of the word "Rache" written on the wall, in letters of blood. When asked what he thinks it means, Lestrade for a second time in three pages jumps to a conclusion: it means, he says, that a woman named Rachel has had something to do with the case.

Holmes now concludes his examination of the room using a tape measure and a magnifying glass. From one place he picks up a bit of dust, and he carefully examines every letter of the word on the wall. At last he puts the tape and glass away in his pocket and asks for the name and address of the constable who found the body. He is informed that it was John Rance of Audley Court, Kennington Park. Then Holmes, for what may be the only time in the entire canon, gives us a detailed account of what he has found early in the story: "There has been murder done, and the murderer was a man. He was more than six feet tall, was in the prime of life, had small feet for his height, wore coarse, squared-toed boots and smoked a Trichinopoly cigar. He came here in a four-wheeled cab, which was drawn by a horse with three old shoes and one new one on his off fore-leg. In all probability the murderer had a florid face, and the fingernails on his right hand were remarkably long." When Lestrade asks how the man was killed in the absence of any wound, Holmes replies, "Poison. One more thing, Lestrade. 'Rache' is the German for 'revenge,' so don't lose your time looking for Miss Rachel."*

No detective character in literature has ever made a more dramatic debut than this. In one paragraph and a couple of lines, Sherlock Holmes has made scientific detection based on observation and deduction a requirement for any credible mystery story—and probably for any real-life exercise in detection as well!

CHAPTER 4: WHAT JOHN RANCE HAD TO TELL

After the brilliance and intensity of chapter 3, this one is easily dealt with. It begins with Holmes sending a long telegram, and

---

* As we come to know, Holmes is a devoted Wagnerian: he would surely recognize "rache" (pronounced "rock-e") from Hagen's killing of Siegfried in the third act of *Gotterdammurung*. But readers of *A Study in Scarlet* could not yet have known of Holmes's attachment to Wagner's music.

immediately afterward explaining to Watson (while they ride in the cab to Audley Court) how he reached the stunning conclusions with which he astonished Gregson, Lestrade, and millions of readers at the end of the last chapter.

With the aid of a half-sovereign, Holmes gets the constable to relate everything that happened during the previous night. Holmes startles the man by interrupting him to ask why, when he reached the front door, he turned back to the street, then astonishes again by telling the constable exactly what he did in the death room. Sherlock finds it necessary to tell the man that Gregson or Lestrade will vouch for him as "one of the hounds and not the wolf." At last he gets a description of the stranger who approached the house, and after telling Rance off, Holmes explains that the drunken stranger was the murderer, who had returned to the house in the hope of finding the ring. Then come the lines explaining the title: "There's the scarlet thread of murder running through the colorless skein of life."

And then Holmes goes off to Halle's concert to hear Madame Norman Neruda play the violin.

CHAPTER 5: OUR ADVERTISEMENT BRINGS A VISITOR

While Holmes is at the concert, Watson, left alone and tired from the morning's activities, tries to get a little sleep. He fails: his mind is too much excited by the experience of visiting the murder scene, and he cannot forget the sinister face of the dead man. He feels nothing but gratitude for whoever killed the simian Mr. Drebber: yet still he recognizes that "the depravity of the victim was no condonement in the eyes of the law."

Here we encounter, in the very first tale in the Holmes canon, a theme which permeates the rest of it down to the last stories: the ambiguity which may often exist between law and justice. Here, it is no more than a thought in Watson's mind. Later, it will have an important effect on Holmes's behavior, as we have already seen in our analysis of the short stories.

Holmes returns late and begins a philosophical commentary on Darwin and his suggestion that music preceded language in the course of human development. This is followed immediately by Holmes's observation that this case has stimulated Watson's imagination and thus disturbed him deeply: "Where there is no imagination there is no terror." These paragraphs point to the mature Holmes of later works—they should not be casually passed over.

The remainder of the chapter is occupied by the advertisement and the remarkable person it brings. While Holmes attempts to follow "the old woman," Watson, still restless, pages through Murger's *Scenes de la Vie de Boheme*, a book we previously encountered in the first Holmes short story, "A Scandal in Bohemia," which was not to be written for several years yet. On Holmes's return he tells how he was hoodwinked by a very good actor, and the chapter ends appropriately enough with more violin music—this time, Holmes himself playing as Watson dozes through the night.

CHAPTER 6: TOBIAS GREGSON SHOWS WHAT HE CAN DO

The author begins this chapter with a satirical account of how the various newspapers treat the story of the "Brixton Mystery" according to their own editorial positions. In the course of discussing this, Holmes quotes La Rochefoucauld: is this the man Watson in chapter 2 accused of having no knowledge of literature?

The noisy entrance of the Baker Street Irregulars breaks into the discussion at this point, though we do not learn what it is that Holmes has directed them to find. Hard on their heels comes Gregson, climbing the stairs three at a time in his hurry to report that he has "made the whole thing as clear as day." For a moment Holmes appears anxious: then he learns the identity of Gregson's suspect (one Arthur Charpentier, a sub-lieutenant in the navy) and gives a sigh of relief and a smile. Holmes invites the Scotland Yarder to take a cigar and a whiskey and soda, and to relate his great accomplishment.

Of course, Gregson begins by putting down his rival, "that fool

Lestrade," who has been tracing Stangerson. Gregson is convinced that Stangerson had nothing to do with the crime: his clue was the hat which was found beside Drebber's body. It bore the name of the hatter who made it (Underwood of Camberwell Road) and Gregson was surprised to find that Holmes had also noted that. But the Scotland Yard man followed up on the address and found that Drebber had bought the hat there. It had been sent to Charpentier's, a boarding house in Torquay Terrace, and thus Gregson learned where Drebber had been staying. Even Holmes is forced to admit that this was a smart piece of detection—the kind of thing he himself might have done, but in this instance failed to follow up on. Gregson visited the house and there learned that Drebber had made advances to the landlady's daughter Alice, trying to get her to run away with him. The scene was interrupted by the appearance of Charpentier's son, Arthur, who drove the drunken Drebber from the house and then went after him with a stick. The young naval officer was found by Gregson and his men, still carrying the cudgel, and arrested on suspicion of murder.

Just as Gregson finishes his story, again chortling over Lestrade's pursuit of Stangerson, Lestrade himself arrives—with news that Stangerson was found murdered at Halliday's Private Hotel early that morning. With this starling news, the chapter ends, and so does subsection 2 of part 1 of the novel, describing the three detectives' investigations of the murder.

NOTE ON SUBSECTION 2

Throughout these four chapters, Sherlock Holmes exhibits a cocksure attitude towards the Scotland Yard detectives, lecturing them like schoolboys and hardly ever showing either of them any respect. The one exception comes when Gregson explains how he located Drebber's boarding house through the clue of the hat, and Holmes actually has a bad moment when it appears that Gregson may have found the criminal. But when he learns that Gregson's suspect is Arthur Charpentier, he "gave a sigh of relief and relaxed into a smile." Obviously, Holmes feared that Gregson might have solved the case, which would have been a terrible blow to his ego. After he knows that Gregson has arrested the wrong man, Holmes resumes his superior attitude. Commenting on Gregson's tale of the doings at the boarding house, he yawns and says, "It's quite exciting." No doubt about it—the young Holmes can be downright boorish, and seems to need taking down a peg. He may be smart, but he is not always nice.

Part 1, Subsection 3

CHAPTER 7: LIGHT IN THE DARKNESS

Inspector Lestrade begins to tell the story of his actions during the past two days, and in contrast to Holmes he starts by admitting that he jumped to the conclusion that Stangerson was concerned in the death of Drebber. (We have seen this tendency in him twice before—over the ring and over the writing on the wall.)

Lestrade continues by explaining that even after he recognized that Stangerson had no part in the murder of Drebber, he still set himself to find out what had become of the secretary, where he was, and what he had been doing after the two Americans were last seen together at Euston Station about 8:30 in the evening of March 3. He evidently did not know about Gregson's finding Drebber's lodging place through the hatter, and so went doggedly from one lodging place to another in the vicinity of Euston. By lucky chance he came to Halliday's about 8 a.m. on the third morning after the murder, to find that indeed Stangerson was staying there and had been waiting for another gentleman to appear for the last two days. In the hope that his appearance would shock Stangerson into disclosing some useful information, Lestrade and the boots went upstairs immediately.* From under the door of Stagerson's room came a trickle of

---

* "The boots" means the hotel worker who handles luggage, shines shoes, and does other chores inside the building.

blood. They broke down the door and found Stagerson's body, dead and cold, near the open window. Above the corpse was written, in letters of blood, the word "Rache." In the room Lestrade found a small box containing a couple of pills.

At this information Holmes sprang from his chair, exclaiming, "The last link. My case is complete." Up to this point, partway through the chapter, we might consider Lestrade's findings part of the second subsection of part 1—the chapters devoted to the detectives and their investigations. Now, however, Holmes takes over the story. He claims to have all the facts in hand and will soon give proof.

There follows the experiment with the sick and aged terrier. Holmes experiences a bad moment when on feeding part of the first pill to the dog, literally nothing happens. For a few seconds he questions whether his whole chain of reasoning could be wrong—and then he seizes the second pill, melts it down in milk, and presents it to the dog, who dies immediately, as if struck by lightning. Holmes goes on to explain that he knows the murderer's identity and hopes to capture him "very shortly." Indeed, Wiggins almost immediately appears at the door to say that he has the cab downstairs. The cab driver is summoned, comes upstairs to help with the luggage, and finds himself handcuffed and introduced to all as Jefferson Hope— the murderer.

A struggle follows, but Hope is finally subdued and taken away in his own cab. The first part of the novel is finished. The second part—the backstory explaining the motive and the long series of events which have led up to the crimes—has yet to begin.

PART 2: THE COUNTRY OF THE SAINTS
Subsection 1: Chapters 1–2
CHAPTER 1: ON THE GREAT ALKALI PLAIN

Here Conan Doyle played fast and loose with North American geography: "From the Sierra Nevada to Nebraska ... is a region of desolation and silence ... an arid and repulsive desert, which for many years served as a barrier against the advance of civilization."

As a matter of fact, there is not now and never was such a "great alkali plain." Moreover, the author omits any specific mention of the great Rocky Mountain chain, and moves the Wasatch Mountains, which are east of the Salt Lake Valley, to the immediate west of it, where in truth the great salt flats are located. But this is a work of fiction—rearranging the landscape to fit the story is the author's prerogative, if it does not threaten the credibility of the tale.

On May 4, 1847, we meet John Ferrier (aged somewhere between forty and sixty) and a little girl of five whose name, we learn, is Lucy. They are the sole survivors of a party of twenty-one people: all the others succumbed to hunger and thirst when the troop became lost while trying to cross the plain.

The irresistible juxtaposition of an older, somewhat cynical man and a carefree little girl commands the reader's interest immediately: we cannot help but want to know what will happen to them. They are rescued when, as if by magic (or divine intervention), the great migration of 10,000 Mormons from their former settlement at Nauvoo, Illinois appears in time to save them. This is our first look at the Mormons, and we are left with a favorable impression: after all, they refer to themselves as "the persecuted children of God—the chosen of the Angel Moroni." That perception will change as the story unfolds. The chapter ends as the caravan with its two new members sets off again on the road to its unknown destination—Zion.

CHAPTER 2: THE FLOWER OF UTAH

Twelve years pass (1847 –1859). On arrival at the site of Salt Lake City, land grants are made and a new settlement established. John Ferrier thrived: "He was a man of a practical turn of mind, keen in his dealings and skillful with his hands. His iron constitution enabled him to work morning and evening at improving and tilling his lands. In three years, he was better off than his neighbors, in six he was well-to-do, in nine he was rich, and in twelve there were not half a dozen men in the whole Salt Lake City who could compare with him." The one thing he refused to do, giving no explanation, was to set up "a female establishment" in the manner of his polygamous neighbors and co-religionists.

Two pages or so suffice to tell his story. The rest of the chapter describes how Lucy grew to young adulthood. One day when she was seventeen, she rode her horse, "Poncho," into town.* The animal panicked in the midst of a herd of cattle, and Lucy was saved from death or serious injury only by the aid of "a tall, savage-looking young fellow, mounted on a powerful roan horse and clad in the rough dress of a hunter, with long rifle slung over his shoulders." He recognizes her as John Ferrier's daughter, and claims that his father and Ferrier were close friends back in St. Louis. His name is Jefferson Hope.

The remainder of the chapter describes Hope's own activities, and the growing affection between him and Lucy. When the time comes for him to return to his silver claim in Nevada, it is with the understanding that in two months he will return to Utah and claim her—with her willing assent—as his bride.**

---

* The author's spelling of "Poncho" rather than "Pancho" may have unintentionally named the horse for a rain cape, rather than for the nickname associated with the Spanish name "Francisco." For those of us who were kids in the 1950s, "Pancho" was the Cisco Kid's sidekick. His horse was called "Diablo."

** This story seems quite in keeping with history. It was in 1859 that a huge treasure of gold and silver ore was discovered on the slopes of Mt. Davidson, fifteen miles from Carson City. One of the first settlers, a miner named Henry Comstock, got drunk one day and named the whole site for himself—"the Comstock Lode." It was the greatest find of precious metal ores ever discovered in the continental United States, but since much of the gold and silver lay deep underground, capital was needed to develop the mines. Young Hope had come to Salt Lake, he said, looking for investors to back the development of his claim. In reality, San Francisco money financed the Comstock boom, and it was San Francisco, not Salt Lake City, which controlled the mines and benefited most from the profits. But at least Hope's search for cash is consistent with Comstock's needs in 1859.

Part 2, Subsection 2: Chapters 3–5

CHAPTER 3: JOHN FERRIER TALKS WITH THE PROPHET

The opening pages of this chapter describe how the Mormon community underwent (at least in fiction) a great and terrible transformation: the formerly persecuted became persecutors themselves. Any questioning of church doctrine, any expression of dissatisfaction with the leadership, any hint of the unorthodox might bring terrible repercussions, including death or disappearance: "Every man feared his neighbor and none spoke of the things which were nearest his heart."

The secret agency which enforced this dictatorship remained shadowed in mystery. No one knew who belonged to it, and no one knew how it carried out its operations. It was called "the Danite Band," or "the Avenging Angels." At first, in the manner of the Spanish Inquisition, its "vague and terrible power was exercised only upon the recalcitrants who, having embraced the Mormon faith, wished afterwards to pervert or to abandon it. Soon, however, it took a wider range."

So far as I am aware, the charge that Dr. Doyle next ascribes to this shadowy secret police has never been proven. But it is not hard to see how non-Mormons living near the Latter-day Saints might come to believe and fear that a shortage of adult women among a group which practiced polygamy might lead to the kidnapping and forcible abduction of local females to fill "the harems of the Elders." The probability that such depredations never occurred did not stop the widespread fear that they did. Thus, the Danite Band acquired an even more grisly reputation than it may have deserved.

So when Brigham Young himself approached John Ferrier's house one morning, Ferrier knew it did not bode well. Clearly the prophet was suspicious of Ferrier's commitment to the church, seeing as how he had not even one wife. Young then brought up status of Lucy, whom he had heard "is sealed to some Gentile." He stated that Ferrier's faith was to be tested on this one point: Lucy was to have a month to choose between the sons of Elders Stangerson and Drebber—one of whom she was to marry. Together, father and daughter plan an escape from the marriage trap. Ferrier says he will get a message through to Hope in Nevada, asking him to return immediately: they will trust in him to take them out of the Salt Lake City territory.

CHAPTER 4: A FLIGHT FOR LIFE

Ferrier arranges for his message to be sent with a party headed for Nevada, but when he reaches his home he finds the two elders' sons there, presenting themselves as candidates for the role of Lucy's bridegroom. Ferrier cannot control himself: he orders them both out of the house. The rest of the chapter describes the campaign of terror to which father and daughter are subjected over the next twenty-nine days; then at last comes the belated arrival of Hope and the midnight escape from the valley.

During the racking tension of the war of nerves waged against him, John Ferrier "had but one hope in his life now, and that was for the arrival of the young hunter from Nevada." With this sentence, Dr. Doyle practically begs us to recognize that "Hope" is no mere casual name, but an aptonym—so far as I can tell the first time in the canon that Conan Doyle employed this device. Of course, having studied the short stories we are by now quite familiar with the author's frequent use of aptonyms, but I must admit (while blushing with embarrassment and shame) that I never caught on to it until I began this book, well over fifty years after first reading *A Study in Scarlet*. I can only wonder how many other readers have missed it since the book first appeared in print. And yet, once one is familiar with Doyle's penchant for the device, aptonyms simply jump off the page. How simple and obvious the device now appears!

CHAPTER 5: THE AVENGING ANGELS

When on the second day of their journey, provisions run low for the travelers, Hope leaves their camp on foot to hunt game. It takes him the rest of the day to kill a big horn sheep and find his way back to the spot where he left the Ferriers that afternoon. He finds only a fresh grave and the signs of many horses trampling the ground and then heading east towards Salt Lake City. On the spot, he dedicates himself to "thorough and complete retribution, brought by his own hand upon his enemies." The rest of the chapter describes his discovery of Lucy's forced marriage to Drebber, Jr., and the fact that it had been Stangerson, Jr., who shot Ferrier. He holds forth in the hills above the town, and when Lucy dies within a month, he breaks in among the mourning women, takes the wedding ring from her finger, and vanishes again among the hills.

For several months he remains in the area, but his efforts to kill Drebber and Stangerson are unsuccessful. Eventually he is forced to return to Nevada, intending to remain there a year. But he is unable to return to Utah for nearly five years, and when he does come back—in disguise and under a false name—he learns that young Drebber and Stangerson had themselves revolted against the Mormon Church and become Gentiles, leaving Salt Lake City and telling no one where they had gone. It takes him years, but at last he finds Drebber in Cleveland. Before he can act against his quarry, Drebber recognizes him as well and has him arrested. Before he is released, the two objects of his revenge leave for Europe.

There the chase resumes: from St. Petersburg to Paris, from Paris to Copenhagen, and finally to London, where Hope at last succeeds in catching them.

This plot reads very nicely—so nicely that it is easy to miss a howling boner. We know that Hope was much changed in appearance over the years which had passed during the long chase. How could Drebber have recognized the man by a single glance through a window, when as far as we can tell they had never met face to face? Even from a photograph of the young Jefferson Hope (if one existed, which is unlikely), it is unlikely that Drebber could have almost instantaneously identified the man who had been chasing him across North America for many years. It is rare to catch Conan

Doyle in such a glaring error in one of his plots—but after all, even geniuses can make mistakes, and this was his first long prose fiction.

Did you catch the mistake? How many others do you think have done so?

There's another observation to make before we leave this chapter. Its title is "The Avenging Angels," and it was surely (as we are told back in chapter 3) the Danite Band which was responsible for the murder of John Ferrier and the kidnapping of his adopted daughter. The chapter title is thus appropriate on its face. However, think about it from a different perspective: which character truly becomes an "Avenging Angel" in this book? He devotes his entire life to revenging the deaths of John Ferrier and Lucy at the hands of Drebber and Stangerson, finally bringing their crimes home to them twenty years later and six thousand miles away across the Atlantic. Yes, the true "Avenging Angel" is Jefferson Hope—a wonderful irony pointed up by the coincidence of the Danite Band being known as the Avenging Angels.

PART 3: A CONTINUATION OF THE REMINISCENCES OF JOHN H. WATSON, MD

CHAPTER 6: (SAME TITLE AS ABOVE)

We are back in London, in the Baker Street rooms, and the story continues from the point where it left off at the end of chapter 7 of part 1. Hope speaks first, addressing Sherlock Holmes: "If there's a vacant place for a chief of police, I reckon you are the man for it," he says. "The way you kept on my trail was a caution."

When at the police station the official in charge informs the prisoner that he will be brought before the magistrate during the week, and he asks if he has anything further to say. Hope replies in the affirmative: he wants to tell the whole story immediately. When asked if he would not do better to reserve his story for his trial, Hope replies "I may never be tried." He asks Watson if he is a doctor, and when Watson confirms that he is, Hope invites him to put a hand on his chest. Watson immediately recognizes the presence of an aortic aneurism. This is important, because it means that the prisoner might die at any time. The inspector in charge (who remains nameless—it is neither Gregson nor Lestrade) recognizes that in the interests of justice, it is their duty to take Hope's statement immediately. This is how we get to hear Hope's remarkable tale from his own lips.

It is easy to overlook the importance of what Watson does here. Until now, he has been a mere observer of the action, an appendage at Holmes's side, who may watch but takes no active part in the investigation. Now he is called upon to make an important contribution to the story: it is his medical knowledge which leads the authorities to take Hope's complete account of his actions at once, rather than take the risk that his death, which may occur at any time, might leave his story untold. To put it another way, Dr. Watson from here becomes a part of what might be called "Team Holmes," participating actively in many future investigations. This is another reason why I contend that *A Study in Scarlet* is primarily Watson's story, a fact which differentiates this novel from Poe's works—infinitely improving the detective story by humanizing the narrator.

Notice, also, how this device allows the author to meet the challenge of having his murderer become more hero than villain through means directly connected with what we have already heard of the story—Hope explains that the origin of his disease was "overexposure and under-feeding among the Salt Lake mountains." He recounts everything, as Lestrade acts as secretary and writes it all down. The only question Hope refuses to answer is the identity of his accomplice—the actor who played the old woman in the episode of the ring, thoroughly hoodwinking Sherlock Holmes. The chapter ends with Hope being escorted to a cell while Holmes and Watson return to Baker Street.

CHAPTER 7: THE CONCLUSION

This remarkable chapter deserves to be read and reconsidered by those who denigrate Doyle's detective stories in general and *A Study in Scarlet* in particular.

It may be conveniently divided into three subsections. First, an introductory series of seven paragraphs in which the author finds a suitable ending for his murderer—Hope, the Avenging Angel, is found "stretched upon the floor of the cell with a placid smile upon his face, as though he had been able in his dying moments to look back upon a useful life and on work well done." If an angel could die, he would probably look like that. This first subsection then merges into the long central part, beginning with the truly brilliant discussion of the distinction between synthetic and analytical reasoning. I am aware of no better dissertation on this topic anywhere in the whole genre of mystery / detective fiction—not to mention in college philosophy classrooms. The benefit of reasoning from effect to cause would seem to be obvious—but it took Dr. Doyle to acquaint me, at least, with the concept.

This discussion is followed by Sherlock Holmes's explanation of each of the steps he took in solving the mystery. Here too there is an important lesson: in sharp contrast to Lestrade, who takes evidence to hand without thinking of alternative possibilities or seeking other data, Holmes is able to solve the Drebber murder because he comes to the scene with no previous biases and observes every possible detail even before entering the death house. Thus, he latches onto the clue of the cab, which neither Gregson nor Lestrade even sees. In other words, Holmes is sensitive to data: observation is essential before deduction can properly begin. No wonder the Scotland Yarders go astray!

The third and final subsection expresses Holmes's frustration at the fact that Gregson and Lestrade get all the credit for the solution when in fact it was his work alone that led to the identity of the killer, his motive, and his capture. Here again, it is Dr. Watson who takes over the tale. "Never mind," he says to his new roommate. "I have all the facts in my journal, and the public shall know them."

"Didn't I tell you so when we started?" says Holmes, with a laugh. "That's the result of all our Study in Scarlet—to get Gregson and Lestrade a testimonial." No, it isn't, I might reply. The real result is to make a writer out of Dr. John H. Watson—or should we say, his alter ego, Dr. Arthur Conan Doyle?

FURTHER COMMENTS ON A STUDY IN SCARLET

While hardly anybody familiar with the later Holmes works would claim that *Scarlet* matches their depth and skill, I cannot agree with those who would demean this quite remarkable book. Aside from the fact that it was the author's first attempt at long fiction, let alone his first mystery / detective story, *Scarlet* has real merit as a work of literature.

First and most important, it passes the acid text for any piece of writing—it entertains and instructs the reader. It contains at least three interesting and involving personalities—Dr. Watson himself, Jefferson Hope, and of course Sherlock Holmes. Its cast of minor characters includes John and Lucy Ferrier; the two Scotland Yard detectives, Gregson and Lestrade; and, in a single short scene, Brigham Young himself—powerful, dangerous, yet able and a strong leader. As Doyle draws him, he might be a study for Professor Moriarty, save for the latter's reptilian, oscillating head.

Scarlet also has suspense—the flight of the Ferriers and Jefferson Hope from Salt Lake towards Nevada; sentiment—the touching scene between little Lucy, five years old, and the old man who becomes her adoptive father; and even dashes of comedy—Watson's catalogue of his new roommate's apparent limits, for example.

From the technical point of view, the structure is symmetrical and efficient; the descriptive language, especially of the death room and the corpse, masterful; and the underlying theme—the difference between the law and moral justice—important enough to be explored throughout the rest of the Holmes canon. We see it raised for the first time when Watson finds himself unable to sleep because of his viewing of Drebber's dead face, and because of his conviction that this was an evil man who deserved to die—even as he realizes that the moral state of the victim does not exculpate the killer under the law. It resurfaces again after the capture of Hope, whose revenge on behalf of the Ferriers is legally criminal but morally justified.

There is more: this novel contains that great discussion of reasoning, and in addition perhaps the best picture ever drawn of Sherlock Holmes investigating a crime. The plot, while it turns out to be simple enough, is so well-handled that the reader feels most baffled when Lestrade reports the death of Stangerson at the end of the sixth chapter. This is significant because it is a perfect illustration of the darkest hour coming just before the dawn—as the title of chapter 7, on the facing page, suggests. When one also recalls the author's use of irony in the words "Avenging Angels," and his first employment of an aptonym ("Jefferson Hope"), it becomes clear that *A Study in Scarlet*, far from being an inferior work, is really an example of an extremely talented young writer beginning to express his talent for longer fiction. It acts as a sort of roadmap toward the things its author will do and the techniques he will perfect in the future.

One last point: it was in this, his first novel-length story, that Conan Doyle displayed his sympathy for the underclasses when he introduced his "Baker Street Boys." Now universally called "the Irregulars," they show that Doyle was able to see real worth in these disdained street kids, and to have them paid for it. Recognizing the humanity and the value of even the most despised members of the human community has been one of the greatest roadblocks to peace and joy in the world. Failure to respect so-called enemies has led to war, slavery, genocide, and unspeakable horrors: in our own country, we had "The only good Indian is a dead Indian" and the enslavement of millions, which ended only with a disastrous conflict in which at least another 700,000 lives were sacrificed. In our own times, at least six million people died in the European Holocaust. Over the centuries, countless lives were lost as Christians killed Muslims, Muslims killed Christians, Christians killed Christians, and Muslims killed Muslims. The recognition by Holmes of the worth of those dirty, uneducated, wild street urchins should be a lesson to the world—a hint to the true depth and worth of the Sherlock Holmes canon. *A Study in Scarlet* thus contains the first key to the uncovering of the unrecognized value in these stories—the hidden Holmes.

CHAPTER 9

The Sign of the Four

CHRISTOPHER RODEN, IN HIS INTRODUCTION TO THE OXFORD WORLD Classics Edition of *The Sign*, writes that the first publication of *A Study in Scarlet* "attracted little immediate public attention: the character of Sherlock Holmes created no great early impression." However, in 1889 Joseph M. Stoddart, managing editor of a new British magazine to be published by the American firm of Lippincotts, was searching for new authors to write for his publication. He hired George Thomas Bettany away from Ward, Lock, and Co., which had bought the manuscript of *Scarlet* three years before and published it in 1887. Bettany promoted Dr. Doyle as a likely prospect, and Stoddart arranged for a luncheon to be held at the Langham Hotel in August 1889. Doyle and another promising young author, Oscar Wilde, were invited. Over the table, Stoddart—who must have been impressed by both his guests—offered each of them one hundred pounds sterling, to write a story of no fewer than 40,000 words to be delivered before January 1890.

Both men accepted: Doyle produced *The Sign of the Four*, while Wilde wrote his masterpiece of horror, *The Picture of Dorian Gray*. Conan Doyle, writing at a feverish pace, finished *The Sign* in barely a month: he signed his contract on August 30, and completed the manuscript by the first of October. Roden writes that "There is nothing to indicate whether or not Conan Doyle had thought of a sequel to *Scarlet* before the Langham Hotel meeting," but the breakneck pace at which *The Sign* was written suggests that its author may well have been storing up ideas and characters for just that possibility. In addition, as I have previously pointed out, the structure and especially the ending of the earlier book positively invite a sequel. It took nearly three years, but sure enough the opportunity to produce one eventually came about. The story was duly published in *Lippincott's Monthly Magazine* for March 1890, and as a book the following October by Spencer Blackett.

In contrast to its predecessor, *The Sign* was an immediate success, and it is not hard to see why. The story has all the elements of a popular hit: a great treasure; exotic scenes in India; a raft of colorful characters including a wooden-legged man and his undersized, bloodthirsty associate; a pair of eerie twins; a blustering if not overly intelligent Scotland Yard detective; a crotchety old naturalist who keeps a remarkable dog; and a beautiful woman who has been wronged. Add to this gallery the lonesome Doctor Watson and the inimitable Sherlock Holmes, throw in the drama of a twilight boat chase down the Thames and a surprising twist at the end, and you have all the ingredients of a bestseller. Why hasn't this incredibly rich and cinematic tale ever been made into a hit movie?*

As popular as *Sign* has been from the beginning, we will discover as we study the structure and execution of the story that it is not mere entertainment. There are deeper meanings beneath the surface, and one way of digging them out is through a letter from Dr. Doyle to Joseph M. Stoddart, written on October 1, 1889—just after the author finished writing the manuscript. Mr. Roden's essay

---

* In fact, it has been filmed at least four or five times, according to my friend Phil Angelo.

quotes this letter as follows: "You promised to collaborate with me on this book, so I want you to name it ... *The Sign of the Four* strikes me as likely to be popular, but a trifle catchpenny. *The Problem of the Sholtos* is more choice, though less dramatic. On you be the burden of choosing."

Stoddart ducked. Instead of opting for one or the other of Conan Doyle's two suggested titles, he used both. When the story appeared first in the magazine and later as a book, it was called, *The Sign of the Four, or the Problem of the Sholtos*. We know well who "the four" are and what they did—but what did Dr. Doyle mean to imply by the title *The Problem of the Sholtos*? We will return to this question in due time: meanwhile, consider how the alternative title may suggest a deeper meaning.

In his essay, Mr. Roden also mentions several influences which may have affected Conan Doyle in the writing of *Sign*. One of these was a former patient of the doctor during his time at Portsmouth: Major General Alfred Greyson. He had formerly commanded a British artillery brigade in India and had been at the great fort at Agra, about which he could supply detailed information. A second possible influence on Doyle was Robert Stevenson's classic adventure story, *Treasure Island*. The original title of that book was *The Sign of the Six*, a reference to the six men Captain Flint took with him when he went ashore to bury his treasure. None of these six ever returned.

Roden also cites as possible influences *The Moonstone* (Wilkie Collins's tale of a stolen jewel, also set partly in India) and Oscar Wilde himself. Roden suggests that Wilde may have served as a model for the peculiar appearance of Thaddeaus Sholto, a character in *Sign*. Personally, I would tend to downgrade the importance of any of these sources: they may indeed have lent touches to Conan Doyle's work, but it seems to me that *The Sign of the Four* is clearly and wholly original.

Let us now discuss the structure of the novel before we proceed to a chapter-by-chapter analysis as we did in *Scarlet*.

THE IMPORTANCE OF STRUCTURE IN READING

Any human creation—be it a building, a painting, a bridge, a piece of music, a ship, or a work of literature—must have some structure, lest it fall apart. The structure is the framework which the creator employs to meld the various elements of their work together into the finished product. In the case of a bridge, for example, the structure determines what materials are to be used; where the abutments and / or piers are to be placed; the length, strength, and type of the span to be used; and the methods employed in the construction. In the case of a work of literature, whether fiction or nonfiction, the structure determines what comes first, what follows, and how the work ends. Paragraphs are placed according to the structure, containing the sentences with which the author tries to best convey his meaning. Pages are made up of paragraphs; chapters are made up of pages; sections comprise related chapters, and the whole work is made up of elements brought together in the complete structure. For this reason, finding the underlying structure and understanding it is the key to fully grasping what the author intends to communicate. Reading for structure enhances comprehension, and that in turn makes for the better retention. Reading for structure also assures that one does not miss any component of the work, nor read something out of context. I would go so far as to assert that one who thinks he or she is reading without ascertaining and understanding the structure of the work is not really reading but skimming. In the discussion of *The Sign of the Four* which follows I shall attempt to point up examples of what I mean.

Let us begin by breaking the novel down into its major component parts, to see how Conan Doyle constructed his story. He employed in this book the same classical three-part structure found in *Scarlet*: exposition, development, resolution, corresponding to the traditional three acts of a play. In the exposition, we are introduced to at least some of the main characters, and the first problem of the play is presented. In the second part (or second act, as you prefer) "the plot thickens;" complications may be introduced, and—as happens in *The Sign of the Four*—the original problem may be resolved only to be replaced by a different and perhaps more difficult one. Finally, in the resolution, all the difficulties come to an end: in a tragedy, often by the death of a leading character or characters; in a comedy, by settling each character in his or her proper place.

The difference between the use of the three-part structure in this book and in *Scarlet* is that in the earlier novel the author presented a partial resolution at the end of the exposition, announcing the identity of the newly captured killer, but without disclosing either his motive or the sequence of thoughts and events which resulted in his arrest. Only after the long flashback, in which the events of twenty years before are presented, does the book end with the rest of the resolution. In *The Sign of the Four*, however, the three-part structure is presented in straightforward chronological order. The only question is about where the exposition ends, and the development begins.

One might consider the exposition to consist of just the first two chapters: the scene of both is Baker Street, and the only event is Miss Mary Morstan's visit to Holmes concerning her invitation to meet an unknown benefactor that night. In that scenario, chapters 3, 4, and 5 would be considered part of the development, on the ground that they begin the investigation that will ultimately lead to the solution.

I considered this idea but rejected it. It makes more sense, I believe, to treat the exposition as a two-subsection unit, and to assign the beginning of the development to the start of chapter 6, when the investigation of the murder of Bartholomew Sholto and the theft of the treasure commences. Of course, this is an arbitrary decision, and matters only as a way of clarifying the structure—but I think it can be justified on two grounds. First: chapters 3, 4, and 5 describe a preliminary investigation, which leads into the story of the murder and the theft of the treasure. Second: placing these chapters as part of the exposition leaves us with an almost perfectly balanced structure.

Consider the following list:

EXPOSITION (Five Chapters—35 pages)*

Chapter 1: The Science of Deduction (8 pages)
Chapter 2: The Statement of the Case (6 pages)
Chapter 3: In Quest of a Solution (5 pages)
Chapter 4: The Story of the Bald-Headed Man (10 pages)
Chapter 5: The Tragedy of Pondicherry Lodge (6 pages)

DEVELOPMENT (Four Chapters—40 pages)

Chapter 6: Sherlock Holmes Gives a Demonstration (9 pages)
Chapter 7: The Episode of the Barrel (12 pages)
Chapter 8: The Baker Street Irregulars (9 pages)
Chapter 9: A Break in the Chain (10 pages)

RESOLUTION (Three Chapters—40 pages)

Chapter 10: The End of the Islander (9 pages)
Chapter 11: The Great Agra Treasure (6 pages)
Chapter 12: The Strange Story of Jonathan Small (25 pages)

In this formulation, each of the three parts of the story (or the three acts, if you prefer) is of virtually the same length; each part concerns a separate stage in the case. First is the mystery of Mary Morstan's father and the gifts of the pearls, cleared up by the end of chapter 5. Second, the murder of Bartholomew and the theft of the treasure—solved by Holmes by the end of chapter 9, but with the case still open. And finally, the capture of Small, the death of Tonga, and disposal of the treasure, followed by Small's story and the romance of Dr. Watson and Mary Morstan, which ends the book. This about as neat and perfect as a structure can be.

Notice how chapter 1, where Holmes and Watson are alone together in the Baker Street house, forms a link to *A Study in Scarlet.*

---

*   Pages are as they appear in my World Classics paperback edition of *The Sign of the Four,* from Oxford University Press.

Once again, Holmes is challenged by Watson to use his powers of deduction—this time on the watch the doctor has recently inherited. Holmes does so, only to discover that Watson is upset because he thinks that his roommate has been digging up dirt about his unhappy older brother, when actually everything the detective says he has learned comes from his observations about the timepiece and the deductions he made from what he saw.

See also how their expedition of the evening clears up the mystery surrounding the death of Mary's father and the yearly gift to her of a valuable pearl, but leads directly to a much deeper set of crimes—the murder of Bartholomew Sholto and the theft of the treasure. Thus, the end of chapter 5 is also the end of the exposition, and the beginning of chapter 6 is the start of the development.

Now that we have laid out the structure of the novel—its genome, to use a contemporary term—it is time to look at *Sign* part by part and chapter by chapter. Afterward, I will make some comments on the story that may be of interest.

PART 1: EXPOSITION

CHAPTER 1: THE SCIENCE OF DEDUCTION

This chapter might be better entitled "Observation and Deduction," since the most important concept in it is that while both faculties are necessary for the detective, they are not the same, and one does not imply the other. Also of interest is Holmes's injection of cocaine to stimulate his brain: "I crave for mental exaltation ... I abhor the dull routine of existence. What is the use of having powers, Doctor, when one has no field upon which to exert them?" He goes on and on in the same vein. The rest of the chapter is largely devoted to Holmes's demonstration of his powers—first in the colloquy of the Wigmore Street Post Office and then over the watch. The arrival of Mary Morstan ends this introductory chapter.

CHAPTER 2: THE STATEMENT OF THE CASE

Miss Morstan instantly attracts Doctor Watson, as is easy to tell from the first paragraph of this chapter. Watson, embarrassed, asks to be excused—but Mary asks him to remain. Does this perhaps hint that she is as interested in him as he obviously is in her?

This suggestion of mutual attraction begs the question I raised in *A Study in Scarlet*—namely, whose story is this? If all we had of this book were the first chapter, the answer would certainly be "Sherlock Holmes." He is the most unusual character in the story, with his great powers of observation and deduction coupled with his immaturity and egotism. As he was in *Scarlet*, so he remains (for the most part) in *Sign*: insensitive to the feelings of others, intolerant of authority, and now addicted to morphine and cocaine because he is a slave to his great brain. In effect, he blames his drug use on the world because it does not supply him with the thrills he seeks—the thrills that arise from being the center of attention and the object of other people's awe. His reaction to Watson's account of the Drebber-Stangerson case is disrespectful and insulting: he wants the spotlight to be on him at all times, as Watson realizes in this chapter.

Yet an opening chapter does not make a book. As you read *The Sign of the Four*, ask yourself some questions: who and what is the story about? To what genre of literature does it belong? What values does the author seek to promote, and what character flaws does he denigrate? Whose life (or lives) are changed by the events of the story? Pondering these questions will give you surprising revelations about what Conan Doyle was writing here.

One further thought generated by this chapter: it strikes me that what Holmes says about observation and deduction applies to all learning and problem-solving. One must start by approaching the data without preconceptions, and with care not to omit anything relevant. From this, one can deduce a theory and follow up by testing it.

In other words, I see the Holmes method as a general philosophy applicable to any field of knowledge in which an individual tries to learn about and understand the unknown. This is in keeping with my theme in *The Hidden Holmes*—that Doctor Doyle's mystery / detective stories are not simply great entertainment, but they have deeper and more serious dimensions that many or most readers miss.

In terms of structure, Chapter 2 consists of four subsections: first, Watson describes Miss Mary Morstan as she enters the Baker Street rooms. He goes into detail about her dress and hat, then goes on to describe her face, her eyes, and her expression. Obviously he is interested: he writes, "In an experience of women which extends over many nations and three separate continents, I have never looked upon a face which gave clearer promise of a refined and sensitive nature."*

As Miss Morstan explains how she came to appeal to Holmes (it seems that her employer, Mrs. Forrester, was a former client of his) the good doctor is embarrassed and uncomfortable. He tries to excuse himself, but Miss Morstan requests that he remain. Is this not an indication that she may be interested in him—literally at first sight?

Subsection two contains Miss Morstan's account of her background, her father's disappearance, her receiving the six pearls over the same number of years from an anonymous source, and

---

* There has been, over the years, a raging debate among Sherlockians about just which three continents Watson was referring to. Clearly Europe and Asia were two, but there has been disagreement about which was the third. Yet the answer has been clear ever since *The Sign of the Four* first saw print, in February 1890. In chapter 5, Holmes, Watson, and Miss Morstan are standing outside Pondicherry Lodge, waiting for the return of Thaddeus Sholto from inside, when Miss Morstan observes how the grounds are all dug up. "What a strange place," she says. Watson then comments, "It looks as though all the moles in England had been let loose in it. I have seen something of the sort on the side of a hill near Ballarat, where the prospectors had been at work."

Ballarat is in Australia, so there is the third continent! There should never have been any argument about it—except that some readers did not read carefully enough, or they failed to remember what they had read. Here is an example of precisely what I meant by the importance of structure in reading: if people had read chapter five with its structure in mind, the presence of Dr. Watson's remark would not have been so easily forgotten.

finally the letter, just arrived, which calls her "a wronged woman" and requests her appearance outside the Lyceum Theatre that same night. It ends with Holmes and Watson agreeing to accompany her to whatever meeting might occur. She promises to meet them again at six o'clock and takes her leave.

In the third subsection, Watson remarks on how attractive Mary Morstan is—and Holmes says, "Is she? I did not observe." Watson's reply is brief and to the point. "You really are an automaton—a calculating machine. There is something positively inhuman in you at times." That may be true of Holmes at this point in his life, but he will grow and change over the years. After a short discussion of handwriting and character, Holmes gets up to leave, promising to be back in an hour. In going, he recommends to Watson a book—*The Martyrdom of Man* by Winwood Reade. We shall encounter this same volume later in the story, and I will comment on it then.

The final subsection of chapter 2 finds Watson, now alone, musing on Miss Morstan, obviously thinking "dangerous thoughts" about her—is she a possible marriage partner? He dismisses the idea at once.

CHAPTER 3: IN QUEST OF A SOLUTION

We can break down this chapter into three clearly defined subsections: Holmes's return to Baker Street with some interesting information; the cab ride to the Lyceum, during which Miss Morstan talks of her father and his friend, Major Sholto, and shows Holmes the strange paper which was found in her father's pocketbook after his disappearance; and the meeting in front of the theater with the coachman who takes them on a second drive deep into South London.

In subsection one we learn what Holmes discovered when he went out: that Major John Sholto died on April 28, 1882—and that within a week, on May 4, Mary Morstan received the first of the six beautiful pearls which she had shown to Holmes and Watson earlier in the day.

Holmes immediately makes the obvious deduction that after the major's death, his heir began to send the pearls as restitution for her father's loss and now wishes to get in touch with her personally. While he does not claim to have solved the case entirely, he does go so far as to remark to Watson, "There is no great mystery in this matter." He—like us—will soon find out how wrong he is.

The second subsection of chapter 3 is devoted to the cab ride to the Lyceum Theatre, during which Miss Morstan shows the peculiar paper which was found in Captain Morstan's pocketbook. It bears the sign of the four and the names of these men—Jonathan Small, Mahomet Singh, Abdullah Kahn, and Dost Akbar. It is after Holmes sees this sheet that he admits that "this matter may turn out to be much deeper and more subtle than I at first supposed."

What follows is another one of those set pieces of descriptive prose that Conan Doyle executes so well. Consider this paragraph:

> It was a September evening and not yet seven o'clock, but the day had been a dreary one, and a dense drizzly fog lay low upon the great city. Mud-colored clouds dropped sadly over the muddy streets. Down the Strand the lamps were but misty splotches of diffused light which threw a feeble circular glimmer upon the slimy pavement. The yellow glare from the shop windows streamed out into the steamy, vaporous air and threw a murky, shifting radiance across the crowded thoroughfare.

Has any other author made better use of d's and p's than Conan Doyle did in these four descriptive sentences?

Once at the Lyceum, the company is eyed by a coachman and questioned briefly. When he is assured that neither Holmes nor Watson is of the police, the three climb in. The driver mounts the box, and off they go at a furious pace—though the passengers have no idea of where they are headed or why. This second ride is the subject of the third subsection, and it ends in South London.

CHAPTER 4: THE STORY OF THE BALD-HEADED MAN

The house at which the three arrive is commonplace on the outside. A Hindu servant leads them through an "ill-lit and sordid" passage, throws open a door—and there they are in "an oasis of art in the howling desert of South London." It's a little piece of India—a thickly carpeted room, decorated with two great tiger pelts and containing a huge hookah and a hanging lamp fashioned like a dove which gives off a subtle odor as it burns.

This is the home of Mr. Thaddeus Sholto, a man as unusual as his apartment. Nervous, a hypochondriac, an art collector— he is all of these. Most important, however, is the information he shares. The first subsection of the chapter is devoted to Thaddeus and the story he tells about his father, Major John Sholto—Captain Morstan's friend. From him, Miss Morstan learns how her father died (maybe), and of the mysteries which surrounded Thaddeus's own father. His most prominent characteristic seems to have been his avarice—a trait also found in Thaddeus's twin brother, Bartholomew. We learn, too, of the "great Agra treasure"—a share of which Mary Morstan was entitled to after the death of her father. She did not get it because Major Sholto could not bear to part with any of it. After the major's death six years before, no trace of the treasure had been found until the previous day. Thaddeus had arranged the evening so Miss Morstan could demand her share.

The second subsection of this chapter describes the ride to Pondicherry Lodge, during which Thaddeus discloses the value of the treasure—"not less than half a million sterling!"

We must not leave chapter 4 without noticing what happens in the last full paragraph.

It is well to quote what Conan Doyle wrote here: "At the mention of this gigantic sum we all started at one another open-eyed. Miss Morstan, could we secure her rights, would change from a needy governess to the richest heiress in England. Surely it was the place of a loyal friend to rejoice at such news, yet I am ashamed to say that selfishness took me by the soul and that my heart turned as heavy as lead within me." Watson does not explain here why he experienced such feeling—although it is explained later in the novel. However, it is not difficult to figure out now why the doctor was crushed and downcast: he was already contemplating marriage to Miss Morstan, but if she were the "richest heiress in England" he could hardly approach her without being seen as a mere fortune hunter—or, worse yet, feeling like one. Here money becomes an impediment to love: with Major Sholto and Bartholomew, it was an impediment to honesty and compassion. This chapter puts money squarely at odds with both love and concern for the rights and feelings of others.

No wonder Watson was relieved when the cab pulled up and the coachman sprang down to open the door!

A MAGNIFICENT DIGRESSION

At this point I beg the reader's pardon, for I am going to interrupt my analysis of the exposition to discuss the names of some of the characters. On the advice of my life partner Rachel, a truly brilliant and trustworthy woman, I decided to place this material here rather than to hold it over and employ it in an essay later.

As we know, Thaddeus and Bartholomew Sholto are the twin sons of Major John Sholto, now deceased. He was Captain Arthur Morstan's best friend and brother officer in the Indian Army and in the Andaman Islands. The first thing we need to know is that "John" and "Sholto" were the given names of John Sholto Douglas, Eighth Marquess of Queensbury. This minor nobleman is famous for two things. First, it was he who was responsible for drawing up the rules of professional boxing still in use today. This includes the use of gloves, and the three-minute round (previously a round ended only when one fighter or the other was knocked down).

Secondly, the Marquess was the father of Lord Alfred Douglas ("Bosie"), the lover of Oscar Wilde. It was Queensbury who ruined

Wilde's life and career after the famous 1895 lawsuit which resulted in Wilde's arrest and imprisonment for having sexual relations with another man—then and for half a century later a crime in the United Kingdom.

Of course, it was Wilde who had shared that famous literary luncheon with Doyle in August 1889, and it was Wilde who probably inspired Doyle's description of Thaddeus (and his twin, Bartholomew) in this novel. However, when *The Sign of the Four* was published in 1890, Wilde's disgrace at the hands of Queensbury was still five years in the future.*

Alerted to Conan Doyle's fondness for aptonyms and remarkable names by my previous study of the short stories, I took the time to look up the origins and meanings of the names of the Sholto twins, Thaddeus and Bartholomew. I found that the brothers were both named after two of the lesser-known apostles of Jesus. The name "Thaddeus" is of Greek derivation—it means "of strong or good heart." This name is remarkably appropriate to Conan Doyle's character. Thaddeus, while small and frail in stature, is goodhearted in seeking justice for Miss Morstan, and strong in standing up to his angry twin brother.

"Bartholomew," on the other hand, is not really a name but a patronymic: it derives from the Hebrew "Bar-Tolomei" or "Bar-Tolomai," meaning simply "son of Tolomei" or "Tolomai." For this reason, and because he is not named in all of the Gospels, some Christian scholars and Biblical historians assert that "Bartholomew" and "Nathaniel," another of the apostles, were actually the same person. If so, may we not think of Bartholomew Sholto as "Nathaniel"?

---

* My Oxford Press World Classics edition of the Sherlock Holmes stories quotes a comment by Mr. Lionel Fredman, which first appeared in the *Journal of the Arthur Conan Doyle Society*. Mr. Fredman wrote, "There is something unmistakably Wildean about Thaddeus Sholto. Both Wilde and Thaddeus were incessant and affected smokers ... Both were constantly passing their hands over the lower part of their faces, self-conscious of discolored teeth, but in fact by so doing drawing attention to them."

Now the Hebrew names "Jonathan" and "Nathaniel" have the same meaning: they both are rendered in English as "God has given." This leads us to a fascinating point in *The Sign of the Four*: Bartholomew (or "Nathaniel") Sholto and Jonathan Small both come into possession of the "great Agra treasure," and neither has any intention of giving it up regardless of anyone's claims. To put that another way, we may assume that both "Nathaniel" Sholto and Jonathan Small have convinced themselves that "God has given" the treasure to him.

As readers, our immediate response is "Neither has any right to it." But really, who else has any more legitimate claim? No person in this novel can show a clear path to the treasure: every claim of ownership derives from murder or theft—or both. Under these circumstances, can we consider Jonathan Small to be a true villain? Were not the greedy and deceitful Sholtos, father and son, more culpable than he—caught in a web of circumstances from which he could not escape?

One more note on the name "Jonathan." The Biblical Jonathan was the son of King Saul and the best friend of David, the young man who was destined to succeed Saul as King.

Jonathan realized that his father, who wished to murder David, was truly unfit to rule the Israelites. Yet even while remaining devoted to his best friend, David, he never left Saul's command, and died beside his father in battle. Jonathan's outstanding quality was his faithfulness in the face of divided loyalties. In this novel, Jonathan Small exhibits the same kind of loyalty to his associates: Singh, Khan, and Akbar, not to mention Tonga. Note that none of these men were white or Christian, yet Small remained true to them all. I simply cannot believe that Conan Doyle gave Small the first name Jonathan by accident, just as I cannot credit the idea that the Sholto twins, one courageous and seeking justice for Miss Morstan, the other determined to keep the whole treasure (rightfully or not), were named Thaddeus and Bartholomew for no serious reason. In all three cases, the names of the characters reflect their personalities and character traits too completely to be accidental.

Let us now return to our chapter-by-chapter study of the exposition.

CHAPTER 5: THE TRAGEDY OF PONDICHERRY LODGE

We can break down this chapter into four subsections with hardly any difficulty. I have designated each by a name:

> *Incident at the Gate*
> *Incident at the Door*
> *Through the Keyhole*
> *In Bartholomew's Room*

Subsection 1: Incident at the Gate

The chapter begins with the arrival of the party at the fortress-like Pondicherry Lodge. The porter (or gatekeeper) McMurdo recognizes Thaddeus's knock and is ready to admit him—but since he has no orders about anybody else, he refuses to let Mis Morstan, Watson, and Holmes pass through the gate until Holmes reminds McMurdo that they had boxed against each other four years before. That is enough: McMurdo lets the whole party pass.* Thaddeus goes ahead to calm the sobbing housekeeper, while outside, Watson and Miss Morstan hold hands.

Subsection 2: Incident at the Door

-Thaddeus Sholto comes running out of the door, "with his hands thrown forward and terror in his eyes." Holmes takes command of the situation and leads the party into the house and to the housekeeper's room, where old Mrs. Bernstone, distraught, is soothed by

---

* For what it may be worth, twenty-five years later, while writing *The Valley of Fear*, Conan Doyle used the name "McMurdo" as an alias of Birdy Edwards— and in the same book, Edwards is also known as "John Douglas"!

Miss Morstan. From the old woman they learn that Bartholomew Sholto had remained behind his locked door all day. At last she went upstairs and peeked through the keyhole. "You must go up, Mr. Thaddeus," she wails now. "I have seen Mr. Bartholomew Sholto in joy and sorrow for ten long years, but I never saw him with such a face on him as that."

Subsection 3: Through the Keyhole

Leaving Miss Morstan to comfort the frightened housekeeper, Holmes, Watson, and Thaddeus climb the three flights of stairs and reach Bartholomew's door. Holmes looks through the keyhole and instantly rises again with a sharp intake of breath. "There is something devilish in this, Watson," he says. "What do you make of it?" The face of Thaddeus was staring at them, seemingly suspended in the air. "The features were set, however, in a horrible smile, a fixed and unnatural grin, which in that still and moonlit room was more jarring to the nerves than any scowl or contortion."

"The door must come down," Holmes says, and the combined weight and strength of Holmes and Watson succeed in getting it to give way.

Subsection 4: In Bartholomew's Room

In Bartholomew Sholto's room, the corpse sits in a wooden arm-chair, still and cold. Clearly, Bartholomew has been dead for several hours. Beside one hand is a stone head lashed to a stick and a torn sheet of paper bearing five words: "The Sign of the Four."

Other aspects of the room include a thorn found in the skin of the corpse, just above the ear; a broken carboy leaking a dark, strong-smelling fluid; and a hole in the lath-and-plaster ceiling "large enough for a man to pass through." There is also a long coil of rope, thrown carelessly together.

Just then, the cry of Thaddeus interrupts the scene. "The treasure is gone!" he says.

Holmes sends him to report both the death and the theft to the police as the chapter ends—and with it, part 1 of the novel, the exposition.

PART 2: DEVELOPMENT
CHAPTER 6: SHERLOCK HOLMES GIVES A DEMONSTRATION

"Now, Watson," says Holmes, rubbing his hands (in anticipation? in delight?), "we have half an hour to ourselves. Let us make good use of it. My case is almost complete, but we must not err on the side of confidence. Simple as the case seems now, there may be something deeper underlying it."

At first glance, we are reminded of the Holmes of *A Study in Scarlet*—he claims to have his case nearly complete within half an hour of first seeing the corpse. Note, however, the caveat he appends to his bragging—"but we must not err on the side of overconfidence." Was he remembering the near embarrassment he felt when the old, sick dog to which he fed the first pill in that story unkindly refused to die immediately? Then notice what he says in the next sentence: "Simple as the case seems now, there may be something deeper underlying it."

For me, this language appears to be a warning to the reader—a wake-up call, suggesting that there is indeed "something deeper underlying it." We should look for what that something might be.

The rest of the chapter, following this significant first paragraph, may be conveniently and easily divided into three subsections: first, there is Holmes's own investigation of the room, under the eyes of Watson, who also acts as foil. The subsection ends with the discovery that the person with the tiny feet has stepped in the creosote, followed immediately by the entrance of the Scotland Yard detective Athelney Jones—"Red-faced, burly and plethoric, with a pair of very small twinkling eyes which looked keenly out from between swollen and puffy pouches." We dislike him even before he says a single word. And when he does open his mouth, the impression we get from his description is simply reinforced. Great writing!

Jones is not one to examine the evidence before forming his ideas about the crime. His first inspiration is based on nothing more than the fact that the two brothers were together on the previous night. His second is based on the fact that there was a quarrel between the two twins; on Thaddeus's clearly disturbed state of mind; and, worst of all, on his appearance, which the detective finds "not attractive." If this is the kind of evidence the police use as the basis for a charge of murder, then God help the citizens. Holmes responds by telling Thaddeus not to worry, and by giving Jones the description and name of Jonathan Small, one of the two men who were in the room. Jones may sneer, but he cannot help being impressed.

Subsection three has Watson sent on the double errand of taking Miss Morstan home and fetching Toby, the dog. It ends with Holmes quoting Goethe—a far cry from the man whom Watson once claimed had no knowledge of literature.

CHAPTER 7: THE EPISODE OF THE BARREL

There are five subsections in this chapter, all quite clearly defined. First, the cab ride to Mrs. Forrester's house, during which Mary breaks down into tears, and Watson dares not say to her all the things he wants to. Her condition—"weak and helpless, shaken in mind and nerve"—makes the doctor refuse "to obtrude love upon her at such a time." Second, he feels that the "great Agra treasure" forms "an impassable barrier between us."

The second subsection is set at Mrs. Forrester's house at two in the morning: "a tranquil English home in the midst of the wild, dark business which had absorbed us."

Subsection 3 describes Watson's visit to Mr. Sherman, the old naturalist, beginning with his review of the case thus far and ending with his return, with Toby, to Pondicherry Lodge. It is now three

THE SIGN OF THE FOUR

in the morning, and Watson finds that Jones has arrested not only
Thaddeus Sholto but also the gatekeeper, McMurdo, the housekeeper, and the Indian servant as well.

In subsection 4, Holmes shows Watson the difference between
the footprint of the small man and his own—his toes are all cramped
together, while the child-size footprint has the toes "distinctly
divided." Holmes says no more at this point, but the reader must see
that the small man was not used to wearing shoes or boots. Then
Holmes has the doctor sniff the odor of creosote on the window sill,
and remarks that if Watson can smell it Toby is unlikely to have any
trouble doing so. Then Holmes sends Watson downstairs with the
dog and works his own way down the outside wall of the house. En
route he finds a little packet containing poison darts, one of which
was the cause of Bartholomew Sholto's death.

Finally, we come to subsection 5, describing the journey of Toby,
Holmes, and Watson across pre-dawn London, in the course of which
Holmes explains his reasoning about the case thus far, concealing
only the identity of the accomplice with the child-sized feet. The trek
is interrupted by Toby's indecision at Knight's Place, but the dog is
soon off again, running hot on the scent—and stopping at the big
barrel of creosote in the lumberyard. The chase has ended in comedy!

CHAPTER 8: THE BAKER STREET IRREGULARS

This is a rather simple chapter to analyze. There are four subsections, all clearly defined. The first follows Holmes, Watson, and
Toby back to the corner of Knight's Place, where the dog picks up a
second creosote trail, this time leading to Smith's Wharf beside the
Thames. Here they learn from Mrs. Mordecai Smith (another wonderful name in the Dickensian tradition) all about the steam launch
Aurora and the wooden-legged man who hired it. On the way back

to Baker Street, Holmes sends a telegram to Wiggins and the crew, calling on them to come to Baker Street at once.*

In subsection 2, having decided that even if finding the treasure would put Mary beyond his reach, Watson is ready "to devote my life" to recovering it. After a bath and a rest he comes down to breakfast and Holmes reads the newspaper account of how the great Jones has handled the case.

In subsection 3, the Irregulars arrive, showing more organization than in *Scarlet*. Holmes gives them their assignment—find the *Aurora*. He gives them each a shilling (a day's pay) and promises a guinea (twenty-one shillings) to the boy who finds the boat. Then off they go.

Subsection 4 includes Holmes's discussion of the mysterious "other man"—an Andaman Islander. Then, seeing that Watson is exhausted, Holmes plays his roommate to sleep with his violin.

CHAPTER 9: A BREAK IN THE CHAIN

Once again, the chapter may be divided into four subsections. In the first, Watson takes off to return Toby and to visit Mrs. Forrester (and, of course, Mary Morstan). He is gratified to see that Mary does not appear excited at the possibility of becoming rich.

Subsection 2 finds the doctor back at Baker Street, where Holmes is frustrated and disturbed because there is no news of the boat. The day passes and Watson once again visits the women. Holmes passes another restless night.

Subsection 3 opens early the next morning with Holmes, in disguise as a sailor, telling Watson to stay home and take any message which may come while he goes downriver to try a new idea. By breakfast, no communication from Holmes has come, so Watson picks up the newspaper to read about the release of both Thaddeus Sholto and the housekeeper. He also sees a missing-persons

---

* I have already pointed out that Holmes must have made a standing arrangement with Wiggins, so that he could call in the Irregulars at any time.

advertisement concerning Mordecai Smith and his eldest son Jim—obviously put in by Holmes, since it gives the Baker Street address. The day passes slowly, with no new word from Holmes, and Watson wonders if for once his friend might be wrong.

The period of inaction ends at three o'clock, when Athelney Jones shows up, "meek and apologetic." His own case has been torpedoed: Thaddeus Sholto has an iron-clad alibi for every moment of his time after he left Bartholomew on the night before he was killed. Jones praises Holmes (to our surprise), admitting that he needs help on the Sholto case—his own professional reputation is at stake. He shows Watson a wire from Holmes, telling him to go to Baker Street and wait there for his return: the showdown in the case will be that very night.

Then enters the old, asthmatic seaman who says he knows everything about the case, but who won't tell anyone but Mr. Holmes. Jones keeps him from leaving—and of course a surprise follows. The development ends with the arrangements for the night's work in place: the stage is set, and there remains only the resolution of the novel.

PART 3: RESOLUTION

It is easy to overlook, but the resolution of *The Sign of the Four* is made up of three related chapters, each of which deals with a different aspect of the story. Chapter 10 concerns the death of Tonga, the actual killer of Bartholomew Sholto, and the capture of Jonathan Small. Chapter 11 deals with the "great Agra treasure," its disposition, and the effects that action has on two of the main characters. And chapter 12 contains Jonathan Small's own account of his life. We will find that his story has an important implication: it points up a deeper meaning of the book, one which has gone largely unnoticed by the reading public ever since this novel was first published back in 1890. A careful study of these three final chapters will, I am convinced, reveal *The Sign of the Four* to be a subtle masterpiece of social criticism.

CHAPTER 10: THE END OF THE ISLANDER

This chapter contains just two subsections—the dinner scene at Baker Street, where the characters are Holmes, Watson, and Athelney Jones; and the action on the Thames that night. There is, however, a remarkable interlude inserted between the two scenes of the second subsection, which I call 2A and 2B. This arrangement appears to be unique in the Holmes canon, and I will discuss each part in its proper place.

Subsection one, the dinner scene, is short—one full paragraph, followed by about eight lines describing the final preparations for the evening after the table has been cleared. Together these few sentences act as an introduction to and compelling contrast with the exhilarating events which follow.

However, that's not the only significant thing about this little scene. Holmes's brilliant conversation at the table indicates a profound change in Dr. Doyle's conception of his character. Gone is the early Sherlock, who talks of keeping his brain free of anything not directly connected to observation and deduction. The Holmes of this scene is clearly a man of wide and differing interests: he talks of no less than five apparently unrelated subjects, "handling each as though he had made a special study of it." In fact, it is often Holmes's great range of knowledge which leads him to the solution of a case. We have already seen a hint of this new Sherlock at the end of chapter 6, when he quotes Goethe, observing that the German master "is always pithy." The dinner party harks back to that earlier glimpse of a different Sherlock Holmes, and it also looks forward to the interlude between the two action sequences of the second subsection of this chapter.

The first of these (2A) begins with the arrival of Holmes, Watson, and Athelney Jones at the Westminster wharf, where they board a police boat. On the trip downriver towards the Tower of London, Holmes smiles with satisfaction at the speed of the boat. "We ought to be able to catch anything on the river," he says. He then explains how he found the *Aurora* in Jacobson's boat yard, the sixteenth place he had visited. Holmes had then arranged to have one of his Baker Street boys stand on watch at the entrance to the yard, ready to signal with a white handkerchief if the *Aurora* came out.

Now Holmes has Jones tell the boat crew to stop opposite the yard, and to cruise back and forth behind a screen of other vessels.

Now we come to the interlude between the two parts of subsection two. It begins as Holmes points out the swarm of people illuminated by the gas lights as they leave their jobs at the yard. It lasts just four paragraphs, two of them only one line long. Yet to me, this little insertion into the text is all-important: it reveals Sherlock Holmes's deepened character. "Dirty-looking rascals," he says, "but I suppose everyone has some little immortal spark concealed about him. You would not think it to look at them … A strange enigma is man!" Watson comments, "Someone calls him a soul concealed in an animal," and Holmes replies with a quote from Winwood Reade.*

---

* This is Holmes's second reference to Reade and his book, *The Martyrdom of Man*: he recommends it to Watson toward the end of chapter 2. The doctor glances at it, but his mind is totally absorbed in thoughts about Miss Morstan, and "far from the daring speculations of the writer."

William Winwood Reade (1838–1875)—he preferred to be called Winwood—is nearly forgotten today. The only information I could find on him was a Wikipedia biography and a single online article by a Princeton professor named John V. Fleming.

According to these sources, however, Reade—Scottish-born and Oxford-educated (though he never got a degree from any college)—was a fervent follower of Charles Darwin. He was an agnostic, though he never was an atheist: he believed in a Creator, but (to quote Professor Fleming) conceived of it as an "ineffable and unapproachable being, far beyond the grasp of the human intellect or the reach of petty human prayers." After leaving Oxford, he tried writing fiction, but with little success. He also wrote a couple of travel books (he spent a good part of his adult life in Africa) and a number of magazine pieces in addition to his most important work, *The Martyrdom of Man*, which has been called a "universal history" purporting to describe the entire story of the human race.

His use of the term "martyrdom" may not be fully understandable, but as Professor Fleming writes, Reade believed that all human history was "a record of a long bloody struggle against malignant forces possessing terrible

The passage comes to a sudden end when Holmes and Watson both spot the handkerchief signal and the boy waving it by the entrance of Jacobson's yard, followed immediately by their spotting the *Aurora*, "going like the devil!" Philosophy is put aside: part 2B, the great chase down the Thames, is on.

Now, unless one is prepared to regard the interlude as totally gratuitous, we must explain its placement and its function at this precise point in the novel. I refuse to believe that a writer as sagacious and as well-organized as Conan Doyle would interrupt the action for no good reason, and I suggest that the "little immortal spark" passage has an important meaning. The key is its placement within the structure of this chapter. Not only does it show Holmes to be a much deeper, more humane, more rounded individual than he was in *A Study in Scarlet*, but it prepares Holmes, Watson, Jones, and the reader for the impending meeting all of us are about to have with just such a person as those leaving the shipyard—Mr. Jonathan Small.

He is certainly guilty of criminal behavior, and yet he is not an evil man. Compare him with Major Sholto, whose greed and utter selfishness are the hallmarks of his character. Who is the villain in this novel, Small or Sholto?

We will find much more to ponder about this subject when we reach chapter 12, in which Jonathan Small relates his life story. For now, let us just remember what Holmes suggested in that offhand

---

powers and tenacity." These forces were ignorance and what stemmed from it—religion and superstition, which he thought caused barbarism of all sorts, mental bondage, and unnecessary material insufficiency.

Apparently, Reade's book attracted Dr. Doyle's interest, as it did that of many intellectuals not rooted too firmly in organized religion. Reade saw in science the way to almost unlimited power and happiness of mankind, even to the eventuality (at some future time) of immortality. His work had so strong an appeal to the creator of the Holmes stories that he refers to it twice in *The Sign of the Four*. One can envision Doyle's Jonathan Small, together with the dockyard workers and the Baker Street Irregulars, as the raw material for the superhuman being of the future!

remark about the apparent simplicity of the case at the beginning of chapter 6: "there may be something deeper underlying it."

Subsection 2-B is simply masterful. To set the scene on the river in the twilight was sheer genius: what reader can ever forget it? Also, note the references to the features and face of Tonga, the Andaman Islander. He is described in clearly menacing terms: the smallest adult man Watson has ever seen, he has "a great, misshapen head and a shock of tangled, disheveled hair." He is described as "a savage, distorted creature," whose face "was enough to give a man a sleepless night. Never have I seen features so deeply marked with bestiality and cruelty. His small eyes glowed and burned with a somber light, and his thick lips were writhed back from his teeth, which grinned and chattered at us with half animal fury."

And after he was felled by Holmes and Watson and their pistols, Watson says, "I caught one glimpse of his venomous, menacing eyes amid the swirl of the waters."

Small is captured when his wooden stump sinks into the mud, and the treasure box is taken aboard the police boat. The chapter ends with the discovery of one of Tonga's poisoned darts just behind where Holmes and Watson had stood. The doctor admits that it turned him sick "to think of the horrible death which had passed so close to us that night."

CHAPTER 11: THE GREAT AGRA TREASURE

This chapter may have the simplest structure of any in the entire book: just two subsections, clearly defined by their location and characters.

Subsection one is set in a cabin on the police boat, and the principal characters are Jonathan Small, Sherlock Holmes, Dr. Watson (in the role of narrator), and Athelney Jones. It begins with a physical description of Small, carefully crafted to leave a reasonably favorable impression of the man. Note Watson's last two sentences: "It seemed to me that there was more sorrow than anger in his rigid and contained countenance. Once he looked up at me with a gleam of something like humor in his eyes."

Small expresses his regrets at the murder of Bartholomew Sholto, and he says how grieved he was when he entered the room and found the man dead. He also relates how he welted Tonga with the slack end of the rope, and he would have killed the islander had he not scrambled away.

During this conversation, Holmes tells the wooden-legged man that if he makes a clean and true account of the whole story, he (Holmes) thinks he can prove that Sholto was dead before Small ever entered the room, and thus absolve him of the murder. Here also Conan Doyle creates sympathy for Jonathan Small.[*]

The prisoner's next paragraph also contains a sort of defense for him, or at least creates more sympathy on his behalf. He says, "It was an evil day for me when first I clapped eyes on the merchant Achmet and had to do with the Agra treasure, which never brought anything but a curse yet upon the man who owned it. To him it brought murder, to Major Sholto it brought fear and guilt, and to me it has meant slavery for life."[**]

Small continues with a complete exoneration of Mordecai Smith

---

[*]   The passage accomplishes its purpose—to ingratiate Small with the reader—but Conan Doyle may stand on weak legal ground here. The law generally states that when a murder is committed during a felony, all participants in the crime are judged to be equally responsible for the murder, whether they were present or not. In this instance, a felony—the theft of the treasure from the dwelling place of another person during the night, the legal definition of burglary—was in process, and by taking the treasure Small became an active conspirator in the burglary. Thus, he was probably also liable to hang for the murder, no matter how quickly the poison acted or when he entered the room.

[**] Blaming the treasure ("a curse") makes good literature but not good sense. Rather, the cause of all the miseries connected with the Great Agra Treasure was the greed of those who wished to possess it for their own benefit. Small and Achmet are perhaps less guilty of avarice than the Rajah, Major Sholto, or Captain Morstan, but the point is that money is not the root of all evil— but the love of money is.

and his son. Smith swore that he knew nothing of the Norwood business (the murder of Bartholomew Sholto and the theft of the treasure) and Small confirms this in no uncertain terms. "I chose his launch because I heard that she was a flier. We told him nothing, but we paid him well, and he was to get something handsome if we reached our vessel, the *Esmerelda*, at Gravesend, outward bound for the Brazils."

The subsection ends with Athelney Jones informing Watson that he had to send an inspector along when the doctor drove to Mrs. Forrester's to deliver the treasure box to Mary Morstan. Then Jones asks Small about the location of the key to the box containing the jewels. "At the bottom of the river," replies the wooden-legged man, and the last lines concern Jones's instructions about bringing the box back to Baker Street where they are all going to meet again.

Subsection two is set at Mrs. Forrester's house. She is out for the evening, but Mary Morstan is in the drawing room. Leaving the inspector in the cab, Watson takes the box into the house. She asks Watson what news he has brought. "I have brought something better than news," he replies with forced joviality. "I have brought you a fortune." The final pages of the chapter describe the surprising discovery and Watson's response. "Thank God," he says, and she repeats the words. Love triumphs over wealth!

CHAPTER 12: THE STRANGE STORY OF JONATHAN SMALL

This, the longest chapter in *The Sign of the Four*, can be divided into four subsections.

The first is very short. It consists of the repartee between Watson and the nameless inspector who had been sent to accompany him. Its subject is the empty treasure box: the inspector laments the fact that neither he nor his partner will get any reward money since the treasure was lost. "Where there is no money there is no pay," he complains. This telling little passage points up once again one of the true subjects of this novel—money and greed.

Subsection two takes place at Baker Street, where Small defends his action in throwing the treasure, jewel by jewel, into the Thames. "It is my treasure," he says, "and if I can't have the loot I'll take damned good care that no one else does." Here too he invokes the compact he made with the three Sikhs. "I know that they would have had me do just what I have done."

Jones then speaks to Small about his "thwarting justice," and stirs up a tirade from the wooden-legged man on the subject of justice—another theme of this novel. All this content in the second subsection leads up to Small accepting Holmes's invitation to tell his whole story from the beginning: until they hear that, they cannot judge how far justice may have been on his side.

This brings us to subsection three—Small's long narrative about his life. Instead of attempting to retell the tale, I wish to focus on the sequence of events which took a young man from Worcestershire to exotic India, and then to the convict barracks in the Andaman Islands, and finally back to England and arrest by Mr. Athelney Jones.

Small begins by telling us that he was unlike his family—"steady, chapel-going small farmers, well known and respected over the countryside." He, on the other hand, "was always a bit of a rover." At eighteen or so, he "got into a mess over a girl"—got her pregnant?—"and could only get out of it by taking the Queen's shilling" (that is, enlisting in the military, in a regiment just going to India). Note that he had no intention of hurting anybody. Once there, he admits "I was fool enough to go swimming in the Ganges," where he lost his leg to a hungry crocodile and survived only because his sergeant, a fine swimmer, got him to shore before he would have drowned. After five months in the hospital he found himself with a wooden lower leg, invalided out of the army, and unfit for any active occupation. Note again that his predicament was not the result of any malicious behavior, but only of foolishness.

Next, Small tells us of his employment by the indigo-planter,

Mr. Abel White, as an overseer on horseback.* He would have been perfectly happy to spend the rest of his life with Mr. White, planting indigo. Not a bit of criminal planning or malicious behavior have we yet seen from Jonathan Small.

But as he says himself, "I was never in luck's way long." Suddenly, the great mutiny broke out: Mr. White and the Dawsons, a couple who worked for him, were killed, and Small, seeing that there were rebels around, took off on his horse until he reached Agra, where there were British troops.

At the great fort, Small was assigned to guard a door in company with two Sikh troopers.

On the third night there, however, his two native companions turned on him and threatened to kill him if he refused to join in their plot. They gave him three minutes to respond, upon pain of death. In the course of his conversation, Abdullah Kahn made a profound remark: "It is nothing against the fort," he told Small. "We only ask you to do that which your countrymen came to this land for. We ask you to be rich."

Small next makes a pertinent remark: "In Worcestershire the life of a man seems a great and a sacred thing; but it is very different when there is fire and blood all round you and you have been used to meeting death at every turn." And then he thought about the great treasure, and how his family back in England would stare when they saw him return with his pockets full of gold. With no time to consider—under extreme duress, with a gun at his head and a knife at his throat, and seduced by the offer of extreme wealth—Jonathan Small surrendered to one of humanity's most tempting sins—greed. He admits that at that moment, he had already made up his mind to join Khan, Singh, and Akbar in the killing of Achmet the merchant, and the taking of the "great Agra treasure."

---

* Here we may have another aptonym: an Englishman named Abel White in a country of dark-skinned people, who suffers death by murder like Cain's brother Abel in the Bible.

Whatever qualms he felt at the sight of Achmet he dispelled with thoughts of the treasure. When Achmet came running away from Akbar, with a chance to escape, Small tells us that "My heart softened to him, but again the thought of his treasure turned me hard and bitter. I cast my firelock between his legs as he raced past, and he rolled over twice like a shot rabbit."

When Holmes, Watson, and Jones give him disgusted looks, Small reiterates an important point. "It was all very bad, no doubt," he says. "I should like to know how many fellows in my shoes would have refused a share of the loot when they knew that they would have their throats cut for their pains. Besides, it was my life or his when once he [Achmet] was in the fort. If he had got out, the whole business would come to light, and I should have been court-martialed and shot as likely as not."

The second part of Small's story—after the discovery of the murder—is largely set on Blair Island in the Andamans. There he was imprisoned, together with his Sikh collaborators. There also he met Major Sholto, Captain Morstan, and the islander, Tonga. Hearing that Major Sholto needed money (to pay off his losses at cards), Small contacted that officer about getting his freedom in exchange for a fifth share of the treasure, the location of which had never been discovered. In the course of their negotiations, Sholto says, "What have three black fellows to do with our agreement?" And it is here that Jonathan Small stands up for his partners. "Black or blue, they are in with me and we all go together." Loyalty is Small's redeeming virtue, whether it is to his three Sikh co-conspirators—or, later, to Tonga, the little black man whom Watson describes in such vicious terms.

Sholto, of course, went off to India, found the treasure, and, instead of carrying out their agreement, left the army (having inherited a fortune on the death of an uncle) and took the whole box of jewels for himself. Small admits that "From that day I lived only for vengeance. I thought of it by day and nursed it by night. It became an overpowering, absorbing passion with me. I cared nothing for the law—nothing for the gallows. To escape, to track down Sholto, to have my hand upon his throat—that was my one thought. Even the Agra treasure had come to be a smaller thing in my mind than the slaying of Sholto."

During his escape from the Andaman Island, with the aid of Tonga and his big canoe, Small committed an act of vengeance against another target—the convict guard who had (in his estimation) "never missed a chance of insulting and injuring me." Small used his wooden leg as a weapon, and "knocked the whole front of his skull in."

Small and Tonga drifted about the world, finally coming to London three or four years before the story begins.* Small made a contact inside the house and was kept aware of anything that happened there, and so he heard of Major Sholto's final illness. He actually witnessed the Major's death through the window, and he got into the room that night hoping to find a clue to the whereabouts of the jewels. He found nothing and came away "bitter and savage as a man could be," but not without leaving "The Sign of the Four" pinned to the corpse.

Small's long narrative finally ends with his account of how he heard from his inside source at Pondicherry Lodge (this source is another individual to whom he remains loyal by refusing to disclose his identity—though it can hardly be anyone but the butler, Lal Rao) that the treasure had at last been found in Mr. Bartholomew Sholto's room at the top of the house. He recounts how he sent Tonga to climb up there, how the islander saw Sholto still in the room and

---

* This is inaccurate: we know that Major Sholto died on April 28, 1882—so Jonathan Small and Tonga must have been in London some time before that date in order to have established contact with an inside source at the lodge. They must have arrived in London six years or more before Sholto's death, rather than three or four. The events of the story can be dated in 1888 by reference to Miss Morstan's pearls and letters, and her recollection of her father's disappearance on December 3, 1878, which she says was "nearly ten years ago."

killed him with a poisoned dart, and then let the rope down so that Jonathan could climb into the room.

Small let the treasure box down by the rope, and then came sliding down himself, leaving Tonga to depart as he had come—by climbing down the outside of the house. Once more Small remains true to his code: for the second time, he exonerates Mordecai Smith from any knowledge of what he had been up to. Subsection three ends with Small asking if there was anything else Holmes wished to ask him, and Holmes's negative reply.

Subsection four consists of Watson's announcement that Miss Morstan has accepted his proposal of marriage, and Holmes's declining to congratulate him about it. Sherlock's character may have changed since *A Study in Scarlet*, but he remains a perfect misogynist here: he will not meet Irene Adler (a.k.a. "The Woman") for another three years yet. As to the final paragraph of the novel—well, I will comment on that at the end of this essay.

ADDITIONAL COMMENTS ON CHAPTER 12

We must not leave this last chapter of *The Sign of the Four* without commenting on the life story of Jonathan Small. He is a remarkable creation—as complex a character as exists in detective / mystery fiction so far as I am aware.

We may start with what he is in the book—the criminal whose actions result in at least three deaths, two of which are clearly homicides. He's also a burglar who stole back the treasure that he regarded as having been stolen from him and his mates years before. Yet he is not by nature an evil person: many of the troubles in his life were the result of happenstance, foolishness, and / or the bad luck to have been in the wrong place at the wrong time. He does indeed succumb to the lure of greed, but he is hardly the only person in the world—or in this novel—who does so.

My observation about Small is that his name reflects him perfectly. He is indeed a small man, buffeted by forces beyond his control—a nearly classic example of the anti-hero who is acted upon rather than acting. The only times he breaks out into violence come when he seeks revenge on others whom he believes to have wronged him—namely, the prison-camp guard whose head he bashes in during his escape from the Andaman convict barracks, and Major Sholto, who dies a natural death despite Small's dreams of murdering him. His first name, too, reflects his outstanding quality—loyalty to those who aid him or show him that they trust him. In this he is like his namesake, the Biblical Jonathan, son of King Saul and bosom friend of the future King David.

There is another aspect to the personality of the wooden-legged man: he comes to truly believe that the "great Agra Treasure" belongs to him and his three Sikh associates, although they murdered a man to get hold of it in the first place. Small feels that his twenty or more years as a convict and a vagabond have earned him the right to the jewels: when he knows that neither he nor his co-conspirators will ever have the use of them he makes sure that no one else ever will either, by emptying the treasure box into the Thames. "There are no rupees for you this journey," he says. When Athelney Jones remarks that if he had helped justice instead of thwarting it, he would have had a better chance at his trial, Small explodes into a rage over the issue of what is justice—an issue that is raised often enough in our own time. At the bottom, one sees in Jonathan Small sincerity in everything he says or does. In this sense, at least, he is an honest man ...

We should also pause long enough to compare Small with Jefferson Hope, who plays a similar role in *A Study in Scarlet*. Both men seek revenge for wrongs done long in the past and far away from London, where both are eventually arrested.

But while there are clearly parallels between these men, they are also very different personalities. Hope is far simpler: he sets out to avenge the murder of John Ferrier and the forced marriage and subsequent death of Ferrier's adopted daughter, Lucy. After years of trying, he runs down his quarry and by his own hand kills Drebber and Stangerson. He dies with a smile on his face and joy in his heart, for he has successfully completed his life's goal. Note that he takes his vengeance not primarily for anything done to him personally (although the loss of Lucy as a wife was certainly a personal hurt), but on behalf of the injured parties.

Small's case is quite different. He seeks revenge only against those who in his eyes have cheated and tormented him. He is a far more complicated character than Hope—a mixture of "schlimazel" and dedicated avenger, whose vehement outbursts against others are tempered by his loyalty to those he sees as his partners and benefactors.* He has in common with Hope only this: whatever his crimes, he is not fundamentally evil. Thus, each of the first two Holmes stories features an ambiguous criminal: we are a long way from the classic villains like Professor Moriarty, Mr. Stapleton, and Baron Adelbert Gruner, whose evil is built into their personalities. Doyle was to create many more sympathetic criminals in the stories to come, but it is interesting to find that he began his career as a detective story writer with two tales in which the killer has at least some claim to sympathy.

Now that we have concluded our close examination of *The Sign of the Four*, I beg your patience as I present my own commentary about the significance and meaning of this book.

ADDITIONAL COMMENTS ON THE NOVEL

In the text of this chapter-by-chapter analysis of *The Sign* I posed three questions. One was to consider the alternative title Conan Doyle suggested for the book—*The Problem of the Sholtos*—which Joseph M. Stoddart employed as if the author had intended the title to be, *The Sign of the Four; or, The Problem of the Sholtos*. A second was,

---

* For those not well-acquainted with the colorful vocabulary of Yiddish, the *schlemiel* is the clumsy oaf who drops the hot iron: the *schlimazel* is the luckless guy on whose foot it lands. Fans of the Three Stooges will surely understand!

"Whose story is this?" The last was "Who is the villain of this novel?" These questions were intended to get readers to think beyond the surface of this terrific adventure-mystery-detective story, and to look for its further implications.

We begin with "the problem of the Sholtos." One can interpret this would-be title in at least two different ways. The first centers on whose problem it was. If that question is asked of Sherlock Holmes and the police, it means: How do we solve the mysteries connected with Major Sholto and his sons? What happened to Captain Morstan? Why did an anonymous person begin sending Miss Morstan a valuable pearl each year, and in 1888 send her a letter calling her "wronged woman" and inviting her to meet someone in front of the Lyceum Theatre? These questions are soon answered, but others are raised next: who killed Bartholomew Sholto, how did they do it, and why? Who stole the treasure box, and where is it? Why did the twin brothers, Thaddeus and Bartholomew, quarrel so violently that Thaddeus chose to move out of the family mansion in Norwood and take up his own quarters in South London? Finally, there remains the triple conundrum: who is the wooden-legged man, who is his odd accomplice, and what does "The Sign of the Four" mean? If one reads the alternative title as a subtitle, "the problem of the Sholtos" must be a challenge to the powers of observation and deduction possessed by Sherlock Holmes, and the powers of the law as wielded by Atheney Jones. Seen this way, "the problem of the Sholtos" is nothing more than a series of mysteries for the detectives to solve.

But the phrase is not unambiguous. "The problem of the Sholtos" can also be read as "What difficulty do the Sholto family members face, and how can they solve it?" In this connotation, the problem (whatever it is) *is for the Sholtos themselves to resolve.* Moreover, once the question is put this way, the family problem becomes immediately apparent—it is greed. Major Sholto is in thrall to the sin of avarice: he admits it himself, but he cannot control it. Even on his deathbed, when he laments his own treatment of his friend Captain Morstan's daughter, he tells his sons to give her a fair share of the treasure—but not a single jewel are they to part with until after he is dead. "After all," he says, "men have been as bad as this and have recovered."

We ought also to recall the death of Captain Morstan. Old Major Sholto tells his sons that his friend had a weak heart, although, he says, that he alone knew it. The Major says that Morstan came to his home to claim his share of the treasure. He admits that they had hot words over the division of the loot, and claims that Captain Morstan, in a fit of anger, sprang out of his chair and had a heart attack, falling backwards and hitting his head against a corner of the treasure box—dying on the spot.

The old major says he was debating what to do when his servant, Lal Chowdar (undoubtedly a relative of the current butler at Pondicherry Lodge, Lal Rao) offered to help him conceal the death. Sholto denies having killed his old friend, but his servant says he heard everything. Sholto raises the question: if his own servant could not believe him innocent, how would he fare before a jury? So he agreed, he says, to allow Lal Chowdar help him hide the body, the crime, and the treasure.

Knowing what we know about Major Sholto's weakness, can we believe this story? Is it not likely that he did indeed kill Morstan, so that he could keep the whole Agra treasure for himself? We cannot dismiss that possibility.

We, of course, can never know whether Major Sholto's account of his friend's death was true. We do know that he had a powerful motive for killing Morstan; that he lied to Mary that he had not known that her father was in London; and that he admitted to his sons that he concealed not only the death of his former associate but also his theft of the treasure. To put it briefly, his greed overcame any scruples he may have had, and while the story he told his sons about the death of Captain Morstan could have been true, it is just as likely to have been false. Indeed, the probability is that he lied through his teeth for the sake of the treasure—of which, he told his sons, he had "made no use ... myself, so blind and foolish a thing is avarice. The mere feeling of possession has been so dear to me that I could not bear to share [the treasure] with another."

Moreover, the old Major is not the only member of the family who suffers from the sin of avarice. We have Thaddeus's account of how he quarreled with his twin brother over giving the pearls to Miss Morstan, and how he moved out of the house because of their disagreement. He is almost certainly understating the case when he says, "Between friends, my brother was himself a little inclined to my father's fault." "The problem of the Sholtos," interpreted this way, is about how to deal with the greed that paralyzes both the old major and his favorite son. Only Thaddeus, who realizes that he has plenty of money, is not crippled or corrupted by greed. Bartholomew cannot see the situation this way, and he pays for his avarice with his life.*

It is, in fact, almost impossible for a thoughtful, careful reader to miss the pervasive greed throughout this novel. "The problem of the Sholtos" is the problem of nearly everyone in the book. Start with the Rajah, who amassed the "great Agra treasure" in the first place: we are told (as Abdullah Kahn first presents the story to Jonathan Small) that this man is rich, despite the fact that his lands are small. This is due to not only his inheritance from his father, but also to his being "of a low nature"—someone who "hoards his gold rather than spend it." From the beginning, then, the treasure is the product of greed.

The three Sikhs are surely motivated by the lust for riches—the plot was hatched by one of them, Dost Akbar, and subscribed to by both his foster brother, Khan, and Singh.** Jonathan Small gives in

---

* There is, in fact, no reason for Conan Doyle to have made the Sholto brothers twins, except that as they are depicted in the book we have the eternal conflict between the good twin (Thaddeus) and the evil one (Bartholomew).

** I have always wondered how a religious Sikh would feel about participating in, let alone devising, a plot to murder a man for the sake of wealth he was carrying while in the service of another. Is it not possible that it was the English who brought this kind of murderous greed to India with them? Or does the impulse to go to any length for wealth transcend culture and religion?

to the sin of avarice as well, and while he is under duress, he admits that his mind was made up from the moment he heard about the treasure—"my heart turned to it, and I thought of what I might do in the old country with it, and how my folk would stare when they saw their ne'er-do-well coming back with his pockets full of gold moidore." Even the nameless police inspector who had been assigned to accompany Watson to Mrs. Forrester's house with the treasure box laments the loss of any reward money for him and his partner, Sam Brown, when he hears that the treasure is lost. "Where there is no money there is no pay," he remarks.

Most surprising of all is Dr. Watson's own admission (at the end of chapter 4) that when he heard that Miss Morstan might become the richest heiress in England, "selfishness took me by the soul and ... my heart turned as heavy as lead within me."

In fact, it seems that the only principal characters in this story who do not suffer from the sin of avarice are Miss Morstan, Thaddeus Sholto, and Holmes himself—though the latter demonstrates an oh-so-human susceptibility to this vice in the case of "The Priory School," many years later.

Greed, then, is more than "the problem of the Sholtos"—it is nearly everyone's problem. Seen in this way, *The Sign of the Four* becomes far more than an adventure story or a detective story: it becomes a morality lesson.

My next question to readers was, "Whose story is this?"

How this poser is answered depends in large measure on how one sees this tale. Today, any long prose work of fiction may be called "a novel." But in the eighteenth century, the term "novel" had a narrower, more specific meaning. Only a work devoted to exploring the manners and mores of a society or segment of society was called a novel: a long piece of prose meant strictly to amuse the reader was called "a romance." (An echo of this distinction survives in the French word "roman," which translates into English as "story." Graham Greene did not use the word "novel" when referring to his suspense / mystery / comic stories; he called them "entertainments.")

The Sign of the Four is ambiguous: it fits with both the contemporary and the eighteenth-century definitions of a "novel," depending on how one interprets the story and views the characters.

It is possible to read *Sign* as a pure piece of detective / mystery fiction: in fact, this is how the general public probably sees it. In this case, one would likely say that Sherlock Holmes is the leading character in the book: he makes all the important observations and deductions which lead to the solution of the case, and is also responsible for the dramatic capture of Small and the death of Tonga. This is a strong argument for the position that this is Holmes's story.

However, potent as that case may be, it clearly ignores another important aspect of the book—the romance between Dr. Watson and Mary Morstan. It can be argued cogently that the real story concerns Dr. Watson and the love affair which changes his entire life—not to mention Miss Morstan's success at finding a loving, caring husband at the age of twenty-seven. This view of *Sign* sees it as primarily a love story: the couple become the central characters, and Holmes and the detective / mystery elements, while both important and entertaining, are peripheral to the main theme of the book.

Nor is that the only alternative answer to my question, "Whose story is this?" After all, the events which drive this novel all involve the life of Jonathan Small: without him there would be no book. In this view Small, the anti-hero, the character to whom things happen far more often than he makes them happen, is by far most important person in the story. Indeed, his narration in chapter 12 consumes about a fifth of the entire book.

There is another point here. What should we make of Abdullah Khan's remark to Small when he outlines the plot against Achmet, the supposed merchant? "We only ask you to do that which your countrymen came to this land for. We ask you to be rich."

This is bitter irony, because Small himself did not come to India to be rich: he only enlisted in the army to get away from Worcestershire and the girl he "got into a mess over." But there is no gainsaying that Britain very definitely established its colonial empire in India with the object of enriching the "mother country." For the better part of two centuries, Great Britain dominated not only Europe but much of the world—and the crown jewel in that empire was India. What did Small do not only to save his life but also to get rich when given the opportunity? He helped to commit murder and grand theft—but isn't that what his countrymen did in India on a colony-wide scale? Also consider Small's commitment to his Sikh partners, and compare that with Major Sholto's racist remark, "What do three black fellows have to do with our agreement?" Sholto, you will recall, was a commissioned officer in the British Army, making his actions and statements at least semi-official expressions of the British government. Indeed, the colonial administration of India by Britain was hardly meant to serve India's interests, and it's no wonder that people like Major Sholto regarded the native population with some degree of disdain. All the more remarkable, then, is Jonathan Small's loyalty to his Sikh partners (and later to the Andaman Islander, Tonga). Race means nothing to Small: loyalty and devotion are more important to him than skin color or religion. In this, Small is admirable today—but just imagine what English readers must have thought about him in 1890!

The point here is that to the extent that *The Sign of the Four* is Jonathan Small's story first, the novel is a subtle but quite apparent attack on the whole British colonial adventure in India, which puts the acquisition of power and wealth ahead of any other values. To put it in the simplest terms, Major Sholto stands "in loco Britannia," and his misdeeds and attitudes are simply those of his country writ Small. (Pun intended!) We know that Sholto lies, steals, betrays his associates and may have committed murder—but did not his country do all of those things during its colonial domination of the subcontinent?

Thus, *The Sign of the Four* is simultaneously a mystery / detective story, a moral fable, a love story, and a work of social criticism—surprising for its time and country of origin. Given that it encompasses four different stories and offers four different possible interpretations, one may wonder if the title of this novel may not refer only to Jonathan Small and the three Sikhs.

Nor are these the only often overlooked dimensions of this novel. It also asks the same question that arises in *A Study in Scarlet*, and which will be posted in a number of other, later Holmes short stories—the question of "What is justice?"

It is abundantly clear from a careful reading of the Sherlock Holmes canon that Conan Doyle early on in his writing career realized that simple obedience to the law is often not just, and that defiance or violation of the statutes may be truer expressions of justice than the law. This theme comes up in stories like "The Abbey Grange," "Charles Augustus Milverton," and "The Devil's Foot," not to mention another Holmes novel—*The Valley of Fear*, which I shall discuss later. This important question—what is justice?—has been asked many, many times in literature, as far back as Classical Greece and the Hebrew Bible, which may have its roots a thousand years before Socrates, Plato, and Diogenes. Many other detective story writers have raised it, and the issue arises often in modern society. It should not be surprising, then, that the first two Holmes stories focus on men who violate the law, yet who have some claim to doing justice. In his life outside literature, Dr. Doyle was acutely aware of the gap between law and justice: recall his intervention in the George Edalji and Oscar Slater cases.

Dr. Doyle's evident compassion for the lower classes, which is clearly demonstrated in each of the first two Sherlock Holmes novels, is probably related to his feelings about justice. So is his work in trying to reform British divorce laws, also reflected in at least two or three of the short stories if not in the first two novels. His depiction of the Baker Street Irregulars in *Scarlet* and again in *The Sign* must not be overlooked. And in this second novel we must pay attention to his two references to the works of Winwood Reade and that wonderful little scene where Holmes observes the dockyard workers on their way home and remarks that each has "some little immortal spark concealed about them." I believe that this aspect of the Holmes canon has been largely ignored, and it deserves more attention from serious readers.

There is yet another aspect to *The Sign of the Four* which, I think, likewise deserves more attention than it usually gets. That is the clear conflict the story raises between love and wealth. Those who seek after money for its own sake cannot have love: only those (like Miss Morstan and Thaddeaus Sholto) who do not seek riches are rewarded with happiness, warmth, and peace. The "great Agra treasure," as Jonathan Small himself says, "never brought anything but a curse...upon the man who owned it." This absolute dichotomy between wealth and love is pointed up in chapter 7, when Watson goes to drop off Mary Morstan at Mrs. Forrester's house. He is touched by the closeness between the two women, and upon leaving he glances back at "the two graceful, clinging figures, the half-opened door, the hall light shining through stained glass, the barometer, and the bright stair-rods. It was soothing to catch even that passing glimpse of a tranquil English home in the midst of the wild, dark business which had absorbed us"—that is, the investigation of the murder of Bartholomew Sholto and the theft of the "great Agra treasure." It is a very short scene—just a single paragraph—but it clearly hints at the impossibility of such a home when the treasure "intervened like an impassable barrier between us."

It is possible that the idea of love and riches being mutually exclusive might have come to Dr. Doyle by way of a set of musical works which received a great deal of attention in the twelve years immediately prior to the composition of *The Sign of the Four* in 1889. I refer to the great cycle of four "music dramas" by Richard Wagner, which was first produced in its entirety in Germany in the summer of 1876. Here, as in Doyle's novel, a great treasure brings nothing but death and misery to its owners, and only when it is returned to its guardians (the Rhine maidens, who inhabit that river) can a new world of human love emerge. We know from other sources that Dr. Doyle was acquainted with Wagner (he actually has Holmes and Watson attend a Wagner night at Covent Garden in one of the later stories) and the fact that in both Wagner's Ring Cycle and Doyle's *Sign*, the treasure is returned to a river leads one to speculate on whether Sir Arthur was influenced by the German work.* It is also possible that Dr. Doyle's attitude toward the wealthy and titled, as it appears in the short stories, may have been reflected by his use of the names of the Marquess of Queensbury, John Sholto (Douglas), for the chief villain of *The Sign of the Four*.

In summary, a close, careful, and intelligent reading of the novel discloses *The Sign of the Four*—undoubtedly a brilliant detective / mystery / adventure story—to be full of deeper meanings. Technically, it validates and elaborates on the author's great stroke of genius in making his narrator, Dr. Watson, a completely delineated character with both intelligence and emotions, far superior to Poe's nameless narrator in the Dupin stories. Indeed, the entire book is full of memorable characters, some drawn with admirable characteristics, no matter how flawed their

conduct. This alone would make the book exceptional. When the use of structure and language is added to the depth of the story, with its detective, moral, romantic, and social criticism aspects, *The Sign of the Four* must be called a great novel.

As for Sherlock Holmes—well, his reward for all his work in solving the case is his bottle of cocaine. Watson, however, comes out with much more satisfaction. In the end, he gets—the heroine!

---

* At the end of "The Red Circle," Sherlock says to Watson, "By the way, it is not eight o'clock, and a Wagner night at Covent Garden! If we hurry, we might be in time for the second act."

CHAPTER 10

The Valley of Fear

THIS, CHRONOLOGICALLY THE FOURTH AND FINAL SHERLOCK HOLMES novel, was begun by Conan Doyle sometime in 1913. We can infer this from the fact that he offered the book to *The Strand Magazine* in January 1914, describing it as a work in progress. As of February 6, the book was about half-finished: Doyle completed the manuscript by summer, and the first chapters were published in the magazine in September 1914—a month after England had declared war on Germany. Doyle is said to have offered to withdraw the story, on the grounds that people had more serious concerns at that moment, but the staff at *The Strand* convinced him that at times of great stress, people would need and want relief. So *Valley* ran in nine consecutive issues of *The Strand*, concluding with May issue of 1915.

The first book publication was not in England at all: George Doran issued it in New York in February 1915—three months before the end of the serial publication in the magazine. The first book edition in Britain appeared on June 3, 1915, under the imprint of Smith, Elder, & Co. But Reginald Smith died not long afterwards, and his firm was acquired by John Murray together with the British book publication rights to this story.

After the publication of the *Return* in December 2004, Dr. Doyle practically ignored Sherlock Holmes for the next eight years, producing just three new stories for *The Strand Magazine* during this period. He busied himself instead by completing all the Brigadier Gerard stories, and began writing the Professor Challenger series. He also wrote *Great Britain and the Next War* at this time, expressing his concern at the rise of Imperial Germany and alerting his readers to the threat Kaiser Wilhelm II posed to the United Kingdom.

It must have come as a pleasant surprise, then, when Herbert Greenhough Smith, the editor of the magazine, heard from Dr. Doyle that he was in the process of writing a new Holmes novel, which he offered to *The Strand* for serial publication. This was in January 1914. Smith immediately responded with a request for more information about this new work in progress, and on February 6 Dr. Doyle sent him a letter which has been published, at least in part, in the introduction to the Oxford World's Classics edition of *The Valley*, which came out in 1993.

Owing to this note, we know some interesting things about the composition of this novel. Dr. Doyle wrote, "The name, I think, will be *The Valley of Fear*. Speaking from what seems to be the present probabilities it should run to not less than 50,000 words. I have done nearly 25,000, I reckon roughly. With luck I should finish by the end of March. As in *A Study in Scarlet*, the plot goes to America for at least half the book while it recounts the events which led up to the crime in England which engaged Holmes's services ... but of course in this long stretch we abandon Holmes. That is necessary."*

At the time he was finishing *Valley*, Dr. Doyle must also have been at work on "Danger!" This short story, which appeared in *The Strand* in

---

* Quoted from the Oxford World Classics edition of *The Valley of Fear*, Oxford University Press, 1993. pp xiii-xiv.

the issue for July 1914, warned the British populace of how a German blockade of the home islands could cripple the country. Then on August 4, just days after "Danger!" was published, war was declared between Germany and Great Britain, and U-boat attacks began. Doyle worried that his new detective story would be found trivial in the face of the war news, but the magazine went ahead with the serial version of the new novel in nine consecutive issues (from September 1914 through May 1915). In fact, *The Strand* went so far as to commission several illustrations for the story—one of them its first color drawing. Since the death of Sidney Paget in 1908, Greenhough Smith had to find another artist to draw Holmes: he assigned the job to Frank Wiles. Les Klinger has reproduced several of Wiles's works in his *New Annotated Sherlock Holmes*, and I have found them quite satisfactory.*

Dr. Doyle's letter to Greenhough Smith also includes an account of how he wrote *The Valley of Fear*. The author reported that he began by writing the first two chapters of part 1 ("The Warning" and "Sherlock Holmes Discourses"), but then abandoned the English part of the book and wrote the American backstory. As of February, 1914, he had done the first two chapters of part 2—"The Man" and "The Bodymaster"—and half of the third ("Lodge 341, Vermissa"). He seems to have finished the remaining American chapters before going back to write the rest of the Birlstone Manor house scenes, completing the story with the epilogue.

According to the *Oxford Sherlock Holmes*, the original manuscript may have been written entirely in the third person, omitting Dr. Watson as both character and narrator. Klinger also believes this to have been the case. Why, when, and how the novel was altered to reintroduce Watson we do not know—but chapters 3 and 4 of part 1 as we now have them show only minimal signs of Dr. Watson's presence and are mainly impersonal.

In any event, Dr. Doyle completed both *Valley* and "Danger" by

---

* See *The New Annotated Sherlock Holmes*, New York: W.W. Norton & Co., 2006.

the middle of April 1914, and shortly afterward left with Lady Doyle for America. They returned to England in July 1914, just as the Sarajevo assassination triggered the falling dominoes that plunged Europe into the Great War.

The threat and eventual outbreak of hostilities affected Conan Doyle. Tensions between England and Germany had been rising for several years, and after the death of King Edward VII in 1911, a major restraining influence on his nephew, Kaiser Wilhelm, was lost. Germany made a strong effort to match Britain's traditional naval superiority, building up a surface fleet capable of at least challenging the United Kingdom at sea. At the same time, a menacing new weapon, the U-boat, gave the Kaiser a new means of destroying Britain's merchant fleet. Dr. Doyle was very concerned about the threat to Britain's commerce—an essential factor in the kingdom's very existence. This may explain one of the unique qualities of *Valley*: virtually from the first page, this novel is characterized by feelings of gloom, uncertainty, apprehension, and—true to its title—fear.

That title derives from the conversation between McMurdo and Brother Morris in chapter 4 of the second (American-based) part of the work, and the chapter bears the same name as the novel—"The Valley of Fear." The two men meet in the park at the top of Miller Hill, overlooking the town of Vermissa. Morris says, "Look down the valley! See the cloud of a hundred chimneys that overshadows it! I tell you that the cloud of murder hangs thicker and lower than that over the heads of the people. It is the Valley of Fear, the Valley of Death. The terror is in the hearts of the people from the dusk to the dawn. Wait, young man, and you will learn for yourself."

Who can read these lines without immediately recalling the words of Psalm 23: "Yea, though I walk through the valley of the shadow of death, I will fear no evil"? The words of Brother Morris specifically equate the "Valley of Fear" with the Biblical "valley of the shadow of death." This cannot possibly be accidental: Dr. Doyle knew that his readers would make the connection. It is up to us, then, to clarify what the author wanted us to get from the words, and why. I suggest that this passage is the seed from which the entire story grows—when we understand it, we will know more about why he wrote this novel in 1913–14, after having practically abandoned Holmes since 1904.

I also insist on using the term "novel" for its eighteenth-century meaning—a story which explores the manners and mores of a society or segment of society. Like its predecessors, *The Sign of the Four* and *The Hound of the Baskervilles*, *The Valley of Fear* invokes deeper meanings than the conventional mystery story, which is written purely to entertain the reader. That sort of book is best thought of by the term Graham Greene coined to describe his own ventures into that form: he called them "entertainments." Dr. Doyle's three long, mature stories in which Holmes appears are true novels.

Moreover, mystery fiction is in general fundamentally optimistic: at the end, the crime is solved, the villain disposed of, and life returns to normal for both the surviving characters and the reader. Not so with *The Valley of Fear*: the crime is solved, indeed, but the ending of the book is ambiguous. There is no clear victory of justice and truth over evil, and the master criminal lives on to taunt Sherlock with his "Dear me, Mr. Holmes, Dear me" note. In fact, *Valley* is unique among the longer stories in the Holmes canon for the powerful atmosphere it creates. It may begin with a joke—Dr. Watson's remark in response to Holmes's "My blushes" line early in the first chapter—but the predominant tone is negative. This is by far the darkest of the four Holmes novels, and only a couple of the short stories ("The Veiled Lodger" comes immediately to mind) share its oppressive atmosphere. It has never achieved the popularity of the other long Holmes stories, and will probably continue to be thought of as "the problematic Holmes book," brilliant as it is.

The origin of the story is historical, as Conan Doyle himself explains in the preface to *Sherlock Holmes: The Complete Long Stories* (1929): "*The Valley of Fear* had its origin through my reading a graphic account of the Molly McQuire [sic] outrages in the coal fields of Pennsylvania, when a young detective drawn from Pinkerton's Agency acted exactly as the hero [of *Valley*] is presented as doing." The account to which he refers was almost certainly Allan Pinkerton's own book, *The Mollie Maguires and the Detectives*, which appeared in 1877.

For those unfamiliar with the story, I give this short explanation. The Molly Maguires were Irish immigrant and first-generation Irish American coal miners, working in the anthracite coal region north of Philadelphia. They experienced not only bad working conditions and low wages in the mines, but also great prejudice from their neighbors and employers, who were mostly English in origin and Protestant by religion. They hated and feared the Roman Catholic Irish—emotions dating to the strife between England and Ireland, going back centuries.

The Irish workers—for the most part members of a social organization called "The Ancient Order of Hibernians"—eventually revolted against the intolerable position in which they found themselves. They used the already existing Order as a means of attacking their oppressors through violence—including beatings, extortion, and even murder.

The man who led a counter operation against the Mollies was Franklin Benjamin Gowen, president of the coal-hauling Philadelphia and Reading Railroad and himself a mine owner. He, like many others of his class and background, saw the unrest in the coal fields as a serious threat not only to his economic interests but also as a challenge to the hegemony of the WASP upper class and the order which it imposed. It was Gowen who hired the Pinkerton Detective Agency with the goal of infiltrating the Mollies and breaking up their organization. The young man chosen for the job was James McParlan, who operated under the alias "Jimmy McKenna." It took him two years, but he succeeded in carrying out his mission. In

1875, nineteen leaders and members of the Mollies were convicted and hanged, mostly on his testimony, and the revolt crushed.*

Given who the Mollies were, we should not forget or ignore Conan Doyle's own heritage. While born into an Irish Catholic family, he never lived in the Emerald Island and grew up in Edinburgh. As a boy he received a Catholic school education. However, he left the Church as a young man and became a political Unionist who opposed any degree of independence for Ireland. He visited his Irish relatives there only once, in 1881, and never went back. He even stood twice (in 1900 and 1906) for parliamentary seats on the Unionist ticket representing Scottish districts. He was defeated both times.

According to the Oxford World Classics Edition of *Valley*, sometime in 1911 Doyle reversed his views. Influenced by Sir Roger Casement, he came out in favor of home rule for Ireland. Two or three years later, the former Unionist wrote this novel about Irish Americans who took to violence in defense of their rights and with the hope of bettering their position in life. While Doyle's treatment of the Eminent Order of Freemen (as the Hibernians are called in American editions of the book: Doyle called the organization "The Ancient Order of Freemen" in the original British text) makes no effort to whitewash the crimes the Mollies (called the Scowrers in the novel) committed, it does give them a chance to present their case— that this was not criminal, but a war against their oppressors—and also makes it clear that not all the members of the organization were bloodthirsty roughs: Mike Scanlan and Brother Morris are examples. The treatment of the Mollies may not be overtly sympathetic, but neither is it totally negative. Could this be because since his conversations with Casement, Doyle had modified his antipathy to the

---

* For more about the Molly Maguires, see Klinger's *New Annotated Sherlock Holmes* (ibid.), which cites several other sources. Contemporary writers have tended to be friendlier about the revolt than earlier critics, who were often notoriously one-sided in support of the mine owners. Klinger also comments on how the Mollies came to be called by that name.

McParlan went further in his career as an anti-labor agent, but Gowen killed himself in 1889, fourteen years after the end of the Molly Maguire revolt.

land and people of his own origins? Did the 180-degree change in his politics reflect a deeper change in his feelings about Ireland and the Irish? I have no evidence that this was the case, but the fact that Sir Arthur's political turnabout and this literary chronicle based on the Mollies came so close together at a critical time in his life and at a trying time for Britain is highly suggestive, at least to me.

And now, having dealt with all these preliminary points, it is time to move on to the intensive reading and study, chapter by chapter, of this most interesting, most challenging, and perhaps most under-appreciated of all the Holmes stories.

STRUCTURAL ANALYSIS

In this, the last-written Sherlock Holmes novel, Conan Doyle returned to the same structural plan he had employed in *A Study in Scarlet* twenty-six years earlier. The book is divided into two large sections, followed by a short epilogue. Each of the two large sections is comprised of seven chapters. The first, entitled "The Tragedy of Birlstone," is set in England "at the end of the Eighties," while the second, called "The Scowrers," takes place in America—specifically the anthracite coal region of Pennsylvania—in or about 1875. The epilogue is set in Holmes's apartment, 221 B Baker Street, two months after the events of the first section—that is, sometime in March of 1887, 1888, or 1889.

Here are the chapters and their titles in each part of the novel.

> *PART I:* The Tragedy of Birlstone
> *Chapter 1:* The Warning
> *Chapter 2:* Sherlock Holmes Discourses
> *Chapter 3:* The Tragedy of Birlstone
> *Chapter 4:* Darkness
> *Chapter 5:* The People of the Drama
> *Chapter 6:* A Dawning Light
> *Chapter 7:* The Solution

PART II: The Scowrers
   Chapter 1: The Man
   Chapter 2: The Bodymaster
   Chapter 3: Lodge 341, Vermissa
   Chapter 4: The Valley of Fear
   Chapter 5: The Darkest Hour
   Chapter 6: Danger
   Chapter 7: The Trapping of Birdy Edwards
PART III: Epilogue

Note that the first chapter of the book is entitled "The Warning," while the next-to-last is called "Danger." I urge readers to think about these bookend terms: who is being warned, and about what? Who is in danger, and from what? Also keep in mind that while writing *The Valley of Fear*, Conan Doyle also produced a polemic with this same title. Remember these questions when after our close study of the novel we reach the section called "Essays on The Valley of Fear": they may be answered there.

PART I: THE TRAGEDY OF BIRLSTONE

CHAPTER 1: THE WARNING

The chapter may be divided into two subsections: the first has Holmes and Watson together at Baker Street, while Holmes discusses the cipher and note from "Porlock" and Porlock's principal, Professor Moriarty. Expecting to receive a key to the cipher, Holmes gets instead a note from "Porlock," resigning from the case in a panic. So full of fear is he that his note is barely legible. Porlock is "evidently scared out of his senses," and thus the theme of fear is introduced on the novel's fourth page.

Notwithstanding this check, Sherlock Holmes undertakes to solve the cipher by pure reasoning, and after a false start (using the new instead of the old almanac), he does so.

Subsection two begins with the arrival of Inspector MacDonald, with his news of the murder at Birlstone Manor during the night.

CHAPTER 2: SHERLOCK HOLMES DISCOURSES

Mostly, he discourses on Professor Moriarty. Then all three men (Holmes, Watson, and the inspector) depart for the scene of the crime.

At this point, permit me to pose a question for the reader: why did Conan Doyle reintroduce Professor Moriarty into this story, more than twenty years after having killed him off at the Reichenbach Falls? Note, also, how the author slips in a second reference to "fear" in the second subsection of chapter 1. As Holmes greets MacDonald, he says, "I fear this means that there is some mischief afoot." MacDonald replies, "If you had said 'hope' instead of 'fear,' it would be nearer the truth, I'm thinking, Mr. Holmes."

Also, for what it's worth, MacDonald uses the word "hope" in this same sentence. Hope is the central emotion in *A Study of Scarlet* and the last name of its hero / killer. I wouldn't bring this up if not for Conan Doyle's use of almost the exact same structure in this first Sherlock Holmes novel. Is this anything more than coincidence? Or was the author suggesting an affinity between the two books? I have no idea—but in any case, he clearly wishes to impress the reader with the emotion of fear, subtly calling attention to the word even when the context is about as unfearful as could be.

CHAPTER 3: THE TRAGEDY OF BIRLSTONE

Again, the chapter can be divided into two subsections. The first describes first the village and area of Birlstone, next, the Manor House, and lastly the people of the household—John Douglas, his wife, and his friend Cecil Barker, "a frequent and welcome visitor." We also hear of Ames, the butler, and Mrs. Allen, the housekeeper.

Subsection two is devoted to the events of the night of January 6: the first alarm; the arrival of the police sergeant, Wilson; and the doctor, Wood. We then hear Barker's account of what he found, and Ames's statement of why the drawbridge was kept down. The shotgun, the card ("V.V. 341"), the hammer, the marks of muddy boots on the carpet behind the window curtain, the brand mark on the right arm of the corpse, and finally the fact that the wedding ring had been taken are all discovered and discussed.* The Sussex detective, Mr. White Mason, is called in.**

CHAPTER 4: DARKNESS

The investigation continues: White Mason arrives, and he wastes no time in sending for MacDonald from Scotland Yard. By noon on January 7, Mr. Mac, Holmes, and Watson are on the scene.

Again, the chapter is made up of two subsections: first, the meeting at the inn; later the walk to the Manor House and the meeting in the murder room. In the first subsection, MacDonald raises objections to the idea that someone from outside the house got in and killed Mr. Douglas, escaping through the window and wading across the moat. It is during this conversation that Holmes makes his first contribution to the investigation—his recognition that the murder gun came from the Pennsylvania Small Arms Company, a "well-known American firm."

---

* If the intruder got into the Manor House over the lowered drawbridge, how did his boots get muddy? Dr. Doyle seems to have slipped up here.

** This incident of the ring bothers me. Why on earth did Dr. Doyle have Douglas and Barker replace the so-called nugget ring on the finger of the corpse? Surely it was not necessary to do so in order to call attention to the missing wedding band: the absence of both rings would surely have been noticed, by Ames if not by Barker or Mrs. Douglas. If both rings were gone, it would probably lead the detective to believe that the intruder wanted the wedding ring: that point could have been emphasized if the nugget were simply tossed away, either in the study or outside where it could be found. Replacing the nugget simply confuses the issue and clouds the argument that the assassin wanted the wedding ring for whatever reason he might have had. Also, mark how the missing wedding band forms still another link between this tale and *A Study in Scarlet*.

Subsection two of chapter 4 begins as the detectives walk through the village from the inn to the 300-year-old Manor House; with its "strange, peaked roofs and quaint, over-hung gables—a fitting covering to grim and terrible intrigue." This is such a fascinating description that it makes me wish to visit the place myself. Holmes looks about the moat and asks if there were any signs that anyone landed on the side opposite the window of the murder room. White Mason replies that he had already looked and found no sign. Holmes asks about the depth of the moat, and learns that it is no more than three feet deep—"a child could not be drowned in it." Then the party meets in the study—the murder room. Sergeant Wilson is sent home and Ames, the butler, left outside the room and told to alert Mrs. Douglas and Barker that they will be asked to come in soon. Then, at last, White Mason lays out his thinking about the crime.

"Is it suicide or murder? That's our first question," he says, and immediately he ticks off the reasons why suicide is "out of the question." The second issue is whether the criminal came from inside or outside the house. White Mason points out how unlikely murder by an insider would be, and Holmes agrees with his reasoning. But when the Sussex detective tries to reconstruct the crime, Holmes calls his idea "Very interesting, but just a little unconvincing." From the evidence of the gun, an American weapon, and the fact that Douglas had lived in America, White Mason also ventures the opinion that the motive for the crime was not burglary but revenge. At this mark MacDonald breaks in with a plea to Holmes for a theory of the crime. Holmes demurs: He wants more data before he will go so far.

In search of more information, Holmes takes over the questioning: he asks Ames about Douglas's mental state the day before the crime. The butler says that his master had been "a little restless and excited." He had cut himself shaving, too—something he did not often do.

Holmes then turns to the brand on the right arm of the body, and he asks Ames if he had seen it before. The butler says he had seen it frequently, but he adds that he does not know what the brand means.

Next, Holmes asks about the card, "V.V.341," and is told that there is no such cardboard in the house: he also finds no ink like that on the card, and no pen like the one used to do the letters. He concludes that the card was not made in the house. Holmes also looks more closely at the marks on the windowsill: he finds them to be remarkably broad, as if left by a splay foot, while the print on the carpet appeared to have been made by "a more shapely sole." Then he crosses to the side table and asks what is kept under there. Ames answers, "Mr. Douglas's dumbbells." Holmes immediately notices that there is only one, and asks about the other, but Ames cannot tell him. "Maybe there was only one," the butler says. "I have not noticed them in months." "One dumbbell," Holmes muses—but just at this moment Cecil Barker enters with news that the bicycle used by the mysterious intruder had been found "within a hundred yards of the hall door." All rush out to look at it, and MacDonald comments about how strange it is that the rider left it there and how he got away without using it. "We don't seem to get a gleam of light in the case, Mr. Holmes," he says. But Holmes says, thoughtfully, "Don't we? I wonder."

Obviously, the "gleam of light" must come from the discovery of the single dumbbell— but at this time, we know no more than that.

CHAPTER 5: THE PEOPLE OF THE DRAMA

An even better title for this chapter might be "The Evidence Given By the People of the Drama," for most of it consists of interviews with each of the four principal witnesses in the case—Ames, the butler; Mrs. Allen, the housekeeper; Cecil Barker, the house guest; and Mrs. Ivy Douglas. Each of these interviews forms a subsection of the chapter, while a fifth subsection takes the story in a different direction.

In subsection one, Ames tells us that Mr. Douglas was "the most fearless man he had ever known." He then recounts how on January 6 he had noticed that Mr. Douglas seemed restless and excited, which was unusual for him. He then tells everything he knows about the events on the night of the killing. Mrs. Allen corroborates what Ames had already said, but adds the fact that while she had heard no shot, she did recall hearing what she took to be a door slammed half an hour before the violent ringing of the bell alarmed the house. She had spent most of the night with Mrs. Douglas upstairs after the discovery of the body, which Mrs. Allen had not seen.

Subsection three is devoted to the testimony of Barker about his life with Douglas as prospecting partners in America. This includes a couple of relevant pieces of information: that Douglas had been a widower when they met; that he had lived in Chicago; and had talked about the coal and iron districts. Shortly afterward, Douglas had abruptly sold his share in their mine and departed for Europe just before half a dozen rough-looking men came asking about him. From Barker, the detectives learn that whatever had happened in the life of John Douglas went back at least eleven years. He also mentions that Douglas always went armed with a revolver, but at home that night he was in his dressing gown (British for "bathrobe"), and so was vulnerable. Inspector MacDonald, who is doing the questioning, then asks Barker about his relationship with Mrs. Douglas. That seems to fascinate him, and he asks about the missing wedding ring. Holmes then inquires about the candle and the oil lamp before the subsection ends.

Mrs. Douglas is the subject of the fourth subsection: she confirms Barker's statements about the events of the fatal night. She contributes the information that Douglas seemed to have had "a danger hanging over him."* Holmes asks her what words of his led her to believe this, and it is she who first mentions "the Valley of Fear" and "Bodymaster McGinty." Subsection five follows the interviews, and it describes Holmes's demonstration about Barker's slippers and the marks on the windowsill. MacDonald, who has been devoted to

---

* She mentions that her husband made the rounds of the house every night because "he was nervous of fire." Notice that she avoids the words "scared of" or "afraid of" fire, adding that that was the only thing he was ever "nervous of."

the idea that Barker and Mrs. Douglas were in cahoots to get rid of her husband, can only ask, after Holmes's experiment with the slippers, "What's the game, Mr. Holmes—what's the game?" And Holmes simply repeats the phrase, saying "Ay, what's the game?" as the chapter ends.

COMMENTS ON CHAPTER 5

"The People of the Drama" suggests that Cecil Barker and Ivy Douglas conspired to kill her husband, opening the way to a romantic relationship between them.

Even Holmes's inspiration about the slippers and the blood on the windowsill may be interpreted as supporting this idea in some way. The conspiracy theory expressed here sets up the scene in the garden in chapter 6, which follows closely upon it. While Holmes remains silent, Inspector MacDonald's thinking must influence the reader to suspect both the wife and the best friend of John Douglas.

CHAPTER 6: A DAWNING LIGHT

We can break this chapter down into four subsections: first, the encounter in the garden between Watson (who we finally see taking an active part in the case), Cecil Barker, and Mrs. Douglas. Second, the discussion between Watson and Holmes, during which the detective offers an alternative theory which accounts for the actions of Barker and Mrs. Douglas. Third, MacDonald and White Mason return after tracing the bicycle, and later Inspector Mac presents his reconstruction of the crime. Finally, in subsection four, Holmes tells his theory.

Subsection three finds MacDonald and White Mason back from their day of chasing down and identifying the abandoned bicycle. They have made great progress, including obtaining a description of the man who called himself "Hargrave" and rented a room at the Eagle Commercial, a hotel in Tunbridge Wells. Inspector Mac than presents his reconstruction of the crime—and Sherlock Holmes replies with "his end of the story"—that the crime was committed half an hour before the first alarm was given; that Barker and Mrs. Douglas are in conspiracy to conceal something; and that they aided the murderer's escape, or at least reached the room before he left, fabricating the evidence of the window escape and probably letting down the drawbridge themselves to let him go.

The fourth subsection is short: Holmes returns to the inn late at night, after spending the evening in the murder room with Dr. Watson's big umbrella. Watson, half asleep, asks him if he found anything out. His reply is a remarkable question, to which Watson answers in the negative. "Ah, that's lucky," says Holmes as he goes to sleep, and the chapter ends.

COMMENTS ON CHAPTER 6

Watson's chance meeting with Barker and Mrs. Douglas leads him to the obvious conclusion—guilty love. He never considers any alternative—even after they ask him about how Holmes relates to the official investigators, a question which ought to suggest that they wish to approach the unofficial detective with some message that they want him to know, as long as he is not bound to disclose it to the police. Again, the author deftly encourages the reader to keep looking at his principal red herring—the "guilty love" theory.

In subsection two, when Holmes offers his alternative outline of the case, he raises the possibility that the missing ring was connected with Douglas's first marriage, rather than his second, and that the decade-old vendetta might be connected with that earlier relationship. I have remarked before on the similarities between the first Holmes detective novel and this, the fourth and last—and here we have another reference to *A Study in Scarlet*, where a missing wedding ring played an important role. If it was the author's intention to present another red herring to his readers, he succeeded, for the missing ring has no importance in this story. However, its presence in this novel may be another suggestion that Conan Doyle was "closing the circle" by deliberately linking elements of his first and last Holmes novels.

It is also in subsection two that we are presented with perhaps the finest depiction of the mature Holmes to be found in the entire canon—the high tea scene. Here is Holmes at his most cheerful as he talks about the missing dumbbell, "with his mouth full of toast and his eyes sparkling with mischief, watching my intellectual entanglement." Later he talks about the importance of imagination: "How often is imagination the mother of truth?" His congenial relationship with Inspector MacDonald is light years distant from his earlier interactions with Lestrade and Gregson—and even later in the canon, when he is much friendlier with them, he never approaches the warmth he shows in his conversations with "Mr. Mac." In *The Valley of Fear*, Sherlock Holmes becomes a warm and charming human being. Who'd have believed it?

When Holmes returns to the inn, he asks the half-asleep Watson, "Would you be afraid to sleep in the same room with a lunatic, a man with softening of the brain, an idiot whose mind has lost its grip?" What does this remarkable question mean? How are we to understand it? Did Holmes perhaps expect to find something other than what he found in the moat? Is he berating himself for not foreseeing what he did find? Does he have trouble believing the truth of his own solution of the murder?

I suggest that Holmes's "insanity" question makes sense only if he had come to the conclusion that he had the answer to the puzzle, but he could not fully accept that solution—it was so out of the ordinary. In any case, Holmes's speech fits in well with the dark world of the novel.

And after all, his solution could not be proved correct until the next night, and he must wonder if he was truly right—or just out of his mind when he conjured it up out of a single clue, the missing dumbbell. Here too we have a different Holmes than the cocksure young man of *A Study in Scarlet*.

CHAPTER 7: THE SOLUTION

Four subsections are found in this chapter, clearly delineated by time and location.

Subsection one is set in the morning of the next day, when Holmes and Watson are in the parlor of Sergeant Wilson's house, talking with the two professional detectives. They now have information about the missing bicyclist from nineteen places, including arrests in three. Hearing this, Holmes invokes his agreement with the police that he would not give them anything less than a complete case solved to his own satisfaction. Because he is not yet sure of his case, he will not yet share it with them, but he does advise them to take the day off rather than waste their time and energy chasing down the man who rode the bicycle. MacDonald points out that, the night before, Holmes was in general agreement with their efforts. What had happened to change his thinking? Holmes explains that he had spent the evening at the Manor House, and that what occurred there had altered his perception of the case. Here he tosses them a broad hint, but neither seems willing to follow up: he mentions the little pamphlet about the old house. He begins to read it, until he is angrily put down by MacDonald. So he does not continue to read it, but mentions some information from it concerning Charles I and George II, both of whom visited the house. "Breadth of view, my dear Mr. Mac, is one of the essentials of our profession." How different is this mature Holmes from the young man who feared overcrowding his little brain attic!

Subsection one concludes with Holmes's humorous advice to the detectives on how to spend their day, followed by his instructions to MacDonald about the note to Barker and his instructions to the inspector to meet in the same room before dusk without fail—"without fail, Mr. Mac." He then dictates the note and orders it to be sent by hand at about four o'clock. The stage is now set for subsection two—the night vigil and its immediate aftermath.

This portion of the chapter contains some of Conan Doyle's best atmospheric writing. He introduces the scene with Holmes's warning that it was going to be cold—but he uses the word "chill," which not only refers to the feeling of cold, but also has connotations of shivering, sickness, and fear. It is surely *le mot juste* for this moment. The words "in the gathering gloom" perfectly give us the feeling of darkness shutting down, and shortly afterwards we encounter these powerful lines: "Slowly the shadows darkened over the long, somber face of the old house. A cold, damp reek from the moat chilled us to the bones and set our teeth chattering. There was a single lamp over the gateway and a steady globe of light in the fatal study. Everything else was dark and still." Don't these words make you feel as if you yourself were crouched in the shrubbery opposite the drawbridge beside Dr. Watson as the minutes turn to hours, waiting for—what?

Subsection two concludes in the study as Holmes unwraps the bundle and turns to Barker for an explanation. He refuses to talk, but the intervention of Mrs. Douglas leads to the emergence through the gloom of a remarkable man.

Subsection three consists of Mr. Douglas's own account of the events of January 6, concluding with his question about his standing under the law of England, and Holmes's warning to him to remain on guard in the future.

Subsection four, just two paragraphs long, forms the transition from part 1 of *The Valley of Fear*—the crime at Birlstone Manor House—and part 2, the American backstory which eventually led to it. Just as the story of the Ferriers and the Mormons was the root of the Drebber and Stangerson murders in *A Study in Scarlet*, so the tale of the Scowrers ends in the English countryside more than a decade later.

COMMENTS ON CHAPTER 7

Conan Doyle never wrote a better piece of Holmesiana than this first part of *The Valley of Fear*. Two things immediately stand out: the personality of Sherlock Holmes, here fully developed and never better portrayed, and the oppressive atmosphere which pervades this whole section of the novel. We can attribute the first factor to Conan Doyle's own maturation over the quarter century which had passed since he created the character, and perhaps the second to his state of mind at a time when clouds of war threatened Britain's hegemony in Europe and the world, if not that nation's very existence.

Imagery of light and dark is central to this first part of *The Valley of Fear*. Nearly every important scene in this half of the book takes place in darkness: the assault on Douglas and the actual killing occurred by candlelight; and chapter 4, in which the investigation of the crime begins, is entitled "Darkness." At the very end of this chapter, MacDonald remarks "We don't seem to get a gleam of light in the case, Mr. Holmes," and Holmes replies "Don't we? I wonder!" He is thinking about the missing dumbbell. Chapter 5 ends with another gleam of light—Holmes's demonstration that it was Barker's slippers that made the footmarks on the windowsill. Chapter 6 is called "A Dawning Light," and contains Holmes's fishing expedition with Watson's umbrella, when, under cover of darkness, he draws the bundle from the moat, and in examining his find, "sees the light." Finally, in chapter 7, Mr. Douglas himself emerges from the gloom and into the light, and the case is solved. But in this novel, unlike nearly all other detective novels, the solution is not the end of the story.

PART 2: THE SCOWRERS

CHAPTER 1: THE MAN

Arbitrarily, I treat this chapter as being made up of two subsections: the mountain scene and the train ride through it, and the town of Vermissa and what McMurdo finds there. Each of the two subsections is itself divided into shorter scenes.

Subsection one appears to have been inspired by the movies. It begins with a panoramic view of the mountains and the valley of Vermissa, through which the train makes its way. Then we see the interior of the first passenger car and its occupants, before the focus narrows to concentrate on a single young man traveling alone, whose appearance and behavior cast him as one "who might conceivably leave his mark for good or evil upon any society to which he was introduced." He looks out of the train window and we see what he sees is "not a cheering prospect. Through the growing gloom there pulsed the red glow of the furnaces on the sides of the hills. Great heaps of slag and dumps of cinders loomed up on each side, with the high shafts of the collieries towering above them. Huddled groups of mean, wooden houses ... were scattered here and there along the line, and the frequent halting places were crowded with their swarthy inhabitants."

There follows another scene in which the young man is drawn into conversation with the miner, Mike Scanlan, during which we learn his name—Jack McMurdo—and we first hear the name of Bodymaster McGinty. After Scanlan leaves the train, we get what I call "the vision of Hell," with leaping flames of the furnaces roaring and dancing in the darkness. McMurdo has a run-in with two policemen, which is overheard by a nameless miner who volunteers to escort the newcomer, McMurdo, through the ugly, depressing town to Shafter's boarding house. This walk through the town is the first scene of subsection two, and it includes further talk about Boss McGinty and "the affairs" of the Scowrers. But when McMurdo knocks on the door of the Shafter house, to find it opened by the beautiful Ettie, the tone of the chapter turns brighter.

I was struck by the cinematic techniques which appear in this chapter, which could be turned into a screenplay with hardly any changes at all. Had Conan Doyle been impressed with movies, which by 1913 were no longer a novelty?

Note also the use of light and dark imagery, which we saw employed to such a great degree in part 1 of the book. As McMurdo rides the train to Vermissa, the evening gloom turns to full dark and the hellish aspects of Vermissa Valley become manifest. The hero arrives in the town of Vermissa as darkness falls over the community, and metaphorically upon him as well.

CHAPTER 2: THE BODYMASTER

This chapter can be broken down into five subsections. The first describes McMurdo's short stay at Shafter's boarding house, the most important part of which was his first meeting Ettie, for whom he fell at first sight. By the end of the sixth paragraph, she too is well on the way to being in love.

The second subsection describes Mike Scanlan's visit to McMurdo, and his advice to McMurdo to go and see Bodymaster McGinty at once.

In the third subsection, the young boarder converses with old Jacob Shafter, who repeats his statement from subsection two—that the Order of Freemen in Vermissa is not the same sort of organization as it is elsewhere. On discovering that McMurdo is already a member of the organization, Shafter bars him from the house after that night.

Things become even tenser when in subsection four McMurdo declares his love to Ettie, who would marry him immediately if he would leave Vermissa. He replies that he cannot leave, but that he has no fear of Baldwin, McGinty, or the Scowrers. Then he relates the response of the Molly McGuires to the charges of criminality—that in fact they are not criminals, but warriors fighting back against oppression with the only weapons they have. At this point Ted Baldwin himself enters, claiming Ettie as his own and nearly provoking a fight. He leaves with a threat, and Ettie tells McMurdo to go to McGinty before Baldwin can get to him first.

Subsection five is set at McGinty's saloon, crowded with those who fear life in the valley without the Bodymaster's good will. Here we get a view of the formidable leader of the Scowrers, who holds a gun on McMurdo—only to hear from the young firebrand that it was he who was most endangered during their interview. The entrance of Baldwin turns the scene into a confrontation between Baldwin and McGinty, and the chapter ends with a passage leading into the initiation of McMurdo into the Vermissa Lodge. This takes place in chapter 3.*

CHAPTER 3: LODGE 341, VERMISSA

Once again, I have arbitrarily chosen to divide chapter 3 into just two subsections.

The first describes McMurdo's move to the Widow MacNama's house on the outskirts of Vermissa, where Scanlan joins him as the only other boarder. He is allowed to come to Shafter's for meals, however, and so draws closer yet to Ettie. He then ingratiates himself with the Scowrers by showing off his counterfeiting moulds and passing out dollars he supposedly made. He also hangs around the saloon socializing and fighting, and one night has his run-in with Captain Marvin, which makes him even more popular with the members of the lodge.

Subsection two describes the events at the Saturday night meeting during which McMurdo is initiated into the lodge. Division Master Windle of Merton County Lodge 249 requests two men from Vermissa for "a job," and Boss McGinty chooses a two-man team for the killing. The treasurer reports that "the funds are good"—that is, that extortion is working. But in answer to a question from Brother Morris, the treasurer reports that seven local firms have been sold to companies in New York or Philadelphia—a step that in time will threaten the hold of the Freemen on the valley.

Then it is time for play—singing, drinking, and carousing. When the members are well liquored up, the Bodymaster calls for volunteers to attack the editor of the local newspaper over his

---

* McGinty's last words in chapter 2 are, "If you come then [to the lodge meeting on Saturday night] we'll make you free forever of the Vermissa Valley." What a terrific irony—the last thing Lodge 341 offers is to be free of the valley!

anti-Scowrers writing.* Baldwin is to lead a party of six, plus two to guard the door.

McGinty orders Baldwin to take McMurdo as one of the posse. Morris reminds the Boss that if the editor, Stanger, is killed the reaction would bring more trouble than the Vermissa Freemen want, so McGinty orders the attackers not to kill the man—just to beat him up.

Subsection two recounts the attack, during which McMurdo holds Baldwin's hand at gunpoint to keep him from killing the man. Note the language here: McMurdo tells Baldwin,

"I'll blow your face in if you lay a hand on me." Years later and thousands of miles away, he does exactly that!

A warning from the sentinel downstairs breaks up the posse, some going back to the saloon to report and others to their own abodes. McMurdo goes home.

CHAPTER 4: THE VALLEY OF FEAR

I count four clearly defined subsections here. Subsection one describes McMurdo's hangover and aching brand: he does not go to his job but writes "a long letter to a friend" (Allan Pinkerton?) and reads in the "Herald" the account of the night's attack on the newspaperman.

Then the Widow MacNamara knocks on his door and delivers as unsigned note requesting him to come to the flagstaff on Miller Hill for an important talk. Realizing from the handwriting that the note comes from a man rather than a woman, and that the author is well-educated, McMurdo decides to go.

Subsection two is the middle section of the American part of the novel. It contains the overlook of "the whole straggling, grimy

---

* The editor's name is James Stanger: was this a conscious reference to Joseph Stangerson in *A Study in Scarlet*? Another tie between the two novels? Another hint that Conan Doyle meant to close the circle of his longer Holmes stories by ending with a tale that had many parallels and references to his first detective novel?

town and the winding valley beneath with its scattered mines and factories blackening the snow on each side of it." This paragraph, I submit, is the daytime twin of the vision of Hell seen from the train in the second part of chapter 1. This panorama presents the sharp contrast between the natural beauty of the area and the man-made ugliness which mars and corrupts it. Symbolically, this might be thought of as telling the entire story in a single sentence.

The figure standing beside the flagpole turns out to be Brother Morris, who risks his life to appeal to McMurdo as a newcomer "whose conscience cannot yet be as hardened" as those of the others. He is trapped in Vermissa, for his store is his only asset: yet he is sickened and appalled by the actions of McGinty and his cohorts. McMurdo restates what he said previously to Jacob Shafter—that what the Freemen are up to is not really crime, but a war against oppression in which they fight back with the only means they possess. While in no way excusing the Mollies for their actions, Conan Doyle subtly gives them a platform for stating their case.

Morris continues in anguish: he was made to participate (as a watchman) in a killing, and now he sees himself as "lost in this world and also in the next," for he has been excommunicated from the Catholic Church.*

What follows is the heart of the novel: Morris explicitly equates the Valley of Fear with the biblical valley of the shadow of death. (I will explain my interpretation of this key identification in the essay which follows our study of the text.) After agreeing on an excuse for their meeting, both men leave the scene.

In subsection three, Boss McGinty comes to McMurdo's rooms: he wants to know what his host spoke about with Brother Morris earlier that day. McMurdo turns the question around: he asks the Bodymaster how he knew that the two men had met and talked? McGinty gives no answer, and he is about to leave when Captain

---

* This Draconian fate befell several of the Mollies; whether it was deserved or not, who now can judge?

Marvin breaks in to arrest McMurdo for his participation in the attack on the editor, Stanger. McMurdo is taken to the town jail.

Subsection Four takes place in the jail, where McMurdo, Baldwin, and three other men are being held. It turns out to be something of a party, as a jailer brings in whiskey, glasses, and cards. They go on trial the next morning, and all are easily acquitted. One onlooker expresses the feelings of many frustrated citizens. He says, "You damned murderers! We'll fix you yet." With that ominous warning, the chapter ends.

COMMENTS ON CHAPTER 4

In my years of reading, writing, and teaching, I first learned and later taught that the weakest part of any structure is the center, unless it is supported in some way. Thus, the creator often plants the key to understanding his creation in the center of the work. In terms of this book, we note that the second subsection of chapter 4 occupies the exact middle of the American part, and what we find here is that identification between the *Valley of Fear* and the valley of the shadow of death. Earlier, I asked my readers to consider why Conan Doyle brought back Professor Mariarty in this novel, after having killed him off twenty-two years before, in "The Final Problem." Now I ask: what meaning can one find in the equation of the two valleys? Why is this paragraph in the center of the second part of the book?

Now we continue our study of the text with chapter 5.

CHAPTER 5: THE DARKEST HOUR

I find four subsections here. The first is made up of the two opening paragraphs, recounting how McMurdo's status within the Scowrers rises like a rocket from his first night as a member of the lodge, while the third describes his rapid decline in status with the Shafters, father and daughter.

Subsection two tells of Ettie's stealthy visit to McMurdo at his home, and how he reacts to being surprised by her. She gets a "sudden glimpse of guilty fear" from his face, and she demands to see the letter he was writing when she interrupted him. He refuses, and she jumps to the conclusion that it must be to another woman—perhaps even to a wife. How can she know that he is not already married? He swears his innocence and tells her that he cannot show the letter even to her, as it is lodge business. On her knees she pleads with him to give up his association with criminals, but he says that he cannot leave, even if the lodge would let him. But he does promise her that in maybe six months, or at the latest a year, they will leave the valley together.

Subsection three is devoted to the incident of the killings at the Crow Hill Mine. The two men sent to carry out the assassinations board with McMurdo and Scanlan, and McMurdo tries to learn who the target would be. But neither of the two will say anything. The scene changes to the site of the action the next morning, and McMurdo and his roommate see the shooting. Scanlan is subdued; murder turns out to be "less funny than he had been led to believe."

In subsection three, we also find that in exchange for having the Hobson's Patch men kill Dunn and Menzies, Ted Baldwin and two others were sent to shoot William Hales of Gilmerton. Now Boss McGinty calls on McMurdo for his first killing assignment—blowing up the house of Chester Wilcox and his family. He carries out the operation, only to learn that Wilcox had moved to some other location. A few weeks later, newspaper reports told that Wilcox had been ambushed and shot at, and it was an open secret that McMurdo was still at work."

Subsection four consists of the final two paragraphs of the chapter, reporting seven other crimes committed by the Scowrers in the early summer of 1875—"the darkest hour" in the Vermissa Valley.

Before leaving chapter 5, I wish to make a point of how the motivating factor in much of what occurs here is fear. When Ettie sneaks up on him, McMurdo's face shows "guilty fear" as he grabs for her throat. Ettie in turn fears that McMurdo may be married—he is "a stranger that nobody knows." She later entreats him to go away: he replies that "the lodge has a long arm. Do you think it could not stretch from here to Philadelphia or New York?" Then she suggests a flight to England or Germany—"anywhere to get away from this Valley of Fear!"* She goes on to say that Baldwin has never forgiven them: "If it were not that he fears you, what do you suppose our chances would be?" Seven paragraphs later we learn that even Boss McGinty fears Evan Pott as "the huge Danton may have felt for the puny but dangerous Robespierre." And the concluding paragraph of the chapter emphasizes the "yoke of terror" which held the Valley of Fear in its grip.

CHAPTER 6: DANGER

I would like to suggest from the beginning that the fact that this chapter bears the same title as the story Doyle was writing at the same time—about the threat of German U-boats to Great Britain— is not accidental. Clearly, the author feared war between Germany and the United Kingdom, just as the Scowrers fear Birdy Edwards and the Pinkerton Agency in the novel.

This chapter may be broken down into four subsections. The first is the opening paragraph, which continues the discussion of McMurdo's rise within the freemen and his corresponding decline of status with the general population. The second contains the account of Brother Morris and his momentous visit to McMurdo, with the information that "Five big corporations and the two railroads have taken the thing up in dead earnest ... Pinkerton has taken hold under their orders, and his best man, Birdy Edwards, is operating. The thing has got to be stopped right now." Morris does not know what to do, and when McMurdo offers to take the matter off his

---

* Of course, years later and without Ettie, "McMurdo" (by then calling himself "Douglas"), does escape to England—where the long arm of the lodge, with local British assistance, eventually tracks him down.

hands he is relieved. The section ends with McMurdo's words, "Why, Brother Morris, we'll have to elect you Bodymaster yet, for you've surely saved the lodge."

In subsection three, McMurdo takes immediate actions—"those of a man who is preparing for the worst." He alerts Ettie that it may soon be time for him to leave: will she go with him? She promises to come with him, day or night, when he sends for her. In subsection four, McMurdo comes to the lodge and presents his information: further, as the only man there who claims to know Birdy Edwards by sight, he proposes his plan to trap the detective. He presents it not to the whole membership but to a committee of seven, including McGinty and his top henchmen. He concludes his speech with these words: "We'll get him in [to the Widow MacNamara's house]. If he ever gets out alive—well, he can talk of Birdy Edwards's luck for the rest of his days."

COMMENTS ON CHAPTER 6

This penultimate chapter in the story of the Scowrers is entitled "Danger." We must ask however, just who is in danger of what? As the tale is presented, the obvious answer is that the freemen (the Mollies) are in danger of arrest and destruction, given the presence of Birdy Edwards in their midst. But if one looks at it from a different perspective, it is Birdy Edwards who is in peril from the organization which he has infiltrated. He knows that these men would kill him if they learned his secret—a secret that we, the readers, as yet do not know. In short, this chapter sets up the stunning ironic twist which will follow in chapter 7.

CHAPTER 7: THE TRAPPING OF BIRDY EDWARDS

Once again, the chapter is divided into four subsections. The first describes the scene of the planned crime—the house, with its secluded location on the edge of town and back from the road.

Also, the Scowrers need to know what Edwards has learned before they kill him, and the lonely house offers a good place to make him talk. Subsection one continues with an account of McMurdo's day, including his trip to Hobson's Patch and his encounter at the station with Captain Marvin, his old adversary from Chicago. On returning to Vermissa he meets Bodymaster McGinty at the Union House saloon where they discuss Edwards, Brother Morris, and the final details of the plan for the evening. The atmosphere of this scene is perfect: a talk between the two most important characters on the eve of a showdown. It is the calm before the storm, and the author conveys that feeling brilliantly.

In subsection two McMurdo returns to the house and makes his own final preparations for the evening. He cleans, oils, and loads his revolver, examines the room with its shutter-less windows covered only by curtains, and speaks to his housemate, Scanlan—advising him to stay away from the house that night.

Subsection three contains the climax of the American backstory. It begins with the arrival of the seven Scowrers, headed by Boss McGinty himself. The other six are described, as is the hot stove and its possible use.

Haraway, the secretary, remarks, "Maybe he won't come. Maybe he'll get a sniff of danger." But McMurdo replies, "He'll come, never fear. He is as eager to come as you can be to see him." He speaks the gospel truth, but of course no one realizes it. Then the expected three loud knocks sound at the door, and McMurdo goes out to answer them. The following five paragraphs ramp up the tension and prepare the reader for McMurdo's reappearance.

The last eleven lines of subsection three must constitute one of the greatest ironic disclosures in literature. Once read, they can never be forgotten.

Subsection four contains the mopping up of the story: the arrests: McMurdo's last address to the Scowrers; Scanlan's mission and its aftermath (the early morning departure of "McMurdo" and Ettie out of the Valley of Fear and into the light of day); the account of the trial and the ten years which followed it, and finally the adventures which came as the former freemen sought vengeance on the man who had destroyed their organization. This chapter ends part 2 of the novel with the link to the Birlstone tragedy.

EPILOGUE

While only three pages in length, the epilogue is the key to understanding the deeper meaning of the novel. Though abbreviated, it is made up of two distinct subsections.

The first four paragraphs tell of Douglas's acquittal on the grounds of self-defense. Holmes writes to Mrs. Douglas, urging her to get her husband out of England at any cost. "There are forces here which may be more dangerous than those he has escaped. There is no safely for your husband in England." One may ask why he addressed this message to the wife and not the man himself, but the obvious answer is that he is so caught up in proving his own fearlessness that only a wife would have a chance of convincing him that he should no longer rely solely on his luck for self-defense. One can only wonder why Douglas, alias McMurdo, alias Edwards, was trying so hard to assert his independence from fear. Was he aiming to convince others of his manhood? Or was it possible that he was trying to prove it to himself?

Two months later comes the enigmatic note to Holmes, pushed into the letter box. It consists of just two words, repeated: "Dear me, Mr. Holmes. Dear me!" From this little message Holmes understands that his old enemy, Professor Moriarty, has had a hand in whatever occurred.

The second subsection takes place—like most evil events of this novel, in which the symbolism of light, dark, blindness, and vision is so prominent—in the night. Mrs. Hudson, the landlady, brings up a message that a gentleman wishes to see Holmes about a matter "of the utmost importance." The gentleman in question is Cecil Barker, who arrives with "bad news— terrible news." "I feared as much," says Holmes, continuing to play on the word which is so important in this book—the word "fear." Barker has had a cable from Mrs. Douglas: their ship reached port at Cape Town, South Africa, that morning, and she reports that "Jack has been lost overboard in gale off St. Helena. No one knows how accident occurred."

Holmes immediately remarks that the death was undoubtedly stage-managed—not an accident at all, but a coldblooded murder masterminded by Professor Moriarty. Hearing Holmes talk about the power of the professor's organization, Barker asks in frustration, "Do you say that no one can ever get level with this king devil?" Holmes replies, "No, I don't say that," as his eyes seem to be looking far into the future. "I don't say that he can't be beat. But you must give me time—you must give me time!" The novel ends on a note of silence and mystery: "We all sat in silence for some minutes while those fateful eyes still strained to pierce the veil."*

What is Holmes straining to see? How he can beat Moriarty? Or how Britain will fare in a conflict of arms with Germany? I can think of no other detective / mystery story which ends on such an uncertain note.

In other words, it is only in the epilogue that we learn that while Holmes has solved the mystery, his solution was not the end of the story: Moriarty accomplished what Baldwin failed to do—bring about the death of "John Douglas." Holmes has lost this battle, but the war between them continues.

THE MERITS OF THE NOVEL

John Dickson Carr, himself an outstanding writer of detective fiction, considers *The Valley of Fear* to be "an almost perfect" example

---

* The phrase comes from Verse 32 of Edward FitzGerald's translation of *The Rubiyat of Omar Khyam*: "There was the door to which I found no key; There was the veil through which I might not see; Some little talk awhile of me and thee there was—And then no more of me and thee."

of the mystery genre. I generally agree with his evaluation. Here are some of my reasons for that opinion.

In examining the structure of the book, we find that each of the two main parts of the story—the murder at Birlstone and the American backstory—consists of seven chapters. Each is about the same length, while the epilogue, or coda, ties the two stories together and informs us that despite Holmes's having solved the case, Moriarty has succeeded in doing what Ted Baldwin failed to do—revenge the Scowrers by killing the man who destroyed their organization. This, I submit, is a perfect structure—efficient, balanced, and emphasizing that the solution of the mystery is not the end of the story.

In terms of plot, *Valley* was, at the time of its original publication, pioneering. If Poe created many of the elements of the modern detective / mystery story, it was left to Dr. Doyle to introduce, as far as I can tell, the "Birlstone Gambit"—an idea which has since been used time and again.

In terms of creating memorable and convincing characters, this novel is unexcelled in the entire Holmes canon, and perhaps in the whole genre of detective / mystery fiction. Consider, first, the formidable Bodymaster McGinty, so masterfully drawn that we feel as if we have actually met him lounging at the bar in his Union House Saloon. McMurdo, too, comes to life, especially in his scenes opposite the boss in chapters 2 and 7. We feel for the tortured, unhappy Brother Morris, trapped by his previous membership in the Freemen on the one hand and his inability to escape the valley because his store is all he owns, on the other.

Ted Baldwin—self-centered, seething with jealousy, and steeped in violence as his solution to every problem—could well be found in any street gang in a big city of today, while his associate, the brutal Tiger Cormac, "was feared even by his own comrades for the ferocity of his disposition." We feel as though we know honest old Jacob Shafter; Mike Scanlan, the basically good-natured Scowrer who discovers that murder is not funny when he sees it close up; and Alec MacDonald, the fine Scots detective whom Holmes treats much like a son. And finally, there is Sherlock Holmes himself, in the best portrait Conan Doyle ever created of him as a mature adult—wise, endearing as never before, and endowed here with more than a touch of humor.

In addition, *The Valley of Fear* stands alone in the Holmes canon for the dark atmosphere it creates. One source of this sensation is the author's use of language. The description of McMurdo's vision of Hell from the window of the train is an example. So are the views of the town of Vermissa, with its rutted streets and tumbledown shanties. One word in particular beats a threnody throughout the novel: "gloom." As a noun, its dictionary definition is "partial or total darkness" or also "a dark or shadowy place." But it is not only the meaning which affects us in this novel: it is also the sound of the word when pronounced out loud, and the look of it on the printed page. That "oo" sound and look is haunting, and Conan Doyle repeats the word over and over in both parts of the story.

But language is only one of the tools the author uses to create the ominous atmosphere permeating the novel. A second major factor is the obsessive use of light and dark imagery throughout the book. I have already commented on its use in part 1; we find it again in part 2. McMurdo's entry into Vermissa is set in the falling dusk, and as he arrives in town, the full darkness of night has come down.

As was the case in part 1, most of the key scenes in part 2 are also nocturnal: McMurdo's initiation into the Lodge, and the subsequent attack on Editor Stanger; the arrival of Lawler and Andrews on their secret mission, during which McMurdo attempts without success to learn who the victims are to be; the post-murderous revels of Ted Baldwin over the killing of William Hales; and of course the trapping of Birdy Edwards. There are exceptions: Ettie's surprise visit to McMurdo's room, the meeting on Miller Hill, and the actual killings of Dunn and Menzies at the Crow Hill Mine take place in daylight. Also, at the end of part 2, Ettie Shafter and McMundo leave Vermissa early in the morning on their special train, suggesting that their departure coincides with the coming of a new day to the valley.

Related to the light / dark imagery is that of vision contrasted with blindness. In part 1, when MacPherson remarks that "We don't seem to get a gleam of light in the case," Holmes, thinking about the missing dumbbell, remarks, "Don't we? I wonder!" He has seen a clue which the other detectives have missed. In part 2, when Birdy Edwards delivers his last speech to the Scowrers, he says, "If you look back, you'll see my work!" (Emphasis added.) Finally, at the end of the epilogue, Holmes's "fateful eyes" strain "to pierce the veil"—that is, to see the future. There are many more such references in the novel.

Nor is this all. Conan Doyle never wrote better dialogue than we find in *The Valley of Fear*. This is true of both parts of the novel: Holmes's conversations in the Birlstone section do much to form the picture of the senior detective—now with the wisdom and respect for others which were often lacking in the earlier stories. The Vermissa section of the book shows a mastery of American slang and Irish cadences worthy of natives of those countries.

Each of these technical factors—structure, plot, characterization, creation of atmosphere through both descriptive writing and the use of imagery, and brilliant use of dialogue—manifests Conan Doyle's mastery of the art of prose at this stage of his career. Each contributes to making *The Valley of Fear* different from any other Holmes work. Yet there are still other unique aspects of this novel which distinguish it from all the other Holmes novels, and from the short stories as well.

One of these is the presence throughout the book of what I call moral ambiguity. In most detective / mystery fiction, there are clearly defined "good guys" and "bad guys," and the detective character or characters serve the purpose of making the good win out over the bad. In this novel, however, there are few such clearly good and bad characters: many, if not most, are both. Take, for example, McMurdo himself. In his work to destroy the Scowrers, he becomes so much like them that the townspeople turn hard against him, while Boss McGinty himself says (in chapter 7), "I guess when I move out of the chair I can put a name to the man that's coming after me." In fact, the real undercover agent James McParlan, on whose experiences McMurdo was modeled, may indeed have crossed the line between innocence and guilt more than once in his two years among the Mollies. Or consider Brother Morris, a member of the lodge in good standing who discovers what murder is really like and shrinks back from it. The Scowrers collectively are the greatest examples of moral ambiguity: are they common criminals? Or are they soldiers fighting a war against oppression, exploitation, and religious discrimination? (To put that question in contemporary terms: are they terrorists or freedom fighters?)

In his later incarnation as "John Douglas," Edwards (alias McMurdo) is also the subject of suspicion. His account of the death of Baldwin is open to question. "Maybe it was I that pulled the trigger," he says. "Maybe we just jolted it off between us. Anyhow, he got both barrels in the face." Well—as to that first "maybe," it is possible that Douglas, having recognized Baldwin at Tunbridge Wells, in fact lured him into a trap and killed his old rival deliberately. It is certain that he had an even better motive to do away with Baldwin than Baldwin had to kill him.

Nor have we yet exhausted the well of moral ambiguities in this novel. How should we regard the mine owners and capitalists whom the Scowrers were fighting? Were they lily-white and pure? Hardly, when they took every advantage of the immigrant workers and made their lives miserable—not only with economic exploitation but also with religious and social repression, and constant torment. We do not know why Franklin Benjamin Gowen killed himself some years after his campaign against the Mollies broke their organization, but it is at least possible that he came to see the evil he had done to them, and to regret his actions.

And what are we to make of the relationship between Cecil Barker and Ivy Douglas? Barker assures us that it was perfectly innocent, but Dr. Watson's observations are persuasive evidence that this may not be true. "I am convinced myself that there must be an understanding between these two people. She must be a heartless creature to sit laughing at some jest within a few hours of her husband's murder," Watson remarks. Holmes answers, "Exactly. She does not shine as a wife even in her own account of what occurred." And even when we know that both Barker and Mrs. Douglas were aware that Douglas was still alive, one can only wonder for how long she would remain a widow after his death, with Barker standing ready to become her next spouse.

What I am suggesting is that Dr. Doyle created in *The Valley of Fear* a world of imperfect human beings much more like the real world than the ordinary world of fiction. In this novel, basically good, ordinary people commit crimes, fall in love with their husbands' best friends or their best friends' wives, get trapped in situations beyond their control, get drunk on power as well as on liquor, take advantage of the weakness of others, and strike out against their frustrations unwisely and too well for their own good. I can think of no other detective / mystery story which goes so far in the direction of emulating real behavior patterns in the context of crime fiction. No wonder readers have a difficult time enjoying this book: whatever it is, it is not a happy reading experience. I think it is fair to assert that *The Valley of Fear* will never achieve the popularity of the other three Holmes novels. Judged strictly as a work of art, however, it may equal or even eclipse one or more of the others.

FEAR, PROFESSOR MORIARTY, AND SHERLOCK HOLMES

Now we come to the questions I have posed to my readers in the course of the text. First: Why did Conan Doyle resurrect Professor Moriarty, his master criminal and Holmes's great nemesis, more than twenty years after he had killed off the Professor and tried to kill off Holmes himself in "The Final Problem"? Second: What did the author want his readers to learn from the clear identification of the Vermissa Valley—the "valley of fear" in this book—with the valley of the shadow of death mentioned in Psalm 23? I believe that the answers to these two puzzling questions are the keys to a more complete understanding of this complex and sometimes daunting book. It seems to me that our best approach is to discuss the second question first.

We know from "The Bruce-Partington Plans" that the idea of submarine warfare was in Doyle's mind at least as early as 1908. We also know that simultaneously with the composition of *The Valley of Fear* he wrote the essay "Danger!"—this alerted the British public to the menace of German U-boats to the maritime commerce that was Britain's life blood. We also have evidence that while he was descended from a family of Irish Catholics, he left the Church while still young, never lived in Ireland, visited there only once, and adopted the political position of opposition to any home rule or independence movements in regard to that country. He held these views for thirty years—but in 1911, "after meeting and talking with Sir Roger Casement," he came out in favor of home rule for Ireland. Can we find traces of his thinking (and his changed political stance) reflected in this novel? I am convinced that we can.

Knowing what was on Dr. Doyle's mind, is it credible that he wrote a novel in which fear and a group of Irishmen are the major factors by mere coincidence? I, for one, simply refuse to believe that idea. My feeling is that he knew exactly what he was doing when he incorporated these elements into his first long Holmes story in more than a decade. No wonder he approached Greenhough Smith of the *Strand* with the offer of a new Sherlock Holmes novel, seemingly out of the blue and after he had nearly abandoned Holmes for ten years or more. He knew that Smith would not be able to resist the offer of the serial rights to *The Valley of Fear*, and so he knew that the new book would reach the public. We must now ask what it was that Conan Doyle so much wanted that public to learn from the new work?

Well, let us review the plot. A gentleman appears to have been the victim of a murder in a quaint English country setting. His butler called him "the most fearless man that he had ever known." His wife described him as "nervous" of fire, but she avoided using the word "afraid." His neighbors were impressed by his "reputation gained for utter indifference to danger," whether it came from falling off a horse or reentering a burning vicarage "to save property, after the local fire brigade had given it up as impossible." Later, we learn that years before in America this same man had undertaken the perilous job of going undercover to break up a gang of dangerous men bent on changing or overthrowing the social order in the coal mining and iron-producing district of Pennsylvania. At the very end of the book, this man, acclaimed as a hero and known for his luck in surviving one danger after another, meets his end at the hands of an agent or agents of Professor Moriarty: fearless and lucky he may have been for many years, but he becomes just another murder victim in the epilogue.

The lesson here is clear: if one plays long enough with fire, one is bound to be burned eventually. *To put it another way, to allow fear to paralyze one into surrender or inaction is self-defeating and costly. Yet to ignore fear is equally senseless. Fear is an emotion which must be respected and met with reason and resolution, not with panic or disdain.

Here is where the McMurdo-Morris conversation, the heart of *The Valley of Fear*, comes into play. By 1913, Conan Doyle saw England already walking through the "shadow of the valley of death"—the looming threat of all-out war with Germany. I believe that he realized that if the British people continued to ignore that menace and

---

* The message here strikes me as remarkably like that found in the works of the American writer, Stephen Crane. In his famous novel, *The Red Badge of Courage*, a young Union soldier in the Civil War by happenstance picks up a falling flag and is hailed as a courageous hero. In a later story, however, the same Henry Fleming dares to enter a burning barn and is killed. Is Fleming truly a hero or just a fool? What is courage—to act in denial of all risk? To gamble with one's very life to prove to someone—or even to oneself— that one is strong and unafraid? I do not know if Doyle ever read Crane's work, but the American author (who died at the impossibly young age of twenty-nine) had written and published his entire body of work years before Doyle began writing *The Valley of Fear*.

allowed it to become a reality, the valley of fear might well become the Biblical "valley of death" for the United Kingdom.

Realizing that a new Holmes book would be bought and read by a large share of the population, he wrote his warning into his new novel. Moreover, he shaped this book so as to alert his readers that it was not just a new entertainment. He gave its first part the title, "The Tragedy of Birlstone."

This nomenclature, like so much more in *The Valley of Fear*, is ambiguous. Did Conan Doyle use the word "tragedy" to mean something unfortunate? Or did he use it to mean what the ancient Greeks meant by it—the downfall of a noble individual caused by a character flaw? If we take the Greek meaning of the word, what happened at Birlstone, and what followed it, is a classic example of the genre. Edwards / McMurdo / Douglas is a man with a tragic flaw— his fearlessness, which leads him "to fight through it alone." This attitude toward danger amounts to the principal tragic flaw in the ancient Greek dramas—"hubris," or overweening pride. This man has it, and it does indeed lead directly to his destruction—though it takes a while before the fatal blow falls.

Now project that feeling of invulnerability onto the British nation as it was in the late nineteenth and early twentieth centuries, and the underlying message becomes clear. Britons must not ignore the serious threat to their existence posed by the rise of Germany: the United Kingdom must not assume its continued hegemony or even its continued existence. It must not fall victim, as Edwards / McMurdo / Douglas does, to another Moriarty.

Now let us turn to my second question: why did Doyle resurrect the professor in this story, after so many years? Why, in fact, did he create "the Napoleon of Crime" in the first place? The answer is simple: he wished to stop writing Sherlock Holmes stories after the first twenty-six, for fear that what he had conceived to be trivial works would lower his status as a "serious" writer. As we know, that was a miscalculation—killing off Holmes only made the public anxious for more stories.

But in 1913, when, as I am suggesting, Dr. Doyle urgently wished to alert the people of Great Britain to the menacing shadow of Germany, he reintroduced Moriarty in *The Valley of Fear* because there could be no other character capable of outdoing Holmes (save, of course, Irene Adler). Metaphorically, Professor Moriarty in this story stands for Germany, while Sherlock Holmes represents the United Kingdom. In this tale, while Holmes solves the mystery, it is Moriarty who ends the saga of its main character. I believe Doyle was saying that Germany might destroy Britain if that nation did not take the threat of war seriously and meet it on its own terms. This, I believe, is the underlying meaning of the book.

Of course, I anticipate cries of anguish from readers who will accuse me of finding a meaning in this novel that the author never intended. I answer with another question: if *The Valley of Fear* was not meant to be a metaphor for the state of Europe just before the Great War, why on earth did Doctor Doyle invoke Moriarty at all? The story would be quite complete without the first two chapters and the Epilogue, and it would showcase the brilliance of Holmes whose solution to the mystery rests (as it does in so many other stories, including *A Study in Scarlet*, "The Bruce-Partington Plans," and others) on a flash of genius which enables him to get the right clue from the first. What other reason can there be for Professor Moriarty's presence as a sort of envelope wrapped around the otherwise completely sufficient story, if Conan Doyle did not mean to use him to send a message to his readers? I challenge anybody to come up with a viable alternative reason for bringing the professor back, and for having him blunt Holmes's triumph so brutally.

The metaphoric interpretation of *The Valley of Fear* explains not only the presence of Moriarty in the book, but also that of Holmes. We must not forget that after the publication of *The Return of Sherlock Holmes*, Conan Doyle wrote and published just three Holmes short stories over the next eight years. Why, then, did he surprise Greenhough Smith and everyone else with his announcement that he was writing a new Holmes novel? This was in January 1914, you will recall— about half the book had already been written, including the first two chapters. In those chapters, Moriarty is revived, and his career discussed by Holmes, with details we had never heard before. Also, Holmes is reintroduced, in such terms that no reader hungry for more of the Great Detective could possibly put the story down. We know that Doyle had been writing pieces to alert the British public to the danger posed by the Kaiser's newly aggressive Germany: why not, the author must have thought, use Holmes to help get my message across? The metaphoric interpretation also gives us an explanation for the dark tone of the novel: the looming cataclysm may or may not come about, but who knows what the future holds? Thus, the gloom, so characteristic of this novel, and so unlike anything else in the Holmes canon!

In addition, the first chapter of the novel bears what might be called an aptotitle: it is called "The Warning." And while that does in fact refer to Porlock's cipher message, might it not also be taken as stating the theme underlying the whole book—the warning to Britain about the dark clouds gathering against her?

Perhaps I have succeeded in convincing you about this aspect of *The Valley of Fear*; perhaps not. But one thing should be perfectly clear to anyone at all versed in the Holmes stories—this one is different.

THE NOVEL OF WARNING

There is yet one more important aspect of *The Valley of Fear* which requires comment: how does the story of the Freemen / Scowrers fit into the picture I have been drawing of a novel of warning? Of course, on the most basic level it provides the background for the events in the Birlstone Manor killing. But there is also a deeper connection.

While the Molly Maguires were active in America, their roots go back to Ireland and its centuries-long history of conflict with England. Even the name came from the Old Country: it was borrowed from a group of young Irishmen who banded together to keep an old woman from being dispossessed of her home. They said of their united efforts, "We're all sons of Molly Maguire," and the Pennsylvania miners adopted the phrase to express unity in their fight against the people and powers who were oppressing them.

The struggle between mostly Protestant England and mostly Catholic Ireland goes back hundreds of years. England had always feared that some other European power would ally with Ireland and use it as a base from which to attack Britannia by way of her back door. For many years the obvious candidate for the role of villain was Catholic France, but after the French Revolution and the final defeat of Napoleon, the rise of Germany as the leading Continental power led the London authorities to fear Teutonic influence in Ireland most. They saw home rule (or worse, independence) for Ireland as a direct and serious threat to the United Kingdom, and intensified their pursuit of the centuries-old policy of seeking ever more control over the neighboring island.

As I have previously noted, while Conan Doyle himself came from Irish Catholic roots, he had been from young manhood oriented more towards Scotland and England than to Ireland and his Irish Catholic family. That seems to have changed about 1911, when Doyle appears to have decided, as he entered middle age, that both British policy and his own beliefs were erroneous. Thus, he became an advocate of home rule for Ireland. When he wrote *The Valley of Fear* (likely begun sometime in 1913) he may have been seeking support for his new political position by using the American Mollies to express the argument for an immediate change in Whitehall's Irish policy. He had been reading about the miners' revolt, and it must have struck him that he could use it as backstory for the Birlstone Manor murder while at the same time allowing the Mollies to speak out against their wealthy, powerful and largely English, Welsh, and Scottish opponents. Of course, he could not go too far in support of the Molly Maguire rebellion: neither his English nor his American readers would have seen the Mollies (i.e., the Scowrers) as anything but common criminals. But in at least three scenes in *The Valley*,

McMundo and others assert that "Sure, it is like a war. What is it but a war between us and them, and we hit back where best we can." (See the conversation with Mike Scanlan in chapter 5.) McMurdo also says, "There are some would say it was war; a war between two classes with all in, so that each struck as best it could." (See the conversation with Brother Morris in chapter 4.) And again, to Ettie: "Well, dear it's not so bad as you think. We are but poor men that are trying in own way to get our rights." (Once more, see chapter 5.)

The references to war, I think, are particularly important, because they loosely but distinctly link the two seemingly unrelated themes in this novel—the need to take seriously the German "Shadow of the Valley of Death," and the Irish struggle against outside oppression. The American Mollies (who stand in for the Irish proponents of home rule) are to England what England might become if Germany defeated her in war. These two aspects of fear come to focus in this book.

Thus, we have in *The Valley of Fear* a novel in which the villains—the Scowrers in America, representing the Irish in Europe—become in a small way also the heroes: they fight back against a hostile and threatening enemy. In the case of the Irish, the enemy is England itself—only adding to the irony of the situation.

There is another irony, but Doyle could not have had it in mind when he published *The Valley of Fear.* England's long struggle to keep Ireland under its control came to an end not because of the actions of any other power but because the London government overreacted disastrously to the Easter Rising in Dublin in April 1916. The Rising itself was a rather pitiful event: there was never a chance that it could win Irish independence by violent means. But when the leaders of the revolt were all shot in the aftermath, many who had never believed that independence was possible, or did not really want it, turned strongly against continued English rule. The result was that within six years, twenty-six of Ireland's thirty-two counties became independent of the British crown.

And why did Britain act so foolishly as to bring on the very outcome its leaders most wished to avoid? Because London feared that Germany would plan or assist an Irish rebellion, opening, as it were, a second front in the war against Britain. Fear brought on panic in Whitehall, and that led to the end of British rule in most of Ireland. Fear can be a useful and necessary emotion, but it cannot be allowed to become irrational panic. This, I believe, is what *The Valley of Fear* is about. The need to deal rationally with fear is the message Conan Doyle was trying to send. The correct response to fear is an intelligent recognition of its double-edged dangers and a well-conceived and well-executed plan to counter the emotion of fear with reason, resolution, and—as in the Psalm—faith.

Am I reading too much into *The Valley of Fear*? Perhaps—but one must pay attention to the words of Professor Owen Dudley Edwards [sic!] of the University of Edinburgh, who notes that "What we find in the book is there by design, and is a different matter from earlier use."[*]

Let me sum up my thoughts about *The Valley of Fear* in a few more paragraphs. We have reason to believe that Conan Doyle made use of the popularity of Sherlock Holmes to gain a wider audience for his message of danger to Britain from the rise of Germany. But the book is no more "about" Holmes than any of the other three novels—or than many of the short stories, for that matter.

And while it has never achieved the popularity of most of Dr. Doyle's other Homes tales, I believe that *The Valley of Fear* is in many ways a great novel, even if it is somewhat complicated and difficult to penetrate. If it lacks cohesion, as some critics have remarked, it remains at least a reasonable synthesis of several themes and elements. Its technical facility is unsurpassed by anything else in the Holmes canon: it has an original plot device so successful that it has been used countless times by other writers since Conan Doyle invented it here; it presents finely drawn, realistic characters—not the least of whom is Holmes himself, here realized so completely as

---

[*] Edwards, Owen Dudley: Introduction to the Oxford World Classics Edition of *The Valley of Fear*. Oxford: Oxford Univ. Press, 1993 p. xiii.

to be the definitive picture of the Great Detective in his maturity. Its use of dialogue and its descriptive passages are letter-perfect: one would not wish a word to be changed. The imagery of light, darkness, blindness, and vision deepens and unifies the book. Above all, the pervasive atmosphere of uncertainty and gloom, coupled with the moral ambiguity of so many of the characters, is unequaled by anything in the canon.

If *The Valley of Fear* is an imperfect book, as so many have claimed, its merits render its flaws insignificant. If it does not stand at the very pinnacle of Dr. Doyle's works, it does not fail to approach that lofty level.

CHAPTER 11

The Hound of the Baskervilles

I SAVED THE BEST FOR LAST. ONLY NOW, AFTER OUR DISCUSSION OF ALL FIF-ty-six short stories and the other three Holmes novels, do we come to that undisputed masterpiece, *The Hound of the Baskervilles*. Les Klinger has called it "the greatest mystery novel of all time," and I would disagree only to the extent that I believe this is not praise enough for this remarkable work.

Doyle began writing *The Hound* in 1899 or 1900, and its first publication in serial form—nine episodes in *The Strand Magazine*—began with the August 1901 issue, and ended in April 1902. Interestingly, the first book publication was by George Newnes, in spring, 1902—before the last episode appeared in the magazine. The first American edition was published by McClure, Phillips & Co., also in 1902.

Full disclosure: I first read *The Hound* when I was eleven or twelve years old, and I have read it, reread it, and taught it on countless occasions since. Yet it was not until ten or fifteen years ago that the full impact and meaning of the story became clear to me. Like Dr. Watson, I had seen without observing. In the course of this study,

I think I will be able to disclose beyond any doubt what this book is really about, and why it deserves a place among the most significant, most entertaining, and best-written novels in the English language. For *The Hound* is not only a great mystery / detective adventure. It is also a chilling horror story, with its weird Dartmoor setting and its spectral killer dog. Even more, it is a true novel in the original sense of the word—an examination of the morals and manners of society. That society is Great Britain at the end of the nineteenth century, the world in which Conan Doyle lived. We must therefore begin with the historical context in which the book was written.

At the time, the island kingdom was the dominant power on the planet. The industrial revolution had turned it into the richest and most productive country in the world, with an empire so far-flung that the sun never set upon it. London had become the greatest metropolis on earth: one third of the world was ruled from there. The great advances in technology were accompanied by similar leadership in science, medicine, and the arts. Profound and rapid social change saw the abolition of slavery everywhere in the empire, and the vestiges of feudalism were disappearing as the dominance of the landed gentry was challenged by the rise of the newly wealthy commercial class. Parliamentary democracy was on the march, spreading from its origins in England to countries around the world. And since the final defeat of Napoleon at Waterloo in 1815, there had been no major war on the continent of Europe: Pax Britannica prevailed, and the Royal Navy policed the world.

It is not surprising, then, that for the most part Britons living in the Victorian Era (1837–1901) felt that they had found the answers to all the problems of life. Increasing technology would produce unending prosperity, moral reform demonstrated real progress in human behavior, and the world could look forward to universal peace under the leadership and power of their own nation. What was there to show that any or all these beliefs were invalid? In 1900—while Conan Doyle was at work on *The Hound*—not very much that optimistic people could see.

Conan Doyle was born in 1859, right in the middle of Victoria's long reign, and he grew up during this extended period of peace, prosperity, and apparent moral improvement. He could hardly have avoided the influences around him, virtually all of which must have reflected the prevailing satisfaction with the present and optimism about the future. It is more surprising then, that we find such great degree of social criticism in the Holmes stories—a quality which finds its most powerful expression in *The Hound of the Baskervilles.* This novel is far and away the author's most successful melding of Holmes / mystery / detective fiction with serious social criticism. Doyle appears to be the first great writer to attempt such a combination, but he was far from the last. Dorothy Sayers, G.K. Chesterton, and Ellery Queen (to name just three) are among other writers who have successfully blended the mystery / detective genre with observations on the societies in which they lived, but no one has ever accomplished that trick with more skill and success than Conan Doyle did in *The Hound.* Indeed, the detective story and the underlying theme of the book are so deftly integrated that the casual reader may not even realize what the author is saying. And yet the message is plainly there, if only one is conscientious and alert enough to see it.

As always, our tools for reading and studying *The Hound of the Baskervilles* are finding the structure, appreciating the characterization, looking for aptonyms, and taking in the nuances in the dialogue and the descriptive passages. With these concerns in mind, let us now tackle the study of Arthur Conan Doyle's greatest accomplishment in the long prose genre. "Come, the game is afoot!" But this time the game is a dog—or is it?

While still in the process of creating *The Hound,* Dr. Doyle remarked, "It is a real creeper!" He meant a story so infused with horror that the reader feels shivers down the spine—that is, feels "creepy." Surely the appearance of the hound, made to look supernatural and diabolical by its glowing phosphorescent paint job, would cause that kind of terror to the aged, superstitious Sir Charles

Baskerville when he saw it approaching across the moor—or even to the hardened murderer Selden when he heard and saw it running on his trail. But we cannot experience that sort of terror at first-hand: we can only imagine what it must have been like. The printed page stands between us and the feelings of the victims.

There is, however, another sort of terror that we can feel ourselves, and I believe that the author intended his readers to suffer shock and awe from its discovery. It is the terror caused by the recognition that everything one has been brought up to believe about one's world is wrong: that far from having advanced both morally and materially in the nineteenth century, we have not really changed internally. The nature of man was no different in 1900 than it was in prehistoric times—still capable of amazing accomplishments aiming towards the common good, but still cursed with the capacity and the inclination to lie, to cheat, to take advantage of others, to steal, to maim, and ultimately to kill. In Hebrew, this side of the human condition is called the *yetzer hara* (the evil inclination), and its face is that of Satan.

The discovery that we are morally no better than the cave man is crushing. Here is true terror—something that each of us wishes to believe is no longer a threat to our lives and souls remains embedded in our humanity, in our very essence, despite what we would like to believe. This discovery, I argue, is what *The Hound* is really all about, and I think I can convince you that it was Dr. Doyle's message in this novel. Let us proceed, then, to our chapter-by-chapter analysis.

THE STRUCTURE OF THE BOOK

The Hound conforms to the traditional three-part structure so common in literature and drama: exposition, development, and resolution. The exposition section comprises chapters 1 through 5 and is set in London—the great city which was and still is the heart of Great Britain. It involves four principal characters: Sherlock Holmes, Dr. Watson, Dr. James Mortimer, and (beginning in

chapter 4) Sir Henry Baskerville. It introduces us to the legend of
the hound, which dates back to the seventeenth century; to the mysterious death of Sir Charles Baskerville; and to the problem of what
to do with his heir, young Sir Henry, who is just about to arrive in
London after having lived in Canada for some time. Holmes undertakes the problem, but his efforts are checkmated. "It is an ugly
business, Watson," he remarks at the end of the section, "an ugly,
dangerous business, and the more I see of it the less I like it." With
these lines, the exposition ends.

Part 2, the development, takes place in Devonshire, on the moor
near the ancestral home of the family, Baskerville Hall. It is six chapters long (chapters 6–11) and for all but a few lines at the end belongs
almost entirely to Dr. Watson, who is not only the narrator, but acts as
detective in the apparent absence of Holmes. Its characters include,
in addition to Watson and Dr. Mortimer, the residents of this weird,
unworldly corner of England. This second section of the novel deals
with the complications of the plot and subplot, and describes the
strange, forbidding atmosphere of the moor. The whole six chapters
are dominated by the traces of Neolithic man, and by the unseen
but ever-present hound. While never visible, its voice is heard—an
eerie and blood-curdling effect. Then there is the escaped convict,
who is at large and threatening; and, later, the other man on the
moor—unknown, and seen only when his brooding figure appears
silhouetted by the rising moon. This second section, the development, ends with a stunning discovery, which leads directly into the
third and final part of the novel: the resolution.

Made up of chapters 12 through 15, the resolution describes the
swift movement towards the conclusion. By the end of chapter 12,
Holmes has already discovered the identity of the criminal, but the
story is not yet finished. A trap is set and sprung, and by the end of
chapter 14, the action of the novel is complete. The final chapter, "A
Retrospection," is what its title says—a "looking backwards"—and it
provides a satisfying close for the work.

Throughout the novel the careful reader will find clue after clue to the underlying theme. Dr. Doyle did a magnificent job of concealing important data by presenting it in ways which disguise its significance: the title of chapter 15 is one example. This aspect of *The Hound* is only one of the things that help to make it a nearly matchless masterpiece.

Let us now go on to look at chapter 1 and its significance in this amazing, terrifying book.

PART 1: EXPOSITION

CHAPTER 1: MISTER SHERLOCK HOLMES

We may divide this chapter into two subsections: the first finds Holmes and Watson alone together in the Baker Street apartment, while the second commences with the entrance of Dr. Mortimer.

The opening scene finds Holmes sitting at the breakfast table, his back to Watson. The doctor picks up the walking stick which a visitor had left in the room the night before, while its two tenants were out and missed his call. Watson notes that it was a thick shaft of wood, banded around with a silver circlet on which the words, "To James Mortimer, M.R.C.S., from his friends at the C.C.H.," and the date 1884. "It was just such a stick as the old-fashioned family practitioner used to carry—dignified, solid, and reassuring," Watson muses.

His reverie is broken by Holmes, who remarks from across the room, "Well, Watson, what do you make of it?" As usual, Watson is astonished. "How did you know what I was doing?" he asks. "I believe you have eyes in the back of your head!" And also as usual, Holmes's explanation is quite simple: "I have, at least, a well-polished, silver-plated coffee-pot in front of me." In short, we understand that Sherlock has seen the reflection of Watson with the stick on the side of the coffee pot. Dr. Doyle might have used the word "reflection" here, but significantly he did not. It is left to the reader to supply the "*mot juste.*"

Why do I raise this seemingly trivial conversation? Because the word "reflection" carries connotations which relate profoundly to the theme of this novel. After all, what does the word mean? The Latin root, *reflectere*, literally means "to bend back," and the current English uses of "reflect" all involve in some way the idea of looking back, or thinking back about something, or of presenting an image of something as in the case of a mirror. As we will see, the idea of reflecting is central to the story and meaning of this novel.

Following up his intrusion into Watson's thinking about this walking stick, Holmes invites his friend "to reconstruct the man" (their missed visitor of the previous night) from an examination of his stick. Watson, with his image of the "old fashioned family practitioner" fresh in his brain, proceeds to do so. "I think," he says, "that Dr. Mortimer is a successful, elderly medical man, well-esteemed, since those who know him give him this mark of their appreciation."

"Good," says Holmes. "Excellent!"

The doctor, encouraged, now goes further. "I think also that the probability is in favor of his being a country practitioner who does a great deal of his visiting on foot." When Holmes asks, "Why so?" Watson for the first time mentions the actual condition of the stick: "Because this stick, though originally a very handsome one, has been so knocked about that I can hardly imagine a town practitioner carrying it. The thick iron ferrule is worn down, so it is evident that he has done a great amount of walking with it." Now this is actual observation, deduction, and imagination. Holmes is quite right to remark, "Perfectly sound!"

Then Watson goes a step too far. With the idea of the old family doctor still in his head, and warmed by his friend's encouraging remarks, he takes up the inscription. From the phrase, "From his friends of the C.C.H.," he conjures up a local hunt whose members the doctor might have helped. Holmes responds with some degree of praise for his friend. "It may be that you are not yourself luminous, but you are a conductor of light. Some people without possessing genius have a remarkable power of stimulating it. I confess, my dear fellow, that I am very much in your debt." Of course, hearing such praise leaves Watson glowing with self-satisfaction—until Holmes himself takes a close look at the stick and announces that most of the doctor's conclusions were erroneous. "Not that you are entirely wrong in this instance. The man is certainly a country practitioner, and he walks a lot."

Then the great detective exposes the falsities of his friend's conclusions.

Watson determines to check just who this James Mortimer may be, and turns to his medical directory. He finds only one Mortimer who could possibly have been their absent-minded visitor. The text quotes the listing as it appears in Watson's volume, and it should not be skipped over. The biographical note mentions Dr. Mortimer's publications as well as his career in practice. It tells us that he was the winner of the Jackson Prize for Comparative Pathology with an essay entitled, "Is Disease a Reversion?"* He was the author of a piece published in the *Lancet* called "Some Freaks of Atavism," and of another essay called "Do We Progress?" published in the *Journal of Psychology* in March 1883. This first subsection of the first chapter concludes with our introduction to Dr. Mortimer's pet curly-haired spaniel, which Holmes sees from the window as its master rings the bell. We are about to meet Dr. Mortimer in person.

Before we leave this first subsection, however, I have some comments to make about what Dr. Doyle wrote into it. I should guess that not one in a thousand readers of *The Hound* has ever stopped to consider the titles of Dr. Mortimer's essays, or to question why he keeps a small dog as a pet. For just as the opening passages of this book, apparently trivial, introduce the theme of reflection—looking backward, thinking of the past—the final five or six paragraphs of subsection one of part 1's chapter 1, which seem to be mere chatter, are actually of cosmic importance in understanding the true meaning of *The Hound*. In them, Conan Doyle may or may not have invented the device of what I call "the concealed clue," but he used it

---

* Pathology may be defined as the study of diseases and the effects they produce.

so skillfully that I have no doubt that no detective story writer before him (and there were few) or after him (and there have been many) has ever employed it better.

The essence of the technique is to conceal important information by presenting it to the reader in an apparently insignificant context. The ultimate effect is similar to the effect of satire: it makes the impact of the story far more powerful. The device of "the concealed clue" also shares with satire the hazard that the reader will skip over or simply not appreciate the message.

Thus, it is important to fathom every paragraph, every line, every word of a serious piece of writing. I must confess that for perhaps thirty or forty years after first reading *The Hound* when I was eleven or twelve years old, I never stopped to look up the meaning of words like "reversion" and "atavism," but simply passed them by. And while I am not a betting man I'd be willing to wager that perhaps 90% of people who read this novel don't know them, either. So in the course of explicating this amazing book, I will give my readers the information they probably lack.

A reversion is a noun whose root is the verb "to reverse," meaning "to go backwards." In law, it means a case in which the owner of property dies, and the property goes back to a former owner or their descendants. (In "The Dying Detective," the fifth story in *His Last Bow*, the evil Culverton Smith murders his nephew Victor Savage because young Savage "stood between this monster and a reversion.") In general, a reversion is a noun describing the return of something to its roots. In "Is Disease a Reversion?" Dr. Mortimer must have discussed the idea that a descendant of a person who had a disease might inherit it at some later—or perhaps much later—time.

Atavism is a similar but more specific term. It describes the reappearance of some characteristic or behavior after one or more generations have passed between the original possessor of the trait and its more recent manifestation.

We can infer from the titles of his writings and from his interest in pathology that Dr. Mortimer was much intrigued by the influence of the past upon the present, and especially in the possible genetic inheritance of illness or behavior. This is a subject which we have encountered before in the Holmes canon—especially in stories like "The Speckled Band," "The Yellow Face," and "The Final Problem."*

The second subsection of chapter 1 begins with the entrance of Dr. Mortimer into the flat at 221B Baker Street.

He is a striking character whose appearance alone makes him unforgettable. He is described as "a very tall, thin man, with a long nose like a beak which shot out between two keen, gray eyes set closely together and sparkling brightly from behind a pair of gold-rimmed glasses. He was clad in a professional but rather slovenly fashion, for his frock coat was dingy and his trousers frayed. Though young, his long back was already bowed, and he walked with a forward thrust of his head and a general air of peering benevolence."**

However, there are at least two other things about this young doctor which make him remarkable. One of these is his last name—Mortimer—with its connotation of death derived from its French root. The second is his strange interest in skulls—a macabre touch which surely takes him out of the ordinary way of surgeons.

---

* We are entitled to link Dr. Mortimer's interest in this subject to that of his creator, I think. Evidently Doyle took the idea seriously, at least for a time—it shows up so often in the Holmes stories.

** It is unusual to catch Doyle in a grammar mistake, but this last sentence has one. The words "he was" are omitted between "though" and "young," so that "his long back" becomes the subject of the sentence. I suspect that this flaw may have been the fault of the printer, and escaped correction by the proofreader or even the author himself.

More importantly, Doyle's description recalls that of Holmes's old enemy, Professor Moriarty—the uber villain of the canon. The professor also walks with his head thrust forward, and the reptilian oscillation of his head from side to side might be compared with Dr. Mortimer's "air of peering benevolence," save for the fact that the professor's look was not at all benevolent. Still, the likeness between the two men makes one wonder if Doyle intended us to distrust Mortimer. If nothing else, his coveting of Holmes's skull makes him a bit creepy. (See "The Final Problem," the last story from *Memoirs*, for the description of the notorious Professor Moriarty.)

Why did Conan Doyle endow this "humble M.R.C.S." with such a bizarre characteristic?

Of course, it serves to emphasize the aura of mystery and oddity which the author wishes us to feel about him. But there is another reason, imparted in the next-to-last sentence of this paragraph. Dr. Mortimer says to Holmes, "A cast of your skull, sir, until the original is available, would be an ornament to any anthropological museum." In short, Mortimer's fascination with the skull serves to introduce the science of anthropology—the study of the development of the human species from prehistoric times to the present. As we will see, this is another piece of the puzzle, which, when it is completed, will disclose more about this truly amazing book. We will find, when we reach the moor in the development part of the story, that skulls, prehistory, and anthropology are all related in that region. Dr. Mortimer's entry into the Baker Street flat thus brings an echo of the wild, perilous, and fascinating atmosphere of Dartmoor into the very center of reason and civilization. Later, first Watson and then Holmes himself will discover and explore the very different world from which Dr. Mortimer has come. This, you will recall, is the formula of the novel as it was originally defined in the eighteenth century—the examination of the manners and mores of a society or segment of society through the device of introducing an outside character or characters.

We get another glimpse of Dr. Mortimer's peculiar character just before the end of the chapter. Holmes asks why he has come to consult. The doctor replies that he has recognized that he is not a very practical man, and that he wants help in dealing with "a most serious and extraordinary problem"—that is, what to do with Sir Henry Baskerville, who is about to arrive in London, as we learn in the following chapter. But Dr. Mortimer now exhibits a lack of good judgement, when he says, "Recognizing, as I do, that you are the second highest expert in Europe ... " Holmes immediately asks, "Who has the honor to be the first?" Mortimer then makes his gaffe even worse by naming Bertillon. Holmes's feathers are ruffled by this glaring lack of tact, and he suggests that Dr. Mortimer state his problem posthaste. With this remark, chapter 1 comes to an end.

Before we go on any further, I wish to emphasize that at least four points which may appear trivial and insignificant—Dr. Mortimer's writings, the fact that he keeps a pet spaniel, his interest in skulls, and his introduction of the science of anthropology—will be found later in the text to play important parts in discovering the full meaning and impact of this book.

CHAPTER 2: THE CURSE OF THE BASKERVILLES

This chapter consists almost entirely of three narratives, each of which may be called a subsection of the whole. The first is Dr. Mortimer's reading aloud the 1742 statement of the legend of the coming of the hound by Hugo Baskerville, a descendant of the seventeenth century cavalier by the same name, whose doings, according to the family legend, brought on the curse of the Baskervilles. The second is Doctor Mortimer's reading of a newspaper account of the recent death of Sir Charles Baskerville, while the third is Dr. Mortimer's own account of the last days of the old gentleman and his private observations about the hound and about the circumstances surrounding Sir Charles's death. These include his recollections of the man's declining health and increasing fear; the sighting of a huge dog at the bottom of the driveway; his observation that Sir Charles had been standing at the moor gate for some time, based on the ashes dropped from his cigar; and finally, the doctor's discovery of something no one else had observed.

"Footprints?" asks Holmes.

"Footprints," replies Mortimer.

"A man's or woman's?"

And then, one of the greatest chapter-ending lines in all literature: "Dr. Mortimer looked strangely at us for an instant, and his voice sank almost to a whisper as he answered: "Mr. Holmes, they were the footprints of a gigantic hound!"

There are several things of importance to note in this chapter. First, the Hugo who lived in 1742—the man who wrote the statement—has the same first name as his ancestor, whom he calls "a most wild, profane, and godless man." The statement is addressed to his own two sons, Rodger and John, "with instructions that they say nothing thereof to their sister Elizabeth." We will find that first names are often repeated generations apart in the Baskerville family: not only do we know of two Hugos, separated by a hundred years, but we also learn of three Rodgers.

Second, we learn from this statement that as of 1742, "Many of the family have been unhappy in their deaths, which have been sudden, bloody, and mysterious." Third, we learn that the event which resulted (according to the family legend) in the first appearance of the hound was the original Hugo's Faust-like oath "that he would that very night render his body and soul to the Powers of Evil if he might but overtake the wench." (A young woman he had kidnapped and locked up at the Hall, but who had escaped her prison by climbing down the ivy clinging to the south wall.) Finally, the 1742 Hugo exhorts his sons "not to fear the fruits of the past, but rather to be circumspect in the future, that those foul passions whereby our family has suffered so grievously may not again be loosed to our undoing," and also "to forbear from crossing the moor in those dark hours when the powers of evil are exalted."

Holmes shows no interest in this remarkable document, which had been given to Dr. Mortimer by Sir Charles Baskerville himself some time before his death. But Mortimer continues with the article from the *Devon County Chronicle*, and this time Holmes pricks up his ears. He recalls having read some newspaper comments at the time, but was busy with another case and lost touch with the Baskerville story. He is eager to hear Dr. Mortimer's catalogue of private facts, things which he did not desire to make public first because he did not wish to seem to endorse the idea that a popular superstition—that is, the hound—had caused Sir Charles' death, and second because he feared that if the heir to the estate heard of the mystery surrounding the old man's death, he would not be likely to come to the Hall to live. So, he said less than he knew—and what he knew he now tells Holmes: "They were the footprints of a gigantic hound!" The chapter ends here.

CHAPTER 3: THE PROBLEM

Structurally, this episode may be divided into two parts. The first contains Holmes's interview with Dr. Mortimer, with Watson present but not participating in the discussion. The second subsection describes what Holmes learned during the day with the aid of a large map of Devonshire and a pound of strongest shag tobacco Mr. Bradley had available in his store—plus two pots of coffee and the silence obtaining when Watson, by Holmes's request, made himself scarce for the day.

Holmes makes two pertinent observations in this second subsection of the chapter. He remarks that "The world is full of obvious things which nobody by any chance ever notices." This sentence might well be used as a motto to appear at the beginning of the book—a clue to the reader to take this novel seriously and to look carefully at its contents. The second point of interest is Holmes's mention of the proximity of the Princetown prison, fourteen miles across the moor. This is our first notice of that institution, which will play an important role in the story.

The remainder of chapter 3 is devoted to Holmes's speculations about the supernatural and its impact on the death of Sir Charles— "The devil's agents may be of flesh and blood, may they not?"—and about Dr. Mortimer's evidence. Holmes suggests an immediate answer to the puzzle of the change in the footprints, and the fact that they indicate that the man who made them was running AWAY from the house instead of towards it. Finally, Holmes puts two of Mortimer's facts together: Sir Charles had been standing at the moor gate on a damp and inclement night for several minutes, contrary to his usual practice of avoiding the moor—and this was on the night before he was to leave for London. "The thing takes shape, Watson. It becomes coherent." Sir Charles was waiting for someone at the gate that night—but who was he waiting for, and why was he waiting outside and not in the house? The chapter ends here.

CHAPTER 4: SIR HENRY BASKERVILLE

In the first part of chapter 3, when Dr. Mortimer explains that his immediate problem is what to do with the heir to the estate, Sir Henry Baskerville, who is on his way to London that very morning, Holmes tells him to meet the young man but not to tell him anything until the next morning, when he will have made up his own mind about whether or not to take Sir Henry back to Devonshire. He asks that both gentlemen come to Baker Street at ten o'clock, and in the opening paragraph of chapter 4 they appear exactly on time.

Their conversation occupies the first of the two subsections in this chapter. Our first glimpse of Sir Henry is calculated to make us both interested in him and sympathetic toward him. He wastes not a moment in mentioning that if Dr. Mortimer had not arranged this meeting, he should have come to see Holmes himself. The occasion was the note he received that very morning—a warning employing printed words from a newspaper advising him as follows: "As you value your life or your reason keep away from the moor." The word "moor" alone was handwritten in ink. The note had been sent through the mail, posted the night before at Charing Cross and addressed to Sir Henry at the Northumberland Hotel. Holmes immediately recognized the source of the printed words by the print—*The Times* for the previous day—and even finds the paragraph from which the words were cut. He also notes that the cutting was done with nail scissors, and the words gummed onto the piece of paper unevenly—perhaps an indication that the message was prepared in a hurry. From the single hand-printed word he deduces that the message was probably written in a hotel.*

---

* Conan Doyle does not play entirely fair with the reader here. We are not told now of what we will learn in chapter 15—that he sniffed a faint odor of

Having extracted so much information from the note, Holmes goes on to ask Sir Henry if anything else of interest had happened to him during his short stay in London—and learns, after a bit of prodding, about the baronet's missing new brown boot. After this, Dr. Mortimer reads the statement of 1742 for Sir Henry, who immediately states that whatever the possible danger, he is determined to go to Baskerville Hall. "There is no devil in hell, Mr. Holmes, and no man on earth who can prevent me from going to the home of my own people, and you may take that to be my final answer." One must admire a man with such fortitude as that, and yet even after asserting his commitment to going down to Devonshire, Sir Henry requests some time to mull over what he has heard from Dr. Mortimer. He invites Holmes and Watson to lunch at the hotel at two o'clock. Mortimer and Baskerville leave on foot, planning to walk back to the hotel, as the first subsection of chapter 4 ends.

The instant the front door bangs shut, Holmes swings into action. He changes his bathrobe for a frock coat, urges Watson to hurry with his hat and boots, and together they begin to follow the doctor and the baronet, who are now about 200 yards ahead of them. Closing the gap to a hundred yards, they follow the two men down Oxford Street and into Regent Street, where they notice a hansom cab with a man inside start to move slowly after the walking pair. The passenger in the cab, a man with a bushy black beard and piercing eyes, spots Holmes and Watson, and instantly tells the driver to get away in a hurry. Holmes berates himself for bad management, but he does not fail to get the number of the cab—2704. This will become one of three leads through which Holmes hopes to identify the strange spy. He sets up another by stopping at a messenger office and hiring a

---

perfume on the note. This proved that a woman was involved, and Mrs. Stapleton was the only one who could have known that Sir Henry was staying at the Northumberland. Then he says "I ... had guessed at the criminal before we ever went to the West Country." Holmes admits to having guessed? The man who asserts so often "I never guess"? Even Sherlock Holmes, at times, has feet of clay!

fourteen-year-old boy named Cartwright to visit twenty-three nearby hotels, searching for the mutilated copy of the *Times* from which the words of the note were cut out. Here the chapter ends.

CHAPTER 5: THREE BROKEN THREADS

This chapter consists of three subsections. The first is set in the lobby and later the dining room of the Northumberland Hotel just before and during lunch. The second subsection takes place in a private sitting room at the hotel just after lunch, while the third subsection finds Holmes and Watson at the Baker Street flat, and it ends prior to dinner.

In the first subsection Holmes learns by consulting the hotel register that the two guests who checked into the Northumberland after Sir Henry were well-known to the staff and could not possibly have been the spy in the hansom. This suggests to the detective that not only was Sir Henry being trailed, but that whoever was doing the trailing did not want the baronet to be aware of their appearance.

The second subsection begins as Holmes and Watson are going up the stairs to the dining room. Sir Henry himself comes to the top of the staircase, livid with anger, and holding an old, dusty boot. The theft of his new brown boot the night before has now been followed by the disappearance of one of his old black ones. Sir Henry considers it a trifle, but Holmes takes the theft of the old boot seriously.

After a pleasant lunch the quartet—Holmes, Watson, Sir Henry, and Dr. Mortimer—go to the private room (apparently part of Sir Henry's suite) where they discuss the baronet's decision to go to his family estate at the end of the week. Holmes approves of the decision and gives a cogent reason for it. "I have ample evidence that you are being dogged in London, and among the millions of this great city it is difficult to discover who these people are or what their object can be." (Note, please, the use of that word "dogged": in the context of this novel it is a classic example of *le mot juste*.) Holmes then asks Dr. Mortimer if anyone he knows on Dartmoor is a man with a full black beard. Dr. Mortimer hesitates for a moment, and then remarks that Barrymore, the butler at the Hall, is such a man. Holmes immediately devises a test to see if indeed Barrymore is at Baskerville Hall, or if he could possibly be in London.

The talk next turns to the Barrymores, and then to the extent of the late Sir Charles's fortune. When it is learned that the total value of the estate was close to a million pounds, Holmes is surprised. "It is a stake for which a man might well play a desperate game." Then, of course, he asks who would inherit the estate if anything befell Sir Henry. Obviously, Holmes is thinking about a motive for murder. Immediately he returns to Sir Henry's decision to go to Dartmoor. Go, he says—but "you certainly must not go alone." He suggests Watson as a companion. The doctor is surprised but readily agrees. Their departure is set for the coming Saturday.

Just then Sir Henry sees and recovers the missing new brown boot. Holmes and Watson return to Baker Street, where Holmes spends the afternoon in silence, wreathed in thought and tobacco smoke. Just before dinner, two telegrams arrive: one from Sir Henry, reporting that Barrymore is at the Hall, and the other from the boy Cartwright, reporting his failure to find the cut-up sheet from the *Times*. Hard on the heels of these two disappointing messages comes a visit from the driver of cab number 2704. John Clayton is his name, and the highlight of his report is his description of his passenger—a detective who says his name is Sherlock Holmes!

When Clayton has gone, the real Holmes says, "Snap goes our third thread, and we end where we began ... I've been checkmated in London. I can only wish you better luck in Devonshire. But I'm not easy in my mind about it."

"About what?" Watson asks.

"About sending you ... Yes, my dear fellow, you may laugh, but I give you my word that I shall be very glad to have you back safe and sound in Baker Street once more." With these words, chapter 5 and the exposition section of the novel come to an end.

My comments on this part of the book:

Note how the last two paragraphs of the exposition function on the technical level: they leave the reader on edge about Dr. Watson's safety, but eager to read the next part of the story. When one recalls that *The Hound* first appeared as a magazine serial, one must admire Conan Doyle's wonderful skill in creating closing lines that virtually guarantee that the reader will not fail to buy the next issue of *The Strand*.

Note also that these last lines not only stress the gravity of the case and its potential danger for Watson, but also draw a line between the apparent security, safety and serenity of London and the wild, untamed moorlands of Devonshire.*

One more comment about chapter 5: note the name of the butler, John Barrymore. He is described as the scion of a family which "has looked after the Hall for four generations now." He and his wife, Eliza (short for Elizabeth) are described by Dr. Mortimer, as being "as respectable a couple as any in the county." But when one pounces on the last name, one finds that it comes perilously close to the sound of "bury more," since the "u" in "bury" when said aloud tends to come out sounding like a long "a." The subplot that dominates much of the development revolves around this couple, and Mr. Barrymore is a suspect. "Barrymore" thus becomes another Conan Doyle aptonym!

Now let us go on to the second part of the story—the development.

PART 2: DEVELOPMENT

CHAPTER 6: BASKERVILLE HALL

This central section of *The Hound* is comprised of six chapters, and coheres partly because all but the beginning of it is set in the peculiar environment of Dartmoor, and partly because, with Holmes in absentia, Dr. Watson is both the narrator and the active investigator.

---

* Not that London is not so safe and serene as it may first appear. After all, it is in the metropolis that the spy operates, tracking the footsteps of both Dr. Mortimer and his charge, Sir Henry. Later in this study I will return to the apparent contrast between "civilized, safe, sane London," and the moor.

In this second role he performs quite creditably: he is no Holmes, but neither is he a bumbling idiot, as Nigel Bruce portrayed him in the classic Basil Rathbone Holmes films. Indeed, few amateurs could handle the case any better than he does, and most would fall far short of his accomplishments.

The structure of chapter 6 is simple and easy to express. There are three subsections which together move the story from London and Holmes to Baskerville Hall and the Barrymores. The first subsection commences with Watson receiving Holmes's final instructions, followed by the scene at Paddington Station, where Dr. Mortimer, Sir Henry, and Watson board the train for the trip to the West Country. Subsection two describes the journey, consisting of two parts. The first, which I'll call 2-A, takes place on the train, culminating with Sir Henry's first sight of the moor from the window of the coach; subsection 2-B tells us of the wagonette ride through the gathering twilight, away from civilization. The third subsection of this chapter covers the arrival of Sir Henry and Watson at the Hall, their dinner in the gloomy dining room, and what Watson heard in the night.

To return now to the beginning: Holmes and Watson driving to Paddington. En route, Holmes asks Watson to gather as many facts as possible about the people of the vicinity, about the death of Sir Charles, and about the relations between young Sir Henry and his new neighbors. He tells Watson that the next heir, an elderly clergyman named Mr. James Desmond, is not the source of any trouble—and that he believes Dr. Mortimer to be "entirely honest." He gives no reason for that opinion, however. Holmes directs Watson specifically to study Mr. Stapleton, the naturalist, and his sister, "who is said to be a young lady of attractions. There is Mr. Frankland, of Lafter Hall, who is also an unknown factor, and there are one or two other neighbors. These are the folk who must be your special study." Then Holmes instructs his friend to "Keep your revolver near you night and day, and never relax your precautions." Subsection 1 ends here, and subsection 2-A begins.

At the station they find that Dr. Mortimer and Sir Henry have already secured a first-class carriage, and there is a short conversation among them before the train departs. Holmes admonishes Sir Henry never to go out alone. "Some great misfortune will befall you if you do. Did you ever get your other boot?"

"No," replies the baronet. "It is gone forever."

"Indeed," says Holmes. "That is very interesting. Well, good-bye." The train begins to glide down the track. One last time Holmes repeats a warning. "Avoid the moor in those hours of darkness when the powers of evil are exalted." Here Watson writes something significant: "I looked back at the platform when we had left it far behind, and saw the tall, austere figure of Holmes standing motionless and gazing after us." What is significant about this sentence? I suggest the use of the words, "I looked back … " They make one recall the coffee pot in chapter 1; Dr. Mortimer's essays, with their references to reversion and atavism; the Hugo Baskerville statement of 1742; and the recurring first names of Baskervilles in different generations. As Holmes remarks at the end of chapter 3, "The thing takes shape, Watson. It becomes coherent." Well, doesn't it?

Watson describes the train trip as "swift and pleasant," and mentions that he spent it in getting to know his two companions better, and in playing with Dr. Mortimer's dog. Sir Henry is eager to see the moor, and gets his first sight of it from afar—"a gray, melancholy hill with a strange, jagged summit, dim and vague in the distance, like some fantastic landscape in a dream."

The railway journey ends at a small wayside station, where the party is met by a coachman driving a wagonette drawn by two horses. In a few minutes they are off down the broad, white road bisecting the "peaceful and sunlit countryside," but behind that scene "there rose ever, dark against the evening sky, the long, gloomy curve of the moor, broken by the jagged and sinister hills."

This paragraph, the beginning of subsection 2-B, gives us a taste of the brilliant descriptive writing to come. Adjectives like "gloomy," "jagged," and "sinister" portend a different atmosphere than that described by the phrase, "the peaceful and sunlit countryside."

Conan Doyle was a virtuoso when it comes to using the sound and sight of English words not only to convey description but also to arouse emotional responses from his readers, and in this three-page account of the drive from the "sunlit countryside" up to the cold and darkness of the moor, he surpasses himself.

Even at the beginning of the wagonette journey, the "peaceful" aura of the country station is jolted by the presence of "two soldiery men in dark uniforms who leaned on their short rifles and glanced keenly at us as we passed." Too, we find in the very next sentence a description of the coachman: he is "a hard-faced, gnarled little fellow" and the adjectives used to paint his picture are quite inconsistent with the placid scene. "Hard-faced" and "gnarled" are words which carry in their appearance on the page as well as in their sounds and meanings emotions quite in contrast with the description of the station as "a sweet, simple country spot."

In the following paragraph the wagonette "curved upward through deep lanes worn by centuries of wheels, with high banks on either side, heavy with dripping moss and fleshy harts- tongue ferns. Bronzing bracken and mottled bramble gleamed in the light of the setting sun." Note the adjectives "dripping" and "fleshy," both of which connote wetness; the alliterative hard "B" sounds of "bronzing," "bracken," and "bramble," and the squishy waterlogged "s" sounds of "setting sun. Still steadily rising, we passed over a narrow granite bridge and skirted a noisy stream which gushed swiftly down, foaming and roaring amid the gray boulders." Coupled with those hard gerund sounds (dripping, sinking, rising, foaming, roaring) and words like "granite," "bridge," and "boulders," you can hear in your mind the sounds of that noisy stream. But the paragraph is not done yet: we learn how Sir Henry "gave exclamations of delight and asked countless questions." (More "s" sounds!) Yet to Dr. Watson "a tinge of melancholy lay upon the countryside, which bore so clearly the mark of the waning year. Yellow leaves carpeted the lanes and fluttered down upon us as we passed. The rattle of our wheels died away as we drove through drifts of rotting vegetation—sad gifts, as it seemed to me, for Nature to throw before the carriage of the returning heir of the Baskervilles." The words "yellow," "passed," "rattle," "died," and "rotting" all invoke thoughts of illness, dying, or death—sad gifts, indeed!*

Next, we see "a mounted soldier, dark and stern, his rifle poised ready over his forearm." In answer to Mortimer's question ("What is this?"), Perkins, the driver, answers, "There's a convict escaped from Princetown, sir. He's been out three days now, and the warders watch every road and every station, but they've had no sight of him yet." We learn that this escapee is no ordinary convict: the locals are scared.

"Who is he, then?" Dr. Mortimer asks.

"It is Selden, the Notting Hill murderer."

Here we have another indication of Conan Doyle's remarkable gift as a writer. No better line could replace this simple identification. The double "t" and hard "g" of "Notting Hill" are perfect vehicles to describe the terror of the nearby farmers. Try any other combination of name and location: I challenge you to come up with a more menacing phrase than this one. "Johnson, the Manchester murderer"? "Williams, the Liverpool murderer"? "Smith, the Plymouth murderer"? Do you see what I mean?

The fifteen lines or so which comprise the following paragraph (describing the ferocity and brutality of Selden's crime, and the commutation of his death sentence, owing to doubts of his sanity) serve a dual purpose. They introduce us to a character who will take a key role in the story as it plays out, and simultaneously, as the wagonette tops a rise and comes out onto the moor, a cold wind sweeps down and chills the party. Thoughts of the fiendish convict hiding out on the moor "complete the grim suggestiveness of the barren waste, the

---

* It must not have been easy for the author to get five words relating to sickness and / or death into two sentences, as Conan Doyle does here. Infusing these lines with such a premonition of mortality is a literary accomplishment deserving of recognition and high praise.

chilling wind, and the darkling sky." Welcome, readers, to the scene of the crime.

But one paragraph remains in subsection 2-B. It describes the fertile country left behind below:

> The slanting rays of a low sun turning the streams to threads of gold and glowing on the red earth new turned by the plow and the broad tangle of the woodlands. The road in front of us grew bleaker and wilder over huge russet and olive slopes, sprinkled with giant boulders. Now and then we passed a moorland cottage, walled and roofed with stone, with no creeper to break its harsh outline. Suddenly we looked down into a cup-like depression, patched with stunted oaks and firs which had been twisted and bent by the fury of years of storm. Two high, narrow towers rose over the trees. The driver pointed with his whip.
>
> "Baskerville Hall," said he.

I can think of few pieces of descriptive writing as good as this, in its ability to make the reader not only see the country but feel the cold, lonely, foreboding of the place, and the danger posed by the terrible murderer hiding somewhere in the vicinity. The second subsection of this chapter makes one feel far more than a few hours from the sanity and safety of London and the epicenter of logic and reason which is 221B Baker Street.

Subsection three of chapter 6 begins with the wagonette's passage through the lodge gates, with Sir Henry standing up and staring "with flushed cheeks and shining eyes." Beyond the gate the party drives through "a somber tunnel" formed by the branches of the old trees. Sir Henry's face turns gloomy in the scary twilight: he promises himself that he'll have electric lights put up inside six months. Then they pull up to the Hall itself—a central block flanked by the two ancient, tall towers, "crenellated and pierced with many loopholes." Beyond the turrets "were more modern wings, built of black granite, and a dull light shone through the heavy mullioned windows and from the high chimneys which rose from the steep, high-angled roof, there sprang a single column of black smoke." Was there ever a better description of a house of horrors than this?

At last a tall man steps from the shadow of the porch to open the door of the wagonette. This is our first glimpse of Barrymore, the butler: he welcomes them to Baskerville Hall as his wife comes out after him to help with the luggage. Dr. Mortimer excuses himself immediately, saying his wife expects him at home, and Sir Henry and Watson enter the old, storied house—the home of the Baskerville family for five hundred years.

The final five paragraphs of the chapter describe first the floor plan of the house and afterwards the great dining room with its black beams and smoke-blackened ceiling. The walls are decorated with portraits of five centuries of Baskerville ancestors; Watson notes that they "stared down upon us and daunted us by their silent company." Then bedtime: Watson looks out the window of his room and sees in the cold light of the half moon "a fringe of broken rocks and the long, low curve of the melancholy moor." Here once again Conan Doyle's mastery of the English language makes his readers not only envision what Watson sees from the window, but also makes us share his feeling about the scene. He finds that sleep will not come. "Far away a chiming clock struck out the quarters of the hours, but otherwise a deathly silence lay upon the old house. And then suddenly, in the very dead of the night, there came a sound to my ears, clear, resonant, and unmistakable. It was the sob of a woman."

What more is there to say about writing like this, other than that its power and ability to make one both see and feel is unsurpassed. This entire chapter is simply masterful. Whoever argues that Doyle is not one of the great English writers ought to be expelled from the society of literary critics.

Before we leave chapter 6, let me call your attention to how Conan Doyle unobtrusively and subtly introduces his readers to the existence of the Baskerville gallery of family portraits. These silent and daunting pictures will play a profoundly significant part in the story later on: here, the reader encounters them in such a context that they seem no more than a triviality. Doesn't every noble house in England have such a collection hanging on the walls? Here is another brilliant use of the device of the concealed clue.

More than that, it is still another instance of the prevalent theme of "looking back" which so pervades this novel. Watson perceives nothing important about the paintings, and at this point in the story neither does the reader. It will take Sherlock Holmes himself to seize upon the portraits in the dining room and to recognize their importance in this case.

CHAPTER 7: THE STAPLETONS OF MERRIPIT HOUSE

We may conveniently break down this chapter into three scenes, defined by where they take place and by the characters who appear in each. Subsection one takes place at Baskerville Hall, during and after breakfast. The people involved are Watson, Sir Henry, and the Barrymores, and the subject is the sobbing of the woman—a sound that both the baronet and Watson heard during the night. Barrymore denies that it could have been his wife, but when Watson meets her in the Hall a bit later, he can tell by her reddened eyes and swollen lids that it was indeed her. Wondering why Barrymore lied about his wife, Watson determines to find out if Barrymore really was at the Hall and not in London when Holmes sent the telegram.

This sends Watson on a walk along the edge of the moor to the village of Grimpen, where the telegraph office is. This walk makes up subsection two of the chapter, and it in turn may be broken down into four scenes. The first is at the telegraph station, where Watson learns that it was possible that Barrymore had not been at the Hall: the telegram had been delivered to Mrs. Barrymore, not to her husband in person. Scene two finds the doctor walking back down the road when he is overtaken by Mr. Stapleton, the naturalist, carrying a butterfly net. They talk, and Stapleton reveals that he knows who Watson is, and asks if Holmes will be coming down. Stapleton then invites Watson to come to Merripit House, and they are on the way when they pass the great Grimpen Mire, where a moor pony is struggling in the ooze. While they watch, they hear "a long, low moan, indescribably sad, which swept over the moor." Stapleton suggests that it might be the call of a bittern, but while he says nothing Watson is clearly not convinced.

Next Stapleton points out the stone huts on the hillside and explains that they are the habitations of prehistoric man with the roofs gone. At this moment he leaves Watson to chase a butterfly.

While he is running across the mire, a most unusual woman appears. She looks nothing like her brother, but Watson realizes that she can be none other than Miss Stapleton. She issues an impassioned warning, then immediately shuts up when she sees her brother, having given up his chase of the butterfly, returning. It is only now that the woman realizes that she had not been talking to Sir Henry, as she had assumed. She repeats her brother's previous invitation to Marripit House, and all three go there together.*

Scene three of the second subsection takes place at the Stapletons' home, which strikes Watson as "mean and melancholy." During the ensuing conversation Stapleton talks about his experiences as the Headmaster of a school in the north of England, and how an epidemic killed three of the students and led to the end of the venture. He goes on to mention his intent to call at the Hall and make the acquaintance of Sir Henry. He invites Watson to see his collection of Lepidoptera, but the latter, thinking of Sir Henry left alone at the Hall, chooses instead to take his leave.

Subsection three begins as Watson resumes his walk, but he is shortly surprised to find Miss Stapleton sitting on a rock by the side

---

* Here we have another example of Conan Doyle's fondness for aptonyms: "Merripit House" turns out to be a "pit" indeed. In this case, however, he did not create the name, but used one which already existed. See Klinger's note on p. 475 of his *New Annotated Sherlock Holmes* for details.

of the road and waiting for him. She apologizes for having taken him for Sir Henry and asks that he forget the words of warning she had uttered. He replies that he cannot forget them and asks her to tell him what she had meant by warning Sir Henry to go back to London. She dodges the question and hurries away before her brother learns that she has been out. Watson, his soul full of vague fears, goes back to Baskerville Hall.

CHAPTER 8: FIRST REPORT OF DR. WATSON

The chapter opens with Watson noting that he will now continue the story by transcribing his letters to Holmes. He writes that he can "show my feelings and suspicions of the moment more accurately than my memory, clear as it is upon these tragic events, can possibly do."

Of course, Watson's reasons for changing the means of telling the story are not Conan Doyle's reasons. We must ask why the author chose to make a change in the narrative. This question should remain in the back of our minds until after we have read the next three chapters.

Looking at the structure of chapter 8, we find it to be made up of six clearly defined subsections. The first of these recounts Watson's observations of the moor and its effects on the souls of those who encounter it. His very first point is that the moor is effectively a time machine: when you are there, you have "left all traces of modern England behind you ... and are conscious everywhere of the homes and work of the prehistoric people." His description of the "skin-clad, hairy man" who you may imagine crawling out of the low door of a stone hut, fitting a flint-tipped arrow into his bow is not only graphic, but as we will see, closely tied to the recurring theme we find in *The Hound*—that is, the relationship of the past to the present.

Watson's imagination here will take on new and deeper significance later in the novel.

Subsection two is devoted to the escaped convict. Two weeks after his flight from the prison he remains at large, and it is thought that he may have left the district. The farmers are sleeping better in the absence of any news, and both Watson and Sir Henry—who were concerned about the vulnerable situation of the Stapletons—are now less fearful. In any event, Stapleton has rejected any idea of having Perkins, the groom, sleep at Merripit House, so the issue is now moot.

Subsection three tells us of how Sir Henry "begins to display a considerable interest in our fair neighbor" (i.e., Miss Stapleton.) Watson speculates on her relationship with her very different brother, of whom Watson suspects "possibly a harsh nature." The subsection continues to describe how Stapleton took the two visitors to the spot on the moor where Hugo Baskerville is said to have been killed by the hound in the seventeenth century. The last paragraph of the section tells of how Stapleton, who might have been expected to be delighted in the baronet's showing interest in his sister, instead disapproves, trying to prevent their being together alone. Watson does not speculate on why Stapleton should oppose a match between Sir Henry and Miss Stapleton: he only reports what he has observed.

The fourth subsection of the chapter is just a single paragraph that updates us on the doings of Dr. Mortimer. We learn that he has dug up a prehistoric skull from an ancient barrow, which "fills him with great joy." His macabre interest in skulls seems to find an echo in his next action: he comes to lunch at the Hall one day, and afterwards, in the company of the Stapletons, takes Watson and Sir Henry (at the latter's request) out to the Yew Alley to show them the exact spot where Sir Charles was found dead, and where he stood at the moor gate and let the ash drop from his cigar before he saw something coming across the moor which sent him running in terror towards the tumbledown summerhouse at the far end. Watson speculates on what that something might have been, but he comes to no conclusion.

In the fifth subsection of chapter 8, Watson recounts his meeting with another neighbor, Mr. Frankland of Lafter Hall. We hear of Frankland's passion for the law and of how he entertains himself by bringing actions for the mere pleasure of fighting cases: he has no convictions, but "is ready to take up either side of a question." In another quixotic manifestation of his penchant for messing things up by legal process we learn that he threatens to prosecute Dr. Mortimer for digging up that prehistoric skull without the permission of the next of kin.

Embedded in all this nonsense we find that Mr. Frankland has recently developed a new pastime: amateur astronomy. He owns an excellent telescope with which he lies on the roof of his house and sweeps the moor all day, looking for the escaped convict. In short, Frankland is a comic character: not for nothing does Conan Doyle call his house *"Lafter* Hall."

The sixth and final subsection of chapter 8 is the longest and most important. Its subjects are the butler, Barrymore, and his wife. It begins with a return to the telegram which Holmes sent from London, with the object of discovering whether Mr. Barrymore was really at the Hall on the day the spy in the hansom was tracking Sir Henry and Dr. Mortimer through the city. This time it is Sir Henry who questions the butler, and who confirms that he did not get the wire from the telegraph boy but had his wife bring it to him. Later in the evening, Barrymore turns the tables and asks Sir Henry if he (Barrymore) had done anything to forfeit his (Sir Henry's) confidence. Sir Henry assures him he hasn't. He pacifies the man by giving him much of his pre-London wardrobe.

Next the spotlight is turned on Mrs. Barrymore, whom Watson describes as "a heavy, solid person, very limited, intensely respectable, and inclined to be puritanical. You could hardly conceive of a less emotional suspect." And yet she sobbed in the night and Watson has more than once seen traces of tears on her face. The doctor sometimes wonders if she "has a guilty memory which haunts her."

Then the focus changes to Barrymore himself. Watson sometimes suspects the man of being "a domestic tyrant." More importantly, the doctor discovers that Barrymore walks the halls at night. Watson follows him one night, and finds him in an empty room with a candle in hand, staring out the window. Watson determines to explore the butler's conduct more thoroughly, and together with Sir Henry devises a plan.

CHAPTER 9: THE LIGHT UPON THE MOOR (SECOND REPORT OF DR. WATSON)

Like its predecessor, this chapter contains six clearly defined subsections, the first of which is an introduction in the form of an opening note to Holmes. The second describes the plan that Watson and Sir Henry resolve to follow Barrymore on one of his nocturnal tours of the house—to see where he goes and what he does. The third subsection begins with Watson's observation about Sir Henry's romantic approaches to Beryl Stapleton and her brother's surprising negative response. It ends with their agreement over the problem.

Subsection four passes on to Watson's account of how he and the baronet tracked Barrymore in the night, discovering the identity of the convict loose on the moor and how he came to be there. This leads into subsection five, when Sir Henry and Dr. Watson venture out onto the moor to capture the fugitive. Their expedition is interrupted by Watson's second hearing of the sound of the hound, emanating from the great Grimpen Mire and chilling Sir Henry both physically and emotionally. Yet the baronet refuses to quit the search, and he and Watson find and actually see Selden, the escaped murderer, looking like one of the prehistoric inhabitants of the moor's stone huts. They chase him, but he outdistances them, and they are forced to admit that they have no chance of catching him this time. Completely winded, they sit down on a couple of rocks and watch their quarry disappear in the distance.

Their evening out concludes in subsection six with Watson seeing the figure of "The Man on the Tor," outlined against the rising moon. Another mystery on the moor has presented itself as the chapter ends.

NOTES ON CHAPTERS 6–9

Why did Conan Doyle put so much emphasis on the prehistoric huts found on the moor?

When, in chapter 7, Dr. Watson asks Stapleton when they were inhabited, the latter answers curtly, "Neolithic man—no date." "Neolithic" means "new Stone Age," so these structures really do date from a period in human development before the beginnings of what we consider to be modern civilization.

And yet in the course of that wagonette drive from the railway station up the rising grade to the moor in chapter 6, the author inserts this sentence: "Now and then we passed a moorland cottage, walled and roofed with stone, with no creeper to break its harsh outline." What, aside from their missing roofs, distances these nine-teenth-century dwellings from the Stone Age huts clustered on the moor? As far as housing is concerned, the people of Watson's time and Baskerville's place are literally in a new "Stone Age." I do not think this subtle but carefully elaborated comparison should be missed; nor should the parallels between the occupants of the roof-less, ancient stone huts and those of the present-day stone cottages be dismissed out of hand.

Here Dr. Doyle employs a device to be found elsewhere in his works as well: a journey into space combined with a trip through time. He uses it in *A Study in Scarlet*, written fourteen years before *The Hound*, and again in *The Valley of Fear*, written roughly fourteen years after. Moreover, this same idea is at the very heart of one of the author's most successful and most popular non-Holmes books— *The Lost World*. There Professor Challenger finds living dinosaurs on an elevated plateau in South America. That story has spawned many, many imitations over the last century or more, but the device it employs is the same combination of travel through both time and space that we find in this book. The treatments may be different, but the idea is the same, and I believe that understanding the implications of this literary trick are crucial to a full understanding of *The Hound of the Baskervilles*.

CHAPTER 10: EXTRACT FROM THE DIARY OF DR. WATSON

This chapter should really be called "Extract*s* from the Diary of Dr. Watson," because there are two of them. I shall treat them separately, beginning with the introduction to the first.

In this single paragraph, Watson writes that he must now abandon his reliance on the reports which he drew up for Holmes and instead trust to his own recollections, aided by the entries in his diary for October 16 (the day after the night of the convict hunt) and October 17. He does not give us any reason *why* he feels compelled to do so, however. My own feeling is that Conan Doyle changed his story-telling method at this juncture because he wished to give the narration a more personal tone, bringing Watson more into focus while at the same time speeding up the pace of the story. These changes prepare us for the startling confrontation which will occur at the end of the next chapter.

The diary entry for October 16 can be conveniently divided into two subsections. The first encompasses four paragraphs, beginning with a mood-setting description of the melancholy feeling brought on by the fog and rain outside the house, and the baronet's "black reaction" to the events of the previous night, and the doctor's own sense of impending danger inside the walls. In the second paragraph, Watson elaborates on the causes of his distress, dismissing the supernatural explanation as "incredible, impossible," but finding the alternative nearly as difficult to credit. He then passes on to the question of The Man on The Tor. Is he friend or enemy?

Who is he? Surely no one Watson has encountered in Dartmoor. "A stranger is still dogging us, just as a stranger dogged us in London." (A nice opportunity to get the canine expression into the reader's mind again!) Then in the final paragraph of this subsection the doctor resolves to track down the mystery man alone, without involving Sir Henry in his quest.

The second subsection of this day's diary entry recounts the interview between Barrymore and Sir Henry, for much of which Watson was present at the baronet's invitation. Satisfied with the resolution of his grievance, the butler turns to go, then hesitates and tells his story about the night Sir Charles died. This scene is of extreme importance to the plot—it represents the first break in the case.

The diary entry for October 17 can likewise be broken down into two distinct subsections. The first describes the all-day pouring rain which sets Watson to think of the escaped convict out on the moor, and then of the other man: "Was he also out in that deluge?" Later, the doctor goes out walking on the sodden moor: he finds the black tor upon which he had seen the mysterious watcher, but there is no sign of him now. As Watson walks back towards the Hall he is overtaken by Dr. Mortimer, driving his dog-cart. (Still another opportunity to keep the word "dog" planted firmly in the reader's cranium!) And indeed, Mortimer is "much troubled" by the disappearance of his pet spaniel, which had wandered out onto the moor and never come back. Watson tries to console him—but recalling the fate of the moor pony in the Grimpen Mire, he is inwardly convinced that the little dog will never be seen again. This incident seems trivial enough, but it will be seen to have enormous importance later, when we recognize how it sets up perhaps the most telling line in the entire novel.

However, it is the conversation which follows that has immediate significance for the plot. Watson asks his fellow physician if he can recall any local woman with the initials "L. L." Mortimer at first demurs, but then thinks of Laura Lyons, who lives in Coombe Tracey. It turns out that she is old Frankland's daughter, who married an artist and was then abandoned by him. Mortimer adds: "The fault from what I hear may not have been entirely on one side." Her father refused to have anything to do with her because she had married without his consent—"and perhaps for one or two other reasons as well."

"How does she live?" Watson inquires. And Mortimer replies, "Whatever she may have deserved one could not allow her to go hopelessly to the bad. Her story got about, and several of the people here did something to enable her to earn an honest living."

This is a curious conversation, which says much less than it appears to mean. What did Mortimer mean when, discussing the artist Lyons's abandonment of his wife, he said that the fault may not have been all on one side? What were the "one or two other reasons" why Mr. Frankland refused to have anything more to do with his daughter? And what was Dr. Mortimer implying when he said, "One could not allow her to go *hopelessly* to the bad" (my emphasis)? I cannot help but read this coded language to mean that Mrs. Lyons may well have been unfaithful to her husband, and that she may have enraged her father and aroused the sympathies of some of her neighbors by occasionally joining the world's oldest profession. What else could Mortimer mean by qualifying "her to go hopelessly [as opposed to just on occasion] to the bad?" On the spot, Watson decides to visit Mrs. Lyons the next day. Her "equivocal reputation" suggests that she might have something of value to contribute to the solution of the Baskerville case. Dr. Watson then closes the Mortimer conversation with an adroit change of subject worthy of Holmes himself.

The third subsection of the diary for October 17 recounts Watson's after-dinner conversation with Barrymore in the library about Selden, and what he had to say about the other man on the moor. Learning that that mysterious personage lived in one of the prehistoric stone huts and had a hired boy bring him his food and other needs, Watson concludes that "The Man on the Tor" seems to be at the very center of the problem, and that another day shall not pass before, as Holmes's agent, he will do everything in his power "to reach the heart of the mystery." This is the end of chapter 10.

CHAPTER 11: THE MAN ON THE TOR

Once again, the chapter begins with a paragraph of introduction: Watson tells us how he can rely on his memory for the rest of the tale, and he recounts his two significant discoveries. First, that on the day of Sir Charles's death, he had received a letter, which he had burned, but from which the postscript was still legible, bearing the initials "L. L." This document explained his presence at the moor gate that night. Second, he relates Selden's comments on the other man on the tor, as passed along by Barrymore. Through this conversation, Watson learned that the other man lived in one of the Neolithic huts on the moor, and that he had employed a boy who brought him food and other necessities. He therefore devotes the day to following up these two clues.

In subsection one, Dr. Watson goes to Coombe Tracey and interviews Mrs. Lyons. Significantly, when the maid shows him into the sitting room, Mrs. Lyons rises from her typewriter "with a pleasant smile of welcome." But when she sees who it is, "her face fell" and she sits down again. Watson makes no further comment here—but clearly, she is expecting someone else. The doctor's first impression of Mrs. Lyons was that she is extremely beautiful, but upon a second look he detects "something subtly wrong with the face, some coarseness of expression, some hardness, perhaps, of eye, some looseness of lip which marred its perfect beauty." Elsewhere in the canon Watson claims wide experience of women: here he proves sensitive to Mrs. Lyons's flaws, which we may well take to reflect imperfections in her character as well as in her appearance. In questioning her, Watson gets her to admit that she wrote to Sir Charles, making an appointment to ask him for help in getting a divorce. She fixed the time and place because she had heard that he was about to leave for London, and because she could not as a woman enter a bachelor's house at ten in the evening. She says that "there were reasons why I could not get there earlier," but never says what they were. Then she admits that she never went to the appointment—but she refuses to tell what kept her from going. She admits only that she did not keep the date because she had received help from another source.

Watson reasons that she is telling the truth about not keeping her appointment, because she could not have gotten to Baskerville Hall without a horse and wagon. If she really had been there, it would be impossible to keep secret. He remains unsatisfied with the interview, reading from Mrs. Lyons's face and manner that she was holding something back—but for the moment he recognizes that he can get nothing more from her. Therefore, he decides to spend the rest of the day tracking down his other clue—the identity and whereabouts of the man on the tor.

Subsection two describes how he goes about it with the chance help of Mr. Frankland and his telescope. He takes advantage of the old rascal's grudge against the local police (which causes him to conceal his discovery of the boy who takes things out to the hut) and with the hint of where to look realizes that while Mr. Frankland believes he has tracked down the lair of the escaped convict, Watson realizes that he has instead stumbled on the key to finding the other man. Wasting no time, he contrives to get away from Lafter Hall, and as soon as he is out of Frankland's range of vision, he sets off across the moor, tracking the boy.

Watson's escape from the old crank leads into subsection three of the chapter, which begins with another of Conan Doyle's beautiful scene-setting paragraphs of descriptive writing. This time colors— golden-green, gray, and blue—are used to underline the sense of loneliness beneath the nearly empty sky and the barren earth. Now Watson finds one in a circle of the prehistoric huts which still has enough roof remaining to offer at least some protection from the weather. Tossing away his cigarette—perhaps in a gesture of defiance—the good doctor, revolver in hand, goes up to the door and looks in. What he sees yields ample confirmation that this is the right place. Surprisingly, a note under the bundle of foodstuffs reads, "Dr. Watson has gone to Coombe Tracey." Was it, then, he and not Sir

Henry who was being "dogged" (there's that word again) by this unknown man?

There follows another paragraph of descriptive prose, which for the first and only time in the novel paints the moor as beautiful and peaceful. In contrast, Watson is on edge, keyed up for the expected confrontation. This paragraph sets up the stunning disclosure which brings both chapter 11 and the development section of *The Hound* to their ironic and startling conclusion.

COMMENTARY ON THE DEVELOPMENT SECTION

There has been some negative criticism of *The Hound*, based on the absence of Sherlock Holmes from the whole center section of the book. I believe such criticism is not only unwarranted, but shows a lack of careful reading, and a misunderstanding of the concept of structure in literature.

Conan Doyle defended the omission of his great detective from this section as "essential," although he did not explain further. It is probable that the original conception of the story did not include Holmes at all. However, as the author developed his plans for the book, he saw how Holmes could be employed in it. His readers had been thirsting for another Holmes tale for years, and Doyle realized that by setting the story before the supposed death of the detective he could satisfy the cravings of his public without having to commit himself to future Holmes stories by presenting him as really still alive. Also, he must have known that sales of the novel would be stimulated if the great detective were in it. Undoubtedly, he supposed that another Holmes book set in the past would assuage the desires of his panting readers so that he could go back to his other literary work. If so, however, he misjudged the fervor of his readers: the demand for more of Sherlock simply increased with the publication of *The Hound*, and not long afterwards Doyle surrendered, and *The Return of Sherlock Holmes* began running in *The Strand Magazine*.

But when Conan Doyle decided to bring Sherlock Holmes into

the novel, he pointedly omitted him from the center. We are entitled to ask why.

I have long emphasized to my English literature students the importance of the center to virtually every human creation. The creator of the work often implants in the center the underlying message they are attempting to impart. They make the center of the work the core from which the whole structure is elaborated.* In keeping Holmes offstage during the entire development section of *The Hound* the author gives us an important piece of information: that while Sherlock Holmes appears in this novel, it is not *about* him.

In fact, this is true about all four of the long stories in the canon. Consider: *A Study in Scarlet* is really about Watson, and how the Jefferson Hope case impacts his life. *The Sign of the Four* is the tale of an anti-hero, Jonathan Small, who is caught up in a series of events, the underlying theme of which is greed and its ultimate expression in Britain's colonial adventure in India. *The Valley of Fear* is at bottom about that powerful emotion—it's a warning that while fear cannot and must not be ignored, neither should it be allowed to bring on panic. In this novel, the absence of Holmes from the core chapters is proof the book is not about him.

What, then, occupies the six chapters which make up the development section—the center of the novel? If one wanted to give this section a title, it might be called "Life on the Moor," for it is devoted entirely to the lonely, wind-swept land and the people who have lived there since pre-history. There are numerous links between the Stone Age inhabitants, those of more recent but still long-ago times, and the residents during Victoria's reign.

The stone huts of the ancients are not much different from the stark moorland cottages of the nineteenth century. This invites

---

* My friend Francis Michael Nevins, a successful mystery writer and critic in addition to his other life as a professor of law, writes frequently about detective stories which fail because of the classic weakness which he calls "the hollow center." When studying a work of human ingenuity, we should pay attention to what occupies the vital middle of any structure.

comparisons between the Neolithic population and the Victorian era residents. In reality, how different are they?

The topography of the moor has not changed in millennia. It remains timeless and basically unchanged since the people Mr. Stapleton calls "our worthy ancestors" eked out a living there.

Baskerville Hall itself, although not from prehistoric times, brings the sixteenth century to life with its ivied walls and crenellated towers pierced with loopholes from a time when the house doubled as a fortress. Inside, its smoke-blackened ceilings, minstrels' gallery, and portraits of long-departed ancestors recall five hundred years of history.

There is also the legend of the hound, handed down from father to son to grandson through many generations. The moor may continue to exist into the Victorian era, but it remains apart from British society while simultaneously inseparable from it.

The few educated residents of the area reflect its weird atmosphere: Dr. Mortimer with his fascination for human skulls; Stapleton and his butterfly net; old Frankland with his comical passion for ridiculous lawsuits; Laura Lyons, his estranged daughter, herself a study in perversity; and the mysterious Barrymores, not to mention the escaped murderer and the unknown man on the tor. The moor is physically elevated above the civilization that lies at its base—but it is even more isolated in its creepy character. Stapleton certainly has it right when he remarks (in chapter 7) "Queer place, the moor!" Contrast this wild, unruly place, where the past is never far from view, with London—the greatest city in the most advanced nation in the world, with its commerce, its arts, its science and technology, and most of all its belief in the triumphs of the times and the nation of which it is the capital. Conan Doyle draws this comparison with such clarity that one can hardly doubt that this was his purpose in creating this development section of the book.

Now it becomes clear why it was necessary to keep Sherlock Holmes, the man of reason, out of sight and out of mind while creating this portrait of the moor as a place apart—more closely linked to both the prehistoric and historical past than to the Britain of the late Victorian era. His presence would have gotten in the way of what Conan Doyle was trying to convey in these six chapters: those links of which I have just written. Allowing Watson to take the spotlight was another stroke of genius: it turns the development section of *The Hound* into a true novel in the original eighteenth-century meaning of the word. That is, a long work of prose fiction which explores the manners and mores of society or a segment of society, usually by bringing into it a perceptive observer from the outside world. In addition, the whole section prepares us for the stunning revelation at the end of chapter 11, which marks the beginning of the resolution, with the solution to the mystery and the powerful (if generally ignored) message of the book. In fact, I would go so far as to argue that if Conan Doyle had brought Holmes to Dartmoor in the conventional manner, this novel would be far less successful in conveying its true message.

Let me add a few more comments on the development section. Notice, first, how while the hound is never seen in these chapters, still it dominates them through its chilling cries. Consider these lines: "There rose suddenly out of the vast gloom of the moor that strange cry which I had already heard upon the borders of the great Grimpen Mire. It came with the wind through the silence of the night, a long, deep mutter, then a rising howl, and then the sad moan in which it died away. Again and again it sounded, the whole air throbbing with it, strident, wild, and menacing."

As regards the three paragraphs which comprise then end of chapter 11—well, they are simply unforgettable. The first of the three sets the scene, with the setting sun turning the moor "sweet and mellow and peaceful in the golden evening light." And yet Watson's soul "shared none of the peace of nature." Rather, "with tingling nerves but a fixed purpose, I sat in the dark recess of the hut and waited with somber patience for the coming of its tenant."

While the first paragraph contrasts the vision of peace with the agitation of Watson, the second is animated by sound. "At last I heard him. Far away came the sharp clink of a boot striking upon a stone. Then another and yet another, coming nearer and nearer." Just as the wailing of the hound struck terror to the people on the moor, Watson here "shrank back into the darkest corner and cocked the pistol in my pocket." The tension rises with the long pause indicating that the unknown occupant of the hut "had stopped. Then once more the footsteps approached and a shadow fell across the opening of the hut."

The line which follows is worthy of standing beside even "Mr. Holmes, they were the footprints of a gigantic hound!"—the famous last line of chapter 2—among Doyle's catalog of remarkable closing sentences. When one recalls that this author was used to serial publication of his works, where the last line must be so dramatic that the reader is left panting to read the next installment, it is easy to understand one reason at least for the way his readers would line up month by month, eagerly awaiting the opportunity to buy and read the new chapter of the current work. In addition to being a master of plotting, characterization, structure, and language, Conan Doyle was a master of the tantalizing closing line. "It is a lovely evening, my dear Watson … I really think that you will be more comfortable outside than in" is indeed unforgettable writing: no wonder the Holmes saga, together with so much more of the author's work, still holds our attention seven generations after it first appeared in print. With the unexpected words uttered by the "well-known voice," the development section of the book comes to an end.

PART 3: RESOLUTION

CHAPTER 12: DEATH ON THE MOOR

My view of the structure of this chapter is that it can be broken down into three subsections. The first, of course, contains Watson's astonishment at finding Holmes to be the mysterious man on the tor, followed by his hurt at finding out how he was used by his friend.

Holmes manages to assuage his anger and disappointment, and

then, as the sun sets and the moor grows dark and cold, Watson tells Holmes of his visit to Laura Lyons. Holmes expresses his appreciation for what Dr. Watson has found out, and then pays his partner back by informing him of the true relationship between the Stapletons. His discovery that they are not really brother and sister but husband and wife is Holmes's most important contribution to the solution of the case.* The two continue to compare notes and Holmes explains what the case is all about ("It is murder, Watson—refined, cold-blooded, deliberate murder") when a terrible scream interrupts their conversation. It introduces subsection two—the moonlit chase across the dark moor, the finding of the body and the belated discovery of its identity, and the discussion of what to do next. The arrival of Mr. Stapleton himself marks the end of the subsection two and the beginning of subsection three, which contains a three-way conversation which occupies the remainder of the chapter. Mainly the subject is Holmes's attempts to keep the naturalist from thinking that he is in any way suspected: Holmes announces that this has

---

* There is another connection to the past in this chapter, although it may easily be forgotten. When Mr. Stapleton passes off his wife as his sister, he is merely repeating events from the Book of Genesis. Both Abraham and his son Isaac used the same trick, although in their cases the purpose was defensive rather than offensive. The Patriarchs feared being killed by powerful men who coveted their wives, so to avoid potential assassination they present Sarah and Rebecca as their sisters. One wonders about the sagacity of this strategy: wouldn't the lustful magnates of whom the husbands are afraid be *more* likely to take the beautiful women into their harems if they were single? One would like to know how the wives thought about what their husbands were doing: after all, it was their bodies and their lives which were imperiled by the ruse. To me, at least, it seems a cruel and selfish idea. Neither Abraham nor Isaac seems to have thought of the fact that a single woman is more likely to attract lecherous males than a married (thus protected) one—although the scheming Mr. Stapleton certainly realized it. The surprising thing is that Beryl Stapleton (alias Vandeleur) went along with the plot at all. Her later actions prove that she did not lack for courage. The only possible reason for her to cooperate with her husband's plot would be that despite his behavior she still thought herself to be in love with him.

not been a satisfactory case, and that both he and Watson will be returning to London in the morning.

American editions of *The Hound* end chapter 12 with this conversation. I understand, however, that English printings push the division between this chapter and the next forward, so that the discussion between Holmes and Watson as they walk across the moor at night on their way to Baskerville Hall—while Holmes explains why an immediate arrest would be a mistake, in that they have little proof to put before a jury—becomes the last part of chapter 12 rather than the opening subsection of chapter 13. While it makes little or no difference to the reader, and is perfectly justifiable either way, the American practice results in two chapters of approximately equal length, while the English version makes chapter 12 appreciably longer.

I wish to call your attention to a couple of tiny points which show just how much attention Conan Doyle paid to details. Both appear in subsection two of chapter 12. Holmes says that his "nets are closing upon" Stapleton, "even as his are upon Sir Henry." Given that Stapleton, the naturalist, chases insects with his butterfly net, this image is delightfully appropriate. Too, in writing about the body on the rocky slope, the author employs the adjective "mangled." The word is perfectly innocent here—but remember it when we come to chapter 15: there we will see how subtle Conan Doyle could be.

I should also register a small complaint about this chapter. Holmes tells Watson of the relationship between Stapleton and Laura Lyons (almost certainly a full-fledged affair) but gives us no hint as to how he found out about it. While it is a minor point, I have always wondered about it: Holmes surely did not get the data from either of the two principals! The source of his information may be a trivial matter, easily overlooked by Watson as well as by generations of readers, but it is a flaw which I would have liked the author to have avoided or corrected.

With all this said and done it is now time to leave chapter 12 behind us, and to move on to its followers.

CHAPTER 13: FIXING THE NETS

The title comes from Sherlock Holmes's comment in chapter 12, and it is even more apropos in this context.

In American editions of *The Hound*, this chapter typically comprises five subsections. In English editions, where the night walk to Baskerville Hall is included in chapter 12, there would be four—with the next chapter beginning when Holmes, Watson, and Sir Henry sit down to a belated supper. It is during this meal that Holmes's gaze is arrested as he looks up at the family portraits hanging on the wall. He asks about the painting of a cavalier in black velvet and lace, and Sir Henry confirms that this is the seventeenth century Hugo whose behavior and Satanic vow brought on the curse of the hound. Holmes remarks, "He seems a quiet, meek-mannered man enough, but I dare say that there was a lurking devil in his eyes. I had pictured him as a more robust and ruffianly person." He says no more until after Sir Henry is gone—then comes the climactic moment when Holmes covers the hat and ringlets, and the face of Stapleton appears.

"Yes, it is an interesting instance of a throwback, which appears to be both physical and spiritual." He does not use the word here, but what we have is a clear instance of atavism. Stapleton surely is a Baskerville, and Watson adds the clinching motive—"with designs upon the succession." With the discovery of the motive, the mystery is solved: it remains only to find evidence enough to bring the villain to trial.

That process begins with subsection three as Sherlock Holmes goes into action. He begins early in the morning by reporting the death of Selden to Princetown, and then he tells of how he communicated with the faithful Cartwright. Note what he says of the boy: "He would certainly have pined away at the door of my hut, as a dog does at his master's grave, if I had not set his mind at rest about my safety." As we have observed, Conan Doyle keeps the idea of dogs before the reader throughout the novel. The remainder of subsection three has Holmes giving his orders for the day, first to Sir Henry (who promises to obey), then to Cartwright, and finally by telegraph to Lestrade, who replies that he is coming. Again, we have the image of the nets closing on the lean-jawed pike—Mr. Stapleton.

Subsection four shows us the interview between Holmes, Watson, and Laura Lyons. Holmes informs her that the woman who has been known as Stapleton's sister is in truth his wife, and when she demands proof he produces both photographic and written documentation.

Confronted with the damning fact, Mrs. Lyons talks. She turns on her lover with all the fury of a woman scorned, saying that she was lied to and betrayed. "If he had kept faith with me I should always have done so with him." The scene ends with Holmes's comment that she has had a fortunate escape.

The chapter ends with the fifth subsection, four paragraphs long. The last three show us again Conan Doyle's brilliance with words. Lestrade is described as "a small, wiry *bulldog* of a man" (my emphasis), who now respects the man he used to belittle. The dialogue between them is short and brilliant:

"Anything good?" asks the Scotland Yarder.

"The biggest thing for years," replies Sherlock Holmes. "Lestrade, we will take the London fog out of your throat by giving you a breath of pure night air of Dartmoor. Never been there? Ah, well, I don't suppose you will forget your first visit."

Could anything be a better lead-in to the climax of the book?

CHAPTER 14: THE HOUND OF THE BASKERVILLES

As one might infer from its title, chapter 14 contains the climax of the story—the first and only time we see the hound. However, Conan Doyle was too savvy a writer to simply show us the creature. Instead, he crafted the chapter into four subsections, with the first and a good deal of the second devoted to building up the tension step by step, constantly ratcheting the pressure on Holmes, Watson, Lestrade and the reader until the last moment.

Subsection one begins this process by describing the journey from Coombe Tracey by hired wagonette to the gate before Baskerville Hall, and subsequently on foot to Merripit House. Holmes is largely silent, Watson nervous with anticipation, and Lestrade attempting nonchalance but clearly disturbed. "My word, it does not seem a very cheerful place," he remarks with a shiver at the sight of the gloomy slope of the hill and the huge lake of fog which lay over the Grimpen Mire.

The second subsection commences as the party takes position beside the road some 200 yards from the house. Holmes assigns Watson (who has been in the house) to go up to the window and look inside. While he does so, the author tightens the screws a bit further: Stapleton and Sir Henry sit at the table, the host chattering away, the guest looking "pale and distrait." As Watson watches from outside, Stapleton gets up and leaves the room. He goes to an outhouse in the corner of the orchard, enters as a curious scuffling sound reaches Watson's ears, and then returns to the dining room. While the author gives us no further data, we can easily gather that Stapleton was visiting the hound (that "curious scuffling noise" from inside the shed), probably with Sir Henry's old black boot in hand to set the animal on the track of the man who had worn it. Seeing Stapleton return to the dining room, Watson creeps back to report on what he has seen, and also who he has not seen—Mrs. Stapleton.

Next, Conan Doyle raises the tension even higher by invoking the fog bank. It is now drifting around the house and toward the three men waiting beside the path. The next two paragraphs describe the contrast between the clear, star-spangled night sky, with the bright cold stars shining and the half-moon giving off "a soft, uncertain light," and the fog gathering around the house. The light in the kitchen goes off: except for the dining room, the house is now in darkness, and increasingly shrouded in fog. The waiting men are forced to move further back from the house, until Holmes says of Sir Henry: "We are going too far. We cannot take the chance of his being overtaken before he can be reach us. At all costs, we must hold our ground where we are." It is now a race between Sir Henry Baskerville and the fog, and Sir Henry wins. They hear his footsteps in the fog, and then he steps out into the clear night.

Holmes cries, "Hist! Look out! It's coming!"

I need write no more about subsection two.

In subsection three, the party enters the house and finds Mrs. Stapleton in great distress. Lestrade is left to guard the premises while Holmes and Watson accompany Sir Henry back to Baskerville Hall, where "before morning he lay delirious in a high fever under the care of Dr. Mortimer. The two of them were destined to travel together around the world before Sir Henry had become once more the hale, hearty man that he had been before he became master of that ill- omened estate."

The fourth and final subsection of chapter 14 is set the next morning. With the fog having lifted, Mrs. Stapleton guides the two detectives and the doctor to the starting point of the pathway leading through the bog to the island where the hound had been kenneled.* The first paragraph of this subsection describes their journey on foot across the mire with words calculated to impress the reader with a sense of corruption, evil, and death. We are told of "green-scummed pits, foul quagmires, rank weeds and lush, slimy water plants which sent an odor of decay and a heavy miasmic vapor onto our faces." The mire is described as "dark and quivering," and Doyle makes the bog seem almost sentient: "It was as if some malignant hand was tugging us down into those obscene depths, so grim and purposeful was the clutch with which it held us." Was Stapleton—the descendent of the first Hugo who had offered his soul to the devil over two centuries earlier, and now himself an acolyte of Satan—a victim of the

---

* Nowhere does the text tell us that Holmes, Lestrade, and Watson all made the trek through the bog to the site of the abandoned tin mine. However, Watson tells us how Holmes sank up to his waist in the ooze when he tried to retrieve Sir Henry's old black boot, and writes that "had we not been there to drag him out he could never have set his foot on firm land again." Since Mrs. Stapleton had been left behind, Lestrade must have accompanied Holmes and Watson on the trek to make Watson write the plural "we" rather than the singular "I." Likewise, he writes "we all" looked for footprints on the island, but saw none. Therefore, not less than three men went through the mire that morning, and the third could only have been Lestrade.

wrath of the deity who prepared for him an appropriate end beneath the earth, in the foul slime which had sucked him down?

There remains the last paragraph of this final subsection. In the hut where the hound had been kept, the party found a quantity of gnawed bones, and the skeleton and pelt of a curly-haired spaniel. One must ask why Conan Doyle ended the action of this book in this grotesque way. Be assured that there is a very good reason, as I shall demonstrate in the essay which concludes this story of the Holmes saga.

CHAPTER 15: A RETROSPECTION

The title of this chapter is significant. "A retrospection" literally means a looking backwards, and in one sense of the word it is what Holmes does after meeting Sir Henry and Dr. Mortimer one late November afternoon in London. That night, Watson asks him to review the Baskerville case—which, as we know, took place in October. Thus, we have a "looking back" by Sherlock Holmes.

However, it is also a retrospection in another sense. Reviewing what happened a few weeks before also involves looking into the background of the action, as far back as the first Hugo Baskerville and his offer to Satan in the seventeenth century. Chapter 15 reinforces the constant theme of the relationship between the past and the present which runs throughout the book. When one recalls that the novel begins with a scene of reflection, and that the entire center section of the story is about the moor in the nineteenth century and its ever-present ties to both history and prehistory, it should come as no surprise that the book ends with still another chapter relating the ties between the past and present.

There is little to say about the structure of this chapter, which is extremely simple. There are just two subsections, and the first consists of a single paragraph which acts as an introduction to the second—Holmes's long discourse on the Baskerville case. All but the last six lines of this second part are devoted to his explanation, and to answers to Watson's questions.

Uncomplicated as it may be, chapter 15 does include some important material. Let us begin with what it tells us about the hound itself. We learn that Stapleton acquired the animal from a dealer called "Ross and Mangles"—said to be in London at an address in the Fullham Road. I have no idea whether such a firm exists or ever existed, or whether Conan Doyle created it from his fertile brain. Either way, however, the name of this establishment is peculiarly appropriate to this story. Recall, if you will, the adjective the author chose to describe the condition of Selden's body when Holmes and Watson found it on the moor in chapter 12: the word was "mangled." What else might one expect from a hound bought from a dealer called "Ross and Mangles?" Once again, Doyle employs an aptonym—whether he created it himself or simply borrowed it from a real dealer!*

A bit more about the dog. Holmes remarks that Stapleton's "use of artificial means to make the creature diabolical was a flash of genius on his part." The literal meaning of the word "diabolical" is "devil-like," and if the phosphorescent hound was diabolical, the adjective applies as much or even more to its owner.

Consider the catalogue of Mr. Stapleton's misdeeds, as Holmes relates it a bit later in the chapter. It includes, in addition to murder and attempted murder, grand theft, armed robbery, burglary, assault and battery, false imprisonment, and wife-beating. His killing of Sir Charles is described a piece of "devilish cunning." This is an unmistakable hint that the naturalist of Dartmoor is like Satan himself.

His treatment of the women in the case is particularly brutal. He deceives and manipulates both, uses them shamelessly, and betrays them. He abuses Laura Lyons emotionally, and his wife both emotionally and physically. We also learn how his self-contained manner "cleverly concealed a fiery soul." He involuntarily exhibited "a passionate outburst" when he witnessed Sir Henry paying court to his

---

* Doyle used the same word ("mangled") to describe what Carlo the mastiff did to Jephro Rucastle in "The Copper Beeches."

wife—even though it was part of his own plan to have her attract him. Conan Doyle's choice of the adjective "fiery" here is telling. Satan and Hell are always associated with fire: is not Mr. Stapleton's "fiery soul" another suggestion of his kinship with the Prince of Darkness?

These are small points, but collectively they hint that Stapleton (born Rodger Baskerville, Junior) is something more than an ordinary criminal. His ancestor, the seventeenth-century Hugo, is said to have offered his soul to the Devil. Is it not possible or even likely that this man, an atavistic clone of his predecessor in the family, made a similar bargain—or even worse, was willingly possessed by Satan in person? He can most certainly be categorized as one who had totally surrendered to "the evil inclination"—the "yetzer hara," which seems to be embedded in some degree or other in the makeup of every human being.

In the final paragraph of the story, Watson raises the issue of how Stapleton might have claimed the estate without causing suspicion and inquiry, if his plot had succeeded. Here Sherlock Holmes's answer ties into the theme of the novel: "The past and the present are within the field of my inquiry, but what a man may do in the future is a hard question to answer ... We cannot doubt from what we know of him that he would have found some way out of the difficulty."

The last sentences of *The Hound* end the book on an upbeat note. Holmes invites his friend to the opera after first stopping at Marcini's restaurant for dinner: the storm and strife is apparently over, and we have returned to the normal course of existence.

Or have we? The book has come to an end, but in the essay which follows I hope to demonstrate, by reviewing the entire novel and fitting the pieces of the jigsaw puzzle together, that the horror is not truly over. Read on!

THE SOLUTION: THE REAL MEANING AND
SIGNIFICANCE OF THE BOOK

No reader, even the most casual, would deny that *The Hound of the Baskervilles* is both a great work of detective fiction and at the same time a superlative story of horror. Yet I believe, and will endeavor to demonstrate, that the true horror of this book is to be found in a different sphere altogether. This novel is to my knowledge the most devastating attack on the smug self-satisfaction of Victorian / Edwardian Britain, written and published in that very era. Even more, it raises questions for our own time and place—questions to which the true answers may not be to our liking.

There are several aspects of *The Hound of the Baskervilles* which merit discussion. Of these, I think the first must be how it fits into the Holmes canon—its relationship to other stories.

I have already pointed out Conan Doyle's interest in the idea that personal and behavioral traits may be transmitted from generation to generation. It first appears in the eighth story of *The Adventures*, "The Speckled Band," written in 1892. It is also present in one form or another in five other tales from *The Adventures* and *The Memoirs* before it culminates in *The Hound.**

In the Baskerville novel this theme finds its apotheosis in the character of Mr. Stapleton, in whom both his appearance and his behavior are clearly throwbacks to his seventeenth-century ancestor, Hugo. However, in *The Hound* Doyle expands the impact of the past from individuals or families to a whole society: the book is permeated by the comparison of the distant past with the present.

Indeed, may we not regard the very creation of *The Hound* as a manifestation of the past's influence on the present? Doyle had killed

---

* These other stories are "The Copper Beeches," "The Yellow Face," "The Reigate Squires," "The Greek Interpreter," and "The Final Problem." It is interesting to note that in both "The Speckled Band" and "The Copper Beeches," the "inheritance" idea is coupled with the traditional horror story—just as it is in *The Hound.*

Holmes in "The Final Problem" and for at least six years had not written a single word about his great detective. But the reading public simply refused to accept the death of Holmes and the end of stories about him, and the growing pressure on the author to write more about Holmes eventually led Doyle to include him as a major character in a book which was originally conceived as a horror story based on a West Country legend in which Holmes was not involved at all.

We should also consider the possible connection between the inheritance theme and Doyle's later conversion to spiritualism—the religious manifestation of the idea that communication with the dead is possible. One has little difficulty in seeing a close connection between the impact of the past on the present and the belief (or at least the hope) that direct personal contact between the two is possible. Seen from this perspective, Doyle's commitment to spiritualism, which seems at first glance to be inexplicable, becomes perhaps less difficult to understand.

If *The Hound* looks backward through the canon, it also points forward to a story that was not to be written and published for another nine years—"The Devil's Foot." Not only do the two tales have in common wild and mysterious settings, they also share Satan as a suspect in cases of murder. However, in both stories Conan Doyle asserts a basic principle of the detective story—that reason and knowledge can explain events and actions which may appear inexplicable save by resort to the supernatural.

Let us now return to the text of *The Hound*, in which we will find any number of clues to its underlying meaning commencing with the very first page.

I have already pointed out, in my analysis of chapter 1, how the book begins with a scene introducing (but without actually employing the word) the concept of reflection—of looking backward. And while the Latin root of the word refers to bending back light, in its larger sense "reflecting" also refers to looking or thinking back into the past. Watson's cliché remark about Holmes having "eyes in the back of his head" simply reinforces the idea of "looking backwards" in another subtle way. By *not* using the word "reflect" or "reflecting," the author makes the reader supply them—a means of stressing the importance of this concept in this novel.

A few paragraphs later, when Watson looks up Dr. Mortimer's biography in his medical directory, we find an account of his essays. There are three titles, each of which refers specifically to the influence of and / or relationship between the past and the present. The first of these, which won for its author the Jackson Prize for Comparative Pathology, is entitled "Is Disease a Reversion?" The second, which appeared in *Lancet* (then as now the journal of the British Medical Society) is called, "Some Freaks of Atavism," while the third and last is called "Do We Progress?" Their importance derives from the theme which is common to all three—again, the relationship between the past and the present, and especially the extent to which the former influences the latter.

I would suppose that not one in a thousand readers of *The Hound of the Baskervilles* stops to think over the content of Dr. Mortimer's essays: they seem to be nothing more than trivia. In truth, these three writings are crucial clues to what the novel is about.

The entrance of Dr. Mortimer, just up from Devonshire, takes us in a new direction. While the opening passages of the book introduce us to the concept of *dichotomy in time* (past vs. present), we now encounter a *dichotomy of place*: Dartmoor vs. London.

Twenty-six previous Holmes stories have created, by their very existence and familiarity, a feeling that the Holmes / Watson apartment at 221B Baker Street in London is the epicenter of all the qualities for which the capital stands—reason, order, justice, and security. But the character of Dr. Mortimer as he is introduced in the first chapter of *The Hound* is calculated to shake up this atmosphere of sanity and safety. He is a striking, unusual, and somewhat disturbing person whose mere looks suffice to upset the serenity of the Baker Street rooms.*

---

* It is nearly impossible for a dedicated reader of the Holmes canon to overlook

Nor is it merely his appearance which makes Dr. Mortimer disconcerting. Before ever getting to his purpose in consulting Sherlock Holmes, this peculiar visitor seizes on Holmes's skull, which fascinates him so much that he admits to coveting it. "A cast of your skull, sir, until the original is available, would be an ornament to any anthropological museum." We can hardly be blamed for thinking, "What sort of crazy man is this doctor from Dartmoor?" Moreover, he completes his strange self-introduction by invoking the name of Bertillon as "the foremost expert in Europe." No wonder that Holmes is upset "just a little."

Dr. Mortimer gives us just a tiny taste of the dichotomy of place, but his visit also yields another view of the dichotomy of time, beyond the titles of his essays. Through his hobby (which today would be called craniology) he introduces the science of anthropology into the book. Anthropology is the study of human development from prehistory to the present, and this discipline certainly covers influence of the past on the present.

Summing up the first chapter, then, we find that the twin themes of dichotomy of time and dichotomy of space are both introduced here, although not much elaborated upon. Each of them will appear many times in the novel, and the author will work them around as a composer reworks his melodies to convey his message to his audience. In this novel, London and the present appear to be superior to Dartmoor and the past, at least in the early chapters. As we penetrate further into the book, however, we will find out much more about the relationships between the capital and the moor, and between the past and the present.

The dichotomy of place is lightly sketched in the first chapter, but

---

the similarities in the description of Dr. Mortimer found here with that of Professor Moriarty in "The Final Problem." Only the latter's reptilian head oscillation is absent in the portrait of Dr. Mortimer. Perhaps the likeness was Conan Doyle's attempt to emphasize the strangeness of the doctor from Dartmoor—highlighting the apparent differences between the city and the wild moor.

it is further explored in the remainder of the Exposition section—
chapters 2–5. We hear the legend of the Hound for the first time
in the second chapter, which also introduces us to the newspaper
account of the death of Sir Charles and then Dr. Mortimer's private
evidence regarding the old man's death. Chapter 2 concludes with
Watson returning from a day at his club to find Holmes, wreathed
in tobacco smoke, pouring over his large-scale map of Dartmoor. In
conversation with Watson, Holmes refers to the moor as "desolate"
and "lifeless." Watson remarks that "It must be a wild place, "and
Holmes returns "Yes, the setting is a worthy one. If the Devil did
desire to take a hand in the affairs of men—" He breaks off here,
but clearly the sentence would end with something like "this would
be the place."

The apparent difference between "safe" London and "dangerous" Dartmoor is further elaborated upon in the later chapters
of part 1, when Dr. Mortimer raises the question of what to do with
the heir, Sir Henry—take him down to Dartmoor, or try to keep him
in the city?

Mortimer, while London-trained and (as Holmes calls him,
"a man of science") is apparently so spooked by the death of Sir
Charles and the atmosphere of Devonshire that he is half ready to
attribute the death to supernatural forces. When asked by Holmes if
he believes that possibility, he answers that he does not know what to
believe. Holmes comments that "A devil with purely local powers like
a parish vestry would be too inconceivable a thing."* He suggests that
Dr. Mortimer call off his spaniel, meet Sir Henry but say nothing
about the question of allowing him to go down to Dartmoor, and
meet again the next day when he (Holmes) will have made up his
mind on the question. In fact, Holmes's comment about a devil with

---

* This remark is doubled-edged: on the surface it seems to say that no devil
with local powers is likely to be found on the moor. But it can also be interpreted as saying that no location is ever safe from devilry, if infernal powers
are not restricted to a single location!

purely local powers more than hints at what his advice will be: yes, take Sir Henry to Baskerville Hall, but do not let him go alone. Thus it is arranged that Watson accompany the baronet to Dartmoor.

The London-Devonshire dichotomy is further stressed by Holmes's comments at the end of chapter 5, when he says, "It's an ugly, dangerous business, Watson, and the more I see of it the less I like it. Yes, my dear fellow, you may laugh, but I give you my word that I shall be very glad to have you back safe and sound in Baker Street once more." It is even more emphasized by Watson's memorable trip to the Hall, as the wagonette leaves the warmth and comfort of the level ground and ascends to the cold and dark of the moor. This passage in chapter 6 is surely one of the finest scenes Dr. Doyle ever created, and it is worthy of comparison with anything similar in the English language.

At this point we must interrupt our discussion of the dichotomy of place issue to raise a different question. Why did the author endow Dr. Mortimer with a pet spaniel which goes with him everywhere? There is no apparent reason for introducing the pet, other than the commonplace fact that many people like and love companion animals, most especially dogs. Yet later in the novel, we will find that the nameless spaniel plays an important (if not the all-important) part in the great scheme of this amazing novel.

Having raised (but not yet answered) the question of why the author gave Dr. Mortimer a pet dog, we can now return to our discussion of the dichotomy of place. We find that thoughtful consideration of the text leads to the surprising conclusion that *The Hound* is riddled with indications that "safe, sane" London is hardly any different from the supposedly "wild, dangerous" moor.

Consider these facts: while London is Holmes's own turf, he must admit to having been checkmated there by the black-bearded stranger in the hansom. This individual not only thwarts every effort Holmes makes to discover his identity—he sends back (through the medium of John Clayton, the cabbie) that audacious and defiant message that *his* name is Sherlock Holmes!

We identify Selden, the escaped murderer, with the moor—but the crime for which he was imprisoned at Princetown—a killing marked by "peculiar ferocity" and "wanton brutality" so shocking that his death sentence had been commuted, due to doubts as to his sanity—took place not in Dartmoor but in the Notting Hill section of London. The hound itself, we learn, had been purchased by Stapleton from Ross and Mangles, "the dealers in the Fulham Road"—in London. The criminal in this case had planned to kill Sir Henry in London. The import of all this is to challenge the illusion that the capital is really any safer or more civilized than the allegedly "wild, desolate, lifeless" moor. People may wish to believe in that idea, but there's a lot of evidence against it.

Moreover, the other supposed dichotomy—that the Britain of 1900 was somehow superior to the Britain of the seventeenth century (or to the country in the Neolithic period, for that matter)—is also exposed as an illusion. Here is where the stone huts on the moor come into play. On that dramatic ride from the train station to Baskerville Hall, Watson notices from the wagonette that the cottages of the local residents which stand beside the road are "walled and roofed with stone, with no creeper to break [their] harsh outlines." How different are these "modern" cottages from the huts of Neolithic man? We also hear of how the "huge russet and olive slopes [are] sprinkled with giant boulders." Where are we, if not in a new "Stone Age?"

When Dr. Watson walks out on the moor and sees the circle of stone huts, he writes (in his first report to Holmes) that,

> the longer one stays here the more does the spirit of the moor
> sink into one's soul, its vastness and also its grim charm.
> When you are once out upon its bosom, you have left all traces
> of modern England behind you but on the other hand you
> are conscious everywhere of the homes and the work of the
> prehistoric people ... if you were to see a skin-clad, hairy man

crawl out from the low door ... you would feel that his presence there was more natural than your own.

And what happens later? In chapter 9, when Watson and Sir Henry are hunting the escaped convict, Selden, he is described just as one would expect a caveman to look (emphases added):

> There was thrust out an evil, yellow face...all seemed and scored with vile passion. Foul with mire, with a bristling beard, and hung with matted hair, it might well have belonged to one of those old savages who dwelt in the burrows on the hillside. The light beneath him was reflected in his small, cunning eyes, which peered fiercely to the right and left through the darkness, like a crafty and savage animal who has heard the steps of the hunters ... At the same moment the convict screamed out a curse at us and *hurled a rock* which splintered up against the *boulder* which had sheltered us. I caught one glimpse of his short, squat figure as he sprang to his feet and turned to run.

Is this not the virtual reincarnation of a Stone-Age man alive in the England of Queen Victoria? What real difference is there between Selden, the Notting Hill murderer, and the prehistoric people who once inhabited the moor on which he now is hiding out? If it is no more than an illusion that London is safer and saner that Dartmoor, then is it not also an illusion that the Seldens and the Stapletons of the late nineteenth century are so very different from the people Stapleton himself calls "Our worthy ancestors?"

As a matter of fact, the past and present are so closely entwined in this novel that I was reminded of William Faulkner's well-known line about the subject: "The past is never dead. It isn't even past."

In short, in *The Hound*, Conan Doyle took two popular and soothing beliefs, both associated with Victorian optimism—and torpedoed them. He saw through the hazy cloud of assumptions and wished-for-but-unsubstantiated changes in human nature, and he saw no evidence that mankind had improved either its morality or its behavior. He demonstrated that Britain (as symbolized by its great capital city, London) had not advanced in sanity, safety, reason, or rule of law, even beyond its own supposedly "wild, dangerous" Western province. And he demonstrated that the passage of millennia had not changed the human race's inbred and ever-present attraction to evil. In this way, he probably hoped to shock his readers out of their illusions. How many (if any) of them perceived his message and were confronted with the true horror to be found in this book—that their cherished beliefs about the world and time in which they lived were no more than shams—neither I nor anyone else can say. The great lesson to be learned from this most anti-Victorian Victorian novel is that humans have always possessed the capacity and inclination to do the greatest good but also the greatest evil— not infrequently at the same time. The Baskerville family produced good men—like Sir Charles, the statesman William who served with distinction in the House of Commons, or the rear admiral who sailed under Rodney in the West Indies. It also produced "the wild, profane and godless" Hugo in the seventeenth century—and his atavistic descendant, Mr. Stapleton, in the nineteenth.

Seen in this light, we are all Baskervilles—each endowed with the potential for good or evil and the free will to choose the courses of our lives. In his time, Conan Doyle saw no evidence that people were choosing the good any more than in the past, while the Seldens and Stapletons continued to appear no less often. In our own day, more than a century after *The Hound* first saw publication, there is no reason to challenge his evaluation of the state of the world, nor to expect anything different in our own present. Great novels show us as we are. *The Hound of the Baskervilles* is just such a book.

Arthur Conan Doyle lived on for nearly thirty years after publishing his masterpiece of horror—long enough to see his vision of the bankruptcy of Victorian-era optimism vindicated. The maiden-voyage sinking of the *Titanic*, Britain's newest and proudest

industrial accomplishment, was the first frightful blow to the kingdom's prestige and self-esteem. Little more than two years later the
onset of what was then called "the Great War" resulted in the complete deflation of the previous climate of overconfidence about the
near future.

Even if Doyle got any satisfaction out of being right about the
smugness of the 1880s and 90s, he was lucky to die before the far
greater catastrophes which were yet to come. The first two-thirds of
the twentieth century saw the unholy triumvirate of Hitler, Stalin,
and Mao, who together were probably responsible for the deaths
of at least sixty or seventy million people. Doyle did not live long
enough to see history's bloodiest decades, but he would not have
been surprised by them if he had.

This observation brings us back to Dr. Mortimer's three essays.
Cited in Dr. Watson's medical directory, their titles were "Is Disease
a Reversion?," "Some Freaks of Atavism," and "Do We Progress?" In
The Hound, his answer to the first question is probably "yes," particularly if the disease is a mental one. He shows us "a freak of atavism"
in his portrait of Mr. Stapleton, the throwback to the first Hugo both
physically and spiritually. And to Dr. Mortimer's third question, "Do
We Progress?" Conan Doyle's response in this novel is an unequiv-
ocal and ringing "No!" The events of the twentieth century, both
before and after the author's death, prove how right he was.

Some readers may question my analysis of and conclusions
about *The Hound*. I answer by simply citing the text: I did not write
this novel. I simply read it and reread it, working to explain what I
found in it. If Dr. Doyle had not meant the story to have its deeper
meaning, then why on earth did he write Dr. Mortimer's remarkably
suggestive essay titles into chapter 1? Why did he create the character of Selden and describe him to look and act like a Stone-Age
savage? Why did he fill the book with references to "the powers of
evil," invoke the supernatural, and create the evil Hugo Baskerville
and his atavistic descendant, if not to attack the simplistic optimism

of his own time and place? I challenge any careful reader to deny the significance of so much of the book.

Moreover, I have not yet written about a terrifying, clinching passage—concealed, so to speak, in broad daylight—which leaves no doubt about Doyle's intended meaning in *The Hound*. I refer to the discovery made by Holmes, Watson, and Lestrade in the last two paragraphs of chapter 14.

On the morning following the death of the hound, Beryl Garcia Stapleton guides the three investigators to the head of a path which leads through the Grimpen Mire, to the island where one of the buildings of an abandoned tin mine served as the kennel and hiding place for the diabolical dog. With all due respect to Joseph Conrad for the borrowing of his great title, this was the true *Heart of Darkness*, the epicenter of evil in Doyle's novel. Inside it, the team comes across a staple and chain showing where the hound had been kept. Around the floor of the hut they found "a quantity of gnawed bones. A skeleton with a tangle of brown hair adhering to it lay among the debris."

"A dog!" said Holmes. "By Jove, a curly-haired spaniel. Poor Mortimer will never see his pet again."

Why did Conan Doyle conclude the action of his masterpiece with this strange and seemingly trivial passage? The answer is simple enough, if only you see it.

Think about what must have happened between the hound and the spaniel, and then think of the three-word phrase expressing this which can also be used to describe the state of the world as Doyle saw it, as contrasted to the way the overoptimistic Victorians wished to believe it was.

Did you get it? The hound ate the spaniel—and it's a dog-eat-dog world in which we live.

Now tell me that the author did not write this deliberately—this little coded phrase summarizes and describes the whole message of the book.

Do you understand now why I call *The Hound of the Baskervilles* a great detective story, a great horror story (although the hound itself is not the true horror), and also a literary masterpiece exposing the false character of a whole nation's beliefs?[*]

There are other implications to be discussed here. How did the tame, domesticated spaniel get to the island in the bog? Mr. Benjamin S. Clark, quoted by Klinger in his *New Annotated Sherlock Holmes*, reasons that the little dog "could not have strayed there by itself"—a conclusion with which I most emphatically agree. However, Mr. Clark's suggestion that Dr. Mortimer, while colluding with Stapleton, delivered his own pet to its doom, cannot, I believe, be credited. Only a completely cold-hearted and cold-blooded individual could be capable of such a terrible act. Dr. Mortimer does not exhibit either of those characteristics. But Stapleton surely does: the most likely explanation by far is that it was he who, having found the spaniel wandering around on the moor, picked it up and carried it to the island. What was his motive? I can think of none other than pure meanness—a desire to deprive Mortimer of his animal companion—or even worse, to sacrifice the spaniel as a means of propitiating his ally and servant, the hound. Only a totally evil man could ever do such a thing—but Mr. Stapleton shows every sign of being just that. Once again, the word "diabolical" comes to mind. Hugo may have created the legend by making a vow to Satan—but his descendent, Stapleton, is no less an acolyte. This little passage, then, completes the profile of Stapleton which the novel draws—man at his most terrible. Have we progressed, if such an individual can be found among the supposedly civilized population of Victorian Britain?

Still more can be drawn from this dog-eat-dog incident. *The Hound* might well be titled *A Tale of Two Canines* (this time the apologies are due to Charles Dickens). Conan Doyle himself observed in one of his Holmes short stories ("The Creeping Man" from *The Case-Book*) that

---

[*]   I taught *The Hound* to a class of high school seniors a few years ago, and during a lecture I used the phrase "dog eat dog." On the subsequent exam, several of them wrote "doggie dog"! Clearly, they had never heard the phrase before, and had no idea what I was talking about. With today's young people you cannot assume that they know much at all—even fairy tales!

dogs tend to reflect the homes in which they live.* "Whoever saw a frisky dog in a gloomy home, or a sad dog in a happy one?" Holmes asks. In this case, the hound, savage by nature and bred from a bloodhound and a mastiff, had been trained by its master, Stapleton, to be vicious. On the other hand, Doctor Mortimer raised a playful, loving spaniel. At least in part, the two animals reflect the personalities of their owners. Thus, the two dogs are symbols representing the unchanging, contradictory nature of mankind, with its capacity for great good, and its inclination to great evil. *A Tale of Two Canines* would be a good subtitle for *The Hound of the Baskervilles*!

I would like to make one more comment about the place of *The Hound* in English literature. With its pessimistic view of human progress, the Doyle novel is in some ways a precursor of another popular British work of fiction, written some fifty years later. I refer to William Golding's *Lord of the Flies*, in which a group of choir boys, cut off from their usual environment, revert to savagery. This popular (if horrifying) book points out how thin and weak the veneer of civilization can be: even choir boys harbor the *yetzer hara*—the inclination toward evil which seems to be universal among the human race, though much stronger and more difficult to control among some people.

Strikingly, the Devil is depicted in both books, though in different disguises. The title, *Lord of the Flies*, is a translation of "Beelzebub," one of Satan's many aliases. In the Golding book, the Devil is depicted by the head of a pig stuck on a stick and surrounded by a swarm of acolytes—the flies. In the Doyle novel, he first appears in the form of the mute, black hound that runs behind the seventeenth-century Hugo Baskerville as he chases the maiden

---

* Alert readers will find serval points in common between "The Copper Beeches" and *The Hound*, the least important of which is the presence of a dangerous dog in each. There are also affinities between this novel and another Holmes short story, "The Devil's Foot," in which Satan does not appear, but an acolyte of his certainly does. In addition, both "The Devil's Foot" and *The Hound* turn in part on contemporary obstacles to divorce—which as we know was a subject of great interest to Conan Doyle.

who had escaped from his Hall. Hugo, you will recall, had vowed that very night that he would surrender his soul to the powers of evil if he were allowed to catch the girl. When he does catch her, she is already dead. Then the hound stands over Hugo's body and tears out his throat as the horrified onlookers watch.

In both novels, the real villain is the untamed nature of man. While often kept well under control, the evil inclination appears never to be completely absent. The Golding book stresses the importance of social mores in combatting the temptations of the *yetzer hara*: in the Doyle novel individuals appear to have to fight off the temptation pretty much on their own, and in some cases (like Mr. Stapleton) the outcome of the battle may be determined by inheritance—what else does atavism mean? In any event, both Doyle and Golding had a shared interest in the wellsprings of human behavior.

HOUNDED? THE TWO LATER-LIFE CONVERSIONS OF CONAN DOYLE

In *The Hound of the Baskervilles,* Dr. Doyle expressed the horror of discovering that the beliefs you have long accepted as gospel may turn out not to be true at all. Now, we may ask if that sensation might have haunted him in his own later life.

For a decade after the publication of *The Hound*, its author was occupied with his historical novel, *Sir Nigel,* his two unsuccessful attempts to win a seat in Parliament as a Unionist, the death of his first wife, his second marriage and the beginning of his second family, and other pursuits—which he deemed far more important than writing more Holmes stories. He remained steadfastly opposed to home rule or independence for Ireland during this period.

But about 1911 he came under the influence of Sir Roger Casement, a leading proponent of these policies. I can just imagine Sir Roger saying something like this: "Arthur, don't you see that your position against Ireland is no more valid than that common Victorian belief you attacked in *The Hound*—that is, that we in England have the answers to everything? To your great credit, you saw through that tomfoolery ten years ago. Now, why don't you rethink your antipathy towards Ireland and the Irish people? You may well come to see that it is no less foolish than the Victorian smugness you demolished in *The Hound*!"

Whether or not that was how it came about, by 1913 Conan Doyle had reversed his position on the Irish question—a political conversion such as is rarely seen.

Now let us advance five years in time—to 1918, when Sir Arthur Conan Doyle, surely among the most respected people in Britain, stunned the world by accepting "The New Revelation"—the belief that communication with the dead is possible, and that spiritualism, its religious manifestation, is a credible and valid belief. In short, having first changed his political thinking about Ireland and its people, he now defied conventional religion and risked his reputation to declare his trust in the reality of fairies, the seances of mediums, and the idea of communicating with the dead. This was in truth a religious conversation, on a par with his political reversal five years before.

Clearly Sir Arthur had become far more philosophical and more open to unpopular opinions during the years following *The Valley of Fear*—the stories in *The Case Book* are clear proof of that. Might not his two great later-life conversions owe something to Dr. Doyle's masterpiece, *The Hound of the Baskervilles*, which may have opened first his eyes and later his mind to political and spiritual ideas far different than the ones he had previously held?

To put it bluntly, was the author of *The Hound* moved to serious life changes by his own novel?

POSTSCRIPT: THE HOUND AND THE KNIGHTHOOD

With our realization of the subject matter of *The Hound*, we may find both irony and humor in the circumstances of the author's knighthood. It was said to be a reward for Doyle's service to Britain during the Boer War, but few people in England would have believed that. The knighthood was really given to the author for bringing back the character of Sherlock Holmes, whom he had killed off in "The Final Problem" back in December 1893. It was eight years before *The Hound* was published in serial and book form, beginning in 1901 and complete by the following spring. Still, the new novel was set before the supposed death of the detective: it was not until "The Empty House" appeared in the *Strand Magazine* in October 1903, that Holmes's resurrection was complete. The knighthood was bestowed upon Doyle on August 9, 1902—before the resumption of the monthly short stories. We can only conclude, then, that the author was really honored for writing and publishing *The Hound of the Baskervilles*.

As to the quality of that novel, it is altogether fitting and proper that its author be raised to knighthood. One wonders, however, what Doyle's inner feelings must have been that day when Edward VII said, "Rise, Sir Arthur." The new knight had been no admirer of the man who spoke those words: just over a decade previously, when Edward had still been Prince of Wales, Conan Doyle had painted an unflattering satiric portrait of him in the first Holmes short story, "A Scandal in Bohemia." Conan Doyle had made no secret of his disdain for titles ("The only title I want is that of doctor, and I have that already"). Moreover, Conan Doyle in time put his feelings about his own new title in print: years later, he had Holmes do what he dared not do himself—decline a knighthood.

The greatest irony about Sir Arthur's knighthood, however, was that the book for which it was bestowed attacked the intellectual, emotional, and social pillars of the society whose monarch had touched his shoulders and bade him rise.

So I come to the end of this study. I set out to prove that the Sherlock Holmes canon contains much important and interesting material that is often ignored by casual readers, and that Arthur Conan Doyle was a deep thinker and perceptive social critic as well as a master storyteller and brilliant literary craftsman. If I have convinced even a small number of readers that Dr. Doyle belongs in the very highest echelon of British writers of the nineteenth and early-twentieth centuries, I shall feel that my work has been well done.

About the Author

IRA FISTELL BEGAN TO TALK IN EARLY INFANCY, WAS READING NEWSPAPERS at age four, and writing editorials for his high school paper at fourteen. He has never stopped talking, reading and writing ever since. After earning a college degree with General Honors from the University of Chicago, he went on to a Law Degree there, and a Masters in U.S. History from the University of Wisconsin—Madison. He began teaching there while still in graduate school. Then in 1968 he began his main occupation—38 years as an on-air personality in radio and television, including coast-to-coast broadcasts on ABC and CBS radio and USA and ESPN television. His wide range of interests (Sherlock Holmes is only one) and store of knowledge fascinated his many listeners. Beginning in 1988 he began writing a personal journal called *TOPICS*, which is now in its 33 year of unbroken monthly commentary.

After retiring from broadcasting in 2006, Ira turned to literature. His book, *Mark Twain—Three Encounters* has been hailed as "the essential book" about the life and works of Samuel Clemens. And now comes *The Hidden Holmes*.

Ira and his brilliant and beautiful life partner Rachel are both native Chicagoans who now divide their time between their old home city and California.

CPSIA information can be obtained
at www.ICGtesting.com
Printed in the USA
FSHW010510220920
73986FS